Fifty Plants

that Changed the Course of

History

A FIREFLY BOOK

Published by Firefly Books Ltd. 2010

Second printing, 2011

Publisher Cataloging-in-Publication Data (U.S.)

A CIP record of this book is available from Library of Congress

Library and Archives Canada Cataloguing in Publication

A CIP record of this book is available from Library and Archives Canada

Published in the United States by
Firefly Books (U.S.) Inc.
P.O. Box 1338, Ellicott Station
Buffalo, New York 14205

Published in Canada by
Firefly Books Ltd.
66 Leek Crescent
Richmond Hill, Ontario L4B 1H1

Conceived, designed and produced by
Quid Publishing
Level 4, Sheridan House
114 Western Road
Hove BN3 1DD
England

Cover and interior design: Lindsey Johns

Printed in China

Fifty Plants

that Changed the Course of

History

written by Bill Laws

FIREFLY BOOKS

Contents

Introduction

What greater delight is there than to behold the earth apparelled with plants, as with a robe of embroidered worke, set with Orient pearles and garnished with great diversitie of rare and costly jewels?

John Gerard, Herbal, 1597

If the world's plants suddenly expired, we would have no tomorrow. Yet it is easy to dismiss plants as the silent witnesses to our progress on the planet. The world nurtures between 250,000 and 300,000 types of flowering plants and they can seem like a pretty backcloth to our remorseless activity: walking a dog through a forest of quiet oaks; driving a car past purple fields of lavender; riding the train across a prairie of wheat.

PLANTS AND PEOPLE

In reality, plants have played a dynamic role in shaping our history. Life on Earth is made possible by the very breath of plants, by the way they absorb carbon dioxide (CO_2) and exhale oxygen. Plants may have even paved the way for us, evolving the process of photosynthesis in response to some prehistoric climate catastrophe and opening the DNA gates for the evolution of terrestrial animals like ourselves.

Grains of pollen frozen beneath the Antarctic ice may yet reveal the secrets of our Earth's own past. They could help predict its future too, solving the puzzle over whether the current hole in the ozone layer, attributed to our use of fossil fuels, was prefigured millions of years ago. Plant history is certainly longer than ours. While plants have been colonizing the planet for 470 million years, our own timeline is huddled into a relatively recent past. If every century counted as a minute on the face of a clock, the Romans conquered Europe twenty minutes ago; Christianity was founded less than a quarter of an hour back; and the first white people only settled in America in the time it takes to turn the beans of *Coffea arabica* into a decent cup of coffee.

LIQUID PERK
The beans produced by *Coffea arabica* have been roasted, ground, and brewed for centuries (see Coffee, p.54).

Plants have always provided us with fuel, food, shelter, and medicines. They have always controlled the rate of land erosion and regulated the amount of carbon dioxide and oxygen in the air that we breathe. They have given us the fossil fuels that we are consuming with such profligacy and they have inspired us to build national botanical gardens, to go garden visiting, and to spend small fortunes on cultivating our own backyard plant collections.

We have self-harmed on plants too, overeating sugar, dosing up on natural narcotics, overindulging in alcohol. An overweight Durban housewife might rue the day that sugar (p.166) was first refined; an inebriate in Adelaide might blame his sorrows on barley (p.104), while some poor patient in a Cincinnati cancer ward could hold tobacco (p.136) responsible for his condition. On the other hand, we can rejoice in a cup of tea (p.26), celebrate with a glass of wine (see Wine Grape, p.202), or simply drink in the scent of the sweet pea (p.118) and the rose (p.162).

GOLDEN CROP
The grains of *Triticum aestivum* have fueled civilizations since the time of ancient Egypt (see Common Wheat, p.190).

FRAGILE EARTH

This is a good time to look at how plants have altered the history of our life on Earth and how they continue to play a pivotal role. We are taking liberties with our plants and, in doing so, with planet Earth. It cannot continue. By consuming the fossil fuels that were made from plants and destroying the plants that make up the rainforests we are, according to the paleoclimatology scientist Professor David Beerling, "undertaking a global uncontrolled experiment guaranteed to alter the climate for future generations. Plants . . . are a major factor in the environmental drama of global warming now as they have been in the recent and more distant past" (*The Emerald Planet*, 2007). The perils of destroying our plants could alter the course of history forever.

FLOWER POWER
The trade in tulip bulbs reached scarcely credible proportions in seventeenth-century Holland, leading to the world's first major financial crash (see p.198).

Agave

Agave spp.

Native range: Southern Mexico and northern South America

Type: Spiny-leaved cactus-like plant

Height: Up to 40 feet (12 m)

+ EDIBLE
+ MEDICINAL
+ **COMMERCIAL**
+ PRACTICAL

Agaves have supplied the raw materials for just about everything from ships' mooring ropes to the high-octane alcohol, tequila. A tequila hangover may not have changed the course of history, but the agave proved to be a life support to one group of Native Americans.

NOBLE AGAVE

The agaves are remarkable plants. They can survive in hot deserts and on the slopes of dry, sunny mountains. They have been consumed for at least 9,000 years, although the agave was not scientifically classified and named until 1753, when Carl Linnaeus borrowed from the Greek word for "noble" and described it as *Agave americana*.

Agave americana was also called the "century plant" because it supposedly took a hundred years to flower. It can actually bloom around three times in a century, the parent plant dying back after flowering and regenerating from offsets or "pups." There are around 136 species of agave, which emerged on the planet around 60 million years ago.

Hard-wearing, sunlight-resistant rugs are made from the agave. In Kenya, Tanzania, and Brazil, the 3-feet (1-m)-long leaf fibers from *Agave sisalana*, or sisal, play a significant economic role. In the early part of the twentieth century, sisal was used to make cords and ropes for everything from tying down ships' cargoes to tying up hop bines. Agaves also possess useful medicinal qualities: although *A. bovicornuta* causes dermatitis and other species are so toxic that they were used to tip poison arrows, some are known for their positive effects, such as helping to relieve inflammation.

In the 1400s, when the Catholic clergy in Spain were persecuting Muslims, Jews, and heretics during the Inquisition, the Aztec civilization, 5,000 miles away in Mexico, was at the zenith of its power. The agave was an essential plant, not least in the case of *A. pacifica*, the fibers of which provided a perfect substitute for cotton clothes. By the early 1500s, the Spanish explorer and soldier, Hernando Cortés, had wrested power from the Aztecs and was bringing booty home to southern Europe. It was a two-way trade: one technology brought into Mexico was the craft of the still. While distilling grains into intoxicating liquor had a long history in Europe, in Latin America the process was unknown—but not for long.

MEXICAN HERITAGE
A *pulque* bar, or *pulquería*, in Tacubaya, Mexico, photographed in 1884 by William Henry Jackson. Sometimes referred to as the national drink of Mexico, tequila is made from the fermented sap of the agave.

Making alcohol from the agave by brewing, however, did have a long tradition. There was *pulque*, made by fermenting the "honeyed water," (*aguamiel*), that collected in the hollowed-out stems of the agave. There was *mescal*, which was made from mashed mescal heads, or *cabeza*—a drink that was doubly distilled and aged in the bottle for up to four years. By the 1620s, Mexicans were cooking the fleshy leaf base of *A. tequilana* in order to convert its raw starches into sugar. Pulping and then fermenting the plant parts in vats caused the sugars to turn into alcohol, creating tequila. For a century and a half the town of Tequila in Jalisco state has been famous for little else.

> **One tequila, two tequila, three tequila, floor.**
>
> *George Carlin, American comedian*

Tequila, with an alcoholic content of up to 50%, was not to everyone's taste. Carlos Herrera, a barman in Tijuana, Mexico, is credited with inventing the margarita cocktail to satisfy a female American barfly who disdained neat tequila.

The agave was central to the lives of one tribe of New Mexican Apache Indians—so central, in fact, that they were known as the *Mescalero*. The tribe ate the mescal agave and turned the leaf fibers into ropes, cords, sandals, and baskets. The dried agave leaves also served as a fuel, while chewed wads of agave, known as "quids," were used in their firearms. The agave even served as a sewing kit: when the needle-sharp tip of the agave was snapped off it came away with a string of vascular tissue that served as thread. The Mescalero barely survived their removal from the ancestral lands under the "reservation period" of the 1870s, but finally settled in south central New Mexico.

ALOE VERA

✦

The unrelated, but similar-looking, *Aloe vera* originated in tropical Africa but was taken to the West Indies around 400 years ago. The sap taken from the fleshy, tapering leaves has extraordinary healing properties, especially in easing dermatitis and eczema, and in the treatment of burns. It has even been used to treat radiation burns.

Onion

Allium cepa

Native range: Uncertain origin

Type: Fleshy bulb

Height: 1 foot (30 cm)

+ **EDIBLE**
+ **MEDICINAL**
+ **COMMERCIAL**
+ PRACTICAL

Onions have changed the course of history? Surely not! Well, it turns out the humble onion has provided science with some tearful revelations, assisted with the classification of the world's plants, and even helped to create the stereotypical image of a Frenchman, with his beret, striped sweater, and string of onions over the handlebars of his bike.

SHEDDING TEARS

Cut into an onion, and a chemical—thiopropanal-S-oxide—is released. It is a substance that reacts on the eye like a pepper spray: we are reduced to tears. Are these onion tears as genuine as the tears of grief? Charles Darwin, after much research, concluded that tears of sadness were no different from those shed by the onion cutter. Tears, he concluded, were a simple device to wet and protect the eye. He was proved wrong when the twentieth-century American biochemist William Frey discovered that while all tears are composed of water, mucus, and salt, tears of sadness contain additional proteins, suggesting that when people cry the body is having an emotional clear-out of stress-related chemicals. Shedding real tears is good for you.

> If the boy have not a woman's gift,
> To rain a shower of commanded tears,
> An onion will do well for such a shift.
>
> *William Shakespeare*, The Taming of the Shrew, *1592*

It was but one of the helpful contributions made to science by the onion. The vegetable may have originated in southwest Asia as long ago as 5,000 years, but it is difficult to really "know your onions." Being one of the oldest of the world's vegetables (the pea, the lettuce, and the onion's cousin, the leek, are close contenders), it seems to have spread through the world, causing confusion in its wake.

The onion was a staple part of the diet in Greek and Roman times, with the Romans naming it *unio*, a word that suggests a singular, pearl-like quality, perhaps a reference to the translucent appearance of the peeled onion. Earlier in history, Egyptian slaves building the Great Pyramid of Cheops were fed on onions, garlic, and leeks; one Egyptian mummy was laid to rest holding an onion and there have even been suggestions of a strange cult devoted to the onion.

Both onion and garlic (*A. sativum*) have traditionally possessed mystical qualities. If garlic could ward off vampires, an onion (carried on the left-hand side) kept disease at bay. Burning an onion on a fire was a charm against bad luck, while just dreaming of an onion brought good fortune. Placing an onion under the pillow on St. Thomas' Eve (December 20) presented the sleeper with a vision of his future wife.

ALL IN THE NAME

The onion acquired as many names as there were different varieties: there were English "jibbles" and French *ciboule*, German *Zwiebel*, and Sanskrit *ushna*. It was a relief when Carl Linnaeus came along to sort it all out.

Linnaeus was born in a turf-roofed timber cabin at Råshult near Lake Möckeln, Sweden, in 1707. He was the eldest child of the parish priest and fanciful gardener, Nils Ingemarsson Linnaeus. Nils once created a curious raised bed in his garden to represent the family dining table, using shrubs to portray the dinner guests at supper. Carl was as intrigued by this horticultural oddity as he was by the natural world. Nils encouraged his son, teaching him the correct plant names and giving the child a plot of his own to cultivate. The garden was a good educator and Carl became a committed naturalist and gardener.

He left home to study medicine at his father's old university in Uppsala at a time when a flood of new plants was reaching Europe from overseas, brought home by adventurous Dutch, French, and English mariners from newly explored corners of the globe. In the ensuing horticultural confusion, some plants acquired several names, making the task of systematically giving them each a single scientific name something of a nightmare. Linnaeus went on to fix the calibration for the garden thermometer (it had been devised by Anders Celsius with the boiling point set at zero, until Linnaeus persuaded the inventor to reverse the calibration). He mastered the craft of growing bananas in the Netherlands and he set the standards for future botanical gardens

GARLIC CHARM
A member of the same family (Alliaceae) as the onion, almost all parts of the garlic plant can be used in cooking, including the leaves and flowers.

ONION JOHNNIES
✦
In northwest Brittany, France, when the onion crop was in, young Breton men would borrow the family bike and, carrying as many strings of onions as they could hang on the handlebars, ride down to the fishing ports of Saint-Brieuc and Tréguier. They were departing on the *journeé d'Albion*, the trip to England to sell early onions door-to-door to English housewives. The Onion Johnnies, as they became known, wore the traditional Breton berets and sweaters just as their forefathers had done before them. It is a practice that has all but died out, although the stereotype of the Frenchman persists to this day.

such as the Eden Project in Cornwall, England. But above all, he cleared up the confusion with the onion and created a system for classifying every living plant and animal.

At Uppsala, Linnaeus befriended a fellow student, Peter Artedi who shared his fascination with the natural world. Together the two young men hatched the ambitious plan of classifying all of God's plants and creatures. They divided the task of classifying the animal and plant kingdoms between them and swore that whoever finished first would come to the aid of his friend. When, in 1735, Artedi drowned after falling into an Amsterdam canal, Linnaeus undertook the whole task himself. When he died in 1778, possibly due to overwork, he had successfully created a system that has lasted to the present day.

> It is the genus that gives the character, and not the characters that make the genus.
>
> *Carl Linnaeus (1707–1778)*

Up until then, plants like the onion went by a variety of vernacular names and several, sometimes conflicting, Latin names. The Greek physician, Dioscorides, had diligently named some 500 plants in his *De Materia Medica* around the time of Christ, but it would be another thousand years before his work was disseminated, first among Arab scholars and then in the Christian world. But Linnaeus, in his two-volume *Species Plantarum* (1753), classified all the 5,900 known plants, each with its own two-word name in Latin. By the 1700s, botanists and naturalists agreed that different plants could be grouped in the same families: the onions, leeks, and garlic in the lily or Liliceae family; beans, peas, and sweet peas in the legume or Leguminosae family; and corn (maize) and bamboo in the grass (Poaceae) family.

These plant families could be subdivided into distinct groups, or genera, and again into different species, and again into subspecies. After throwing out or shortening some of the old Latin names, Linnaeus used the genus for the first name (as with *Pisum*) and the species for a second name

HEALTHY BALANCE
The *Tacuinum Sanitatis* (1531) was a guide to health that included a summary of the hazards and benefits of various plants and foodstuffs. The print below, which featured in the original publication, shows farm laborers picking garlic.

(as with *P. sativum*, or the garden pea). The convention is to use a capital letter for the genus (*Pisum*), the lower case for the species (*sativum*), abbreviating it when it was repeated (*P. sativum*) and adding a deferential "L" if it had been published by Linnaeus himself, as with *P. sativum L*. Additional varieties, cultivars (plants that are cultivated for particular traits), or subspecies were noted with an additional name: *P. sativum* "Kelvedon Wonder," for example.

A degree of order was brought to the rather confused world of the onion when Linnaeus began to divide the genus *Allium* into various species, such as *A. porrum* (leek), *A. schoenoprasum* (chive), *A. sativum* (garlic), and *A. fistulosum* (Welsh onion). He classified the genus and species of plants within families according to the number of stamens and stigmas they have—an approach known as a "sexual system" of classification. One of his contemporaries was Johann Siegesbeck, a St. Petersburg academic after whom Linnaeus named the *Siegesbeckia orientalis* plant. When Linnaeus published his findings, Siegesbeck denounced his work as "lewd." How, he ranted, could onions be up to such vegetative immorality? Even worse, how could young people be taught "so licentious a method" of classification? Despite its "loathsome harlotry," Linnaeus' system was adopted universally and the Swedish naturalist became a household name.

Linnaeus was a modest man and stipulated for his funeral arrangements: "Entertain nobody . . . and accept no condolences." But when he died in January 1778, his instructions were ignored. Even the King of Sweden came to pay his respects at the funeral of the man who gave a name to the onion, and to every other plant in the world.

OLD AS ONIONS?

✦

The leek, *Allium porrum*, may be older than the onion. It was listed as an ingredient in one of the world's oldest recipes, a lamb and leek stew inscribed on a 4,000-year-old Babylonian tablet. The Greeks called it *prasa*, the Arabs *kurrats*, and the Romans, who brought the leek into northern Europe, *porrum*. The Celtic Welsh, who did their best to resist the invading Romans, called it *cenhinen* and adopted the leek as their national plant. The reason for this is something of a mystery, although, given their love of song and oration, it may have been associated with the leek's throat-soothing, mucilaginous qualities. Another legend is that soldiers fixed leeks to their hats before a battle so that they could identify one another.

Pineapple

Ananas comosus

Native range: Tropical South America

Type: Tropical fruiting plant

Height: 5 feet (1.5 m)

+ **EDIBLE**
+ MEDICINAL
+ **COMMERCIAL**
+ PRACTICAL

ROYAL GIFT
This painting from 1675, by the Dutch artist Hendrick Danckerts, shows King Charles II being presented with a pineapple by the royal gardener John Rose.

Take a train and spy on the gardens of any northern European city suburb. Where once there were neat rectangles of grass and a row or two of vegetables, there now stand row upon row of plastic conservatories, boiling in the sun and filled with exotics plants. In an exercise of gigantically unsustainable proportions, thousands of miles of extruded plastic are produced each year to satisfy the demand. The one plant that could be held responsible for starting the conservatory craze is the king of fruits: the pineapple.

GARDENER'S DELIGHT

Most jobbing gardeners like to please their masters, to produce a prize-winning chrysanthemum for the annual horticultural show, or present the household with some exotic vegetable dish. None did a better job than John Rose, gardener to the English King Charles II (1630–1685). In 1675, Rose, in his frock coat and tumbling wig, was pictured by the court painter Hendrick Danckerts kneeling on one stockinged knee before his king. He is proffering his master a curious, knobbly fruit, the like of which had scarcely been seen in Europe before. The dandy king, with one of his favorite namesake spaniels barking at his feet, looks a little sour-faced at the offering. This was, nevertheless, something very special: an early, homegrown pineapple.

"Discovered" by the Spanish when they landed in the Americas, the pineapple proved as much a delight to the invaders as it had done to the indigenous people. Since the fruit is formed from a conglomeration of a hundred or so individual flowers that coalesce into one giant sugary fruit, it is as packed with flavor as it is with vitamins A and C. Propagated by planting its sprightly green crown, or striking its side shoots, or slips, in compost, the pineapple grows easily in a tropical climate. The Spanish, who brought it home to Europe, could just about find sufficient heat to grow it. It was to flourish in pineapple plantations in Northern Africa and South Africa, and eventually Malaysia and Australia; and one of the world's most productive pineapple regions turned out to be Hawaii. However, in the dour, cold northern European countries, the pineapple was a problem. Presented with the challenge of domesticating the "pine," Europe's gardeners eventually set to producing single fruits in wooden tabernacles warmed by stoves on hot beds of the best horse manure.

The garden writer John Evelyn had outlined his method of harnessing natural energy when he delivered his "Philosophical Discourse on Earth" to the Royal Society—the organization established by Charles II to promote science and the arts. Evelyn explained how forcing pits, deep enough for a man to stand in, could be filled with steaming dung. Plants grown in portable wooden trays over the pits positively thrived with this natural bottom heat. (The idea was not new; in the 1000s, celebrated Muslim gardeners such as Ibn Bassal had advocated using the manure of corn-fed stallions rather than that of some tired pack horse grazed on poor hay, and advised that laborers be encouraged to urinate on the compost to help matters along.)

WARDIAN CASE

✦

Shipping home exotic plants from the Americas in the early days was a hit and miss affair. One solution came from Nathaniel Bagshaw Ward (1791–1868), who invented what he hoped would be a moth cage. Consisting of a sealed glass container set in a foldable, wooden frame, the device—when filled with the appropriate plants—was designed to improve the study of moths, a particular fascination for the Victorians. But the Wardian case proved to be a self-contained, self-sustaining little plant world: the plants transpired at night and their condensation watered the soil by day. Nathaniel's cases were soon being transported throughout the world and used to bring exotic plants and ferns back home from the New World where they could be studied and, wherever possible, propagated for commercial gain.

MULTIPLE FRUIT
Despite appearances, the pineapple is in fact a collection of individual fruits pressed together to form a whole. They are arranged helically, with each row running diagonally along the shape of a spiral.

THE GREENHOUSE EFFECT

The early pineapple "stoves," as these horticultural hothouses were known, sparked a passion for special houses to shelter other tender greens including citrus fruit, myrtles, bay trees, and pomegranates. In 1705, the English Queen Anne commissioned a vast structure to be built at Kensington Palace by Nicholas Hawksmoor. It was dubbed a "green house," to distinguish it from Evelyn's design, and worked to "conserve" the tender exotics from the winter's chill. Evelyn's "conservatory" also inspired a number of other famous horticultural architects, Sir Christopher Wren, James Wyatt, and John Vanbrugh among them, to try their hands at glass palaces and "pine house" for the aristocracy. This mania for glasshouses was spurred on as nations competed to erect the most prestigious "winter garden." In 1847, the 295-foot (90-m)-long Jardin d'Hiver on the Champs Elysées in Paris rose up almost three stories high, while a vine house at Buffalo, New York, was built large enough to house more than 200 vines in its 689-foot (210-m) length.

He is the very pineapple of politeness.

Richard Brinsley Sheridan, The Rivals, *1775*

The glasshouse genius of the time, or the man who happened to be in the right place at the right, technological time, was a farmer's boy from Bedfordshire, England: Joseph Paxton. He knew that ventilation was critical; that the reflective quality of whitewashed walls helped raise the temperature inside; and that a glass roof set at a precise slope of 52 degrees would maximize the effects of the sun, which, at midday, struck the glass exactly at right angles. The choice of the glass was critical too. Patenting the first curved iron glazing bars, the Victorian gardener and writer John Loudon had declared that "economy, as to the quality of glass" was self-defeating and resulted in "the sickly pale etiolated appearance of plants more painful than agreeable to the eye of any who take an interest in the vegetable kingdom." Broad or cylinder glass (blown into a cylinder and then opened out flat to be cut into sheets) and plate glass (molten glass poured out onto a casting table and then laboriously polished smooth) were too expensive for horticultural use. The solution was crown glass, which was spun into a large disc and then cut into squares and diamonds.

GREAT GREENHOUSE
The transept of the Crystal Palace, London, during the Great Exhibition. The palace covered an area of 990,000 square feet (92,000 sq m) and accommodated 15,000 visitors during the inaugural exhibition.

Combining these elements with an invention of his own—a cast-iron glazing bar with a rainwater channel outside and a condensation channel inside (he based his design on the leaf of a giant water lily)—Joseph Paxton built his celebrated Crystal Palace in London in 1851. The Palace opened the floodgates on a frenzy of greenhouse building for the common man. There were double-span cucumber houses and meloneries, modest plant preservers, "lawn" conservatories that were "invaluable for the use of Amateurs in the forwarding of . . . various seeds" as the horticultural trader William Cooper's catalog promised, pit frames, lean-to green-houses, and lean-to forcing houses calculated to "convince all practical minds of the importance and utility of this class of House for Gentlemen, Nurserymen, Market Gardeners, and, in fact, all those who require a cheap, strong House for Forcing, or growing Cucumbers, Tomatoes, Melons, &c, &c." Thanks to the pineapple stove, the popularity of the conservatory and greenhouse grew. The nineteenth-century garden writer James Shirley Hibberd regarded the greenhouse as a thing of beauty: "A houseful of melons or cucumbers, showing a rich screen of foliage between the eye and the sun, and the fruits hanging below it, as they would natu-rally if the plants were twining among the trees of their native soils, is one of the finest sights in the whole range of horticultural exhibitions."

SEED CONTROL

Seeds in a pineapple are considered detrimental to the fruit's quality. In Hawaii, where pineapples are an important export crop, measures are in place to restrict pollination, including a ban on bringing humming-birds into the country.

In time, the cast iron gave way to timber and then, thanks to a New York immigrant, Leo Baekeland, to plastic. Working on the science of polymers (from the Greek *polus*, "many," and *meros*, "parts"), Baekeland had developed his first plastics in 1907. Eventually he created a new and unpronounceable polymer: polyoxybenzylmethylenglycolanhydride. It was a hard, black plastic that could be shaped in a mold, and he called it Bakelite. He used to tell journalists that he chose the field of polymers in order to make money, although it did not make him happy: he died in a New York sanatorium in 1944 after living as a recluse, living on nothing but tinned food. In a tragic twist of fate, his grandson is thought to have suffocated himself with a plastic bag in 1981, having murdered his own mother. But Bakelite paved the way for a plethora of plastics, including polypropylene (separately "invented" nine times, the legal patents were finally awarded to two American scientists working for Phillips Petroleum in Bartlesville, Oklahoma) and polyvinyl chloride (PVC). The PVC summerhouse would eventually grace (or deface, depending on taste) hundreds of thousands of homes across the world. The humble pineapple stove has a lot to answer for.

FRUIT IN A CAN

✦

Sales of pineapples boomed after a Mr. Dole of Hawaii mastered the craft of canning the fruit. Mean-while, pineapple juice was taken for a range of folk remedies ranging from ridding the body of intestinal worms, easing the pain of labor, fractured bones, hemorrhoids, and sore throats.

Bamboo
Tribe: Bambuseae

Native range: Most hot, tropical regions, especially East Asia

Type: Woody evergreen grass

Height: Up to 100 feet (30 m)

✦ EDIBLE
✦ **MEDICINAL**
✦ **COMMERCIAL**
✦ **PRACTICAL**

O ne of the fastest-growing plants on the planet, bamboo's influence has been widely felt. As well as being used in construction, it has also played an important role in Asian arts, including in ink drawing and painting.

THE GENTLEMAN

Aside from rice, no other plant has played such an important role in the history of China and the East as the bamboo. The spear-like blades grow into edible shoots, and bamboo has been used for everything from the world's first wheelbarrow to airplane models, but the bamboo was also responsible for creating some of the most distinctive art on the planet. If William Wordsworth's "host of golden daffodils" changed forever the literary form of the poem in the nineteenth century, bamboos produced some of the most striking paintings that would influence artists such as the Impressionist Claude Monet (1840–1926).

So useful was the bamboo to Chinese society it even demonstrated the model behavior of the gentleman. A gentleman, wrote Bai Juyi (772–846), should always be as upright as the bamboo and equally as strong. And, just as the bamboo culm was hollow, so should the perfect gentleman keep his mind open and never entertain prejudice or secret thoughts.

There are over 1,400 species in the world. While they can adapt to different environments, thriving at high altitudes and low plains, they prefer to avoid alkaline soils, dry desert conditions, and marshlands.

As far back as 2,000 years, bamboo groves were providing a healthy income for foresters. Since then, there has been no area of life in China in which the bamboo failed to figure. Official records in ancient China were inscribed on strips of bamboo, *jian*— records that continued to be kept for some time after

Ascending the winding path through bamboo groves brings the coolness of the hall. Your slanting shadow and whistling sound linger long with meaning.

Wang An-shi (1021–1086)

the invention of silk books. It was just as well: modern scholars are still able to read and interpret their prehistory from the *jian* that have been unearthed by archaeologists.

Buddhism arrived in China in the first century CE. Its followers were forbidden to commit any acts of cruelty to their fellow creatures, which ruled out meat, fish, and eggs from their diet. The tender bamboo shoot, at least, was permitted. One Buddhist monk, Zan Ning,

in the tenth century naturally devoted his "Manual of the Bamboo Shoot," *Sun Pu*, to detailed descriptions and recipes for 98 different shoots. When the legendary "Yellow Emperor," Huang Ti, ordered his court musician Ling Lun to set a standard for Chinese music, Ling turned to the reliable bamboo: he cut 12 bamboo pipes to different lengths to accurately reproduce the six female and six male voice notes. There was no area of life into which the bamboo did not intrude. This Victorian commentator was astonished by the impact of the plant on everyday Chinese life in the nineteenth century. "The bamboos of the Celestial Empire are more valuable than her mines, and, next to rice and silk, yield the greatest revenue." He went on to describe its many uses including "waterproof coat and hat, each wrought out of leaves of bamboo . . . agricultural implements . . . the fishing net, baskets of diverse shapes, the paper and pens, the grain-measures, the wine-cups, water-ladles, the chopsticks, and finally the tobacco-pipes, are all of bamboo."

TEA FOR TWO?

Bamboo was an essential element in the ritual of the tea ceremony (see Tea, p.26). Tea, so it was said, had arrived after Bodhidharma—the founder of Zen Buddhism—found himself nodding off while he was trying to meditate. In frustration, the sage tore off his very eyelids, casting the offending body parts onto the floor, where they were transformed into the eye-shaped leaves of the tea plant. The tea ceremonies that evolved subsequently demanded the stirring of powdered tea, *matcha*, with a whisk composed of a bamboo culm, three quarters of an inch (2 cm) in diameter, which was split into no less than 80 fine prongs. The tea ladle, too, was made from bamboo.

ARTIST-IN-LAW

✦

One of the most famous practitioners of *sumi-e* art was the polymath Su Tung-p'o, who lived from 1037 to 1101. As a city planner, he created the largest bamboo water systems ever built at Hangchow (1089) and Canton (1096). One day, Su Tung-p'o was acting as a magistrate in a case against a peasant debtor. Taking pity on the poor man, Su Tung-p'o took up his brush and paper and dashed off a sketch of a bamboo, which he presented to the man to be sold to repay his debts.

Tea drinking in Japan was elevated into an art form by Rikyu (1522–1591), who was befriended (and unfortunately later condemned to death) by his emperor, Hideyoshi. For Rikyu, the very "art of being in the world" revolved around the 10 x 10-foot (3 x 3-m) bamboo tea room (*chashitsu*), large enough to seat five people. While tea was washed and arranged in the side room, the *mizuya*, the guests waited in the bamboo *machiai*, before they were invited to walk the tea garden path, the *roji*, and finally, with great respect and ceremony, enter the tea room itself.

As Confucius (551–479 BCE) put it: "People become thin without meat. But without bamboo they become vulgar." It was to be in the arts, above all, that the slender bamboo triumphed.

China has the longest continuous history of art in the world. Painting and calligraphy, which are closely allied, have developed for more than 2,000 years. Central to it is a simple, soft bamboo brush, a pot of black ink made from pine soot, and, after a period of deep meditation, the execution of the work in minutes, or even seconds, without any corrections or delays.

The style of painting most closely associated with the bamboo was *sumi-e*—a form of ink and wash painting—not least because the act of painting so closely mirrored the tremulous *chi* of the trembling bamboo leaf. The invention of the bamboo brush was attributed to a military general, Meng Tian, who around 221–209 BCE produced his brush (*pi*) composed of *chu*, the bamboo, and *yu*, the stylus or brush. If brush it was, the hairs might be taken from any number of animals including deer, goat, sheep, sable, wolf, fox, or rabbit or, for infinitesimally fine detail, the whiskers of a mouse. The *sumi-e* artist, working with paper so fragile it easily tore, took up his bamboo brush and "fenced" with the ink. This was required to be "the color of the heart," black. The artist's aspiration was not to represent his subject, but to eliminate the inessentials; to capture the moment of seeing with only a few minimalistic brushstrokes.

BAMBOO AND THE ARTS

China's art greatly influenced that of its neighbors, Japan, Korea, and Tibet, as well as the regions of Manchuria, central Asia, and also more distant Islamic nations. But it was through Japan, busily opening its borders during the mid-1800s, that it came to influence one of the best-known art movements of the nineteenth century: Impressionism.

The movement's greatest exponent was Claude Monet, the big, bluff, bearded artist who purchased a second house in the neighborhood of Giverny because it had a fine vegetable garden. He insisted on visiting each day to select the vegetables that would be picked the following morning and served with his supper at the end of his hard day working from dusk until dawn.

Before he made the big time and could command decent prices for his many paintings of the famous Japanese-style bridge in his garden at Giverny, he had exhibited with Camille Pissarro in Paris in 1874. One art critic, Louis Leroy, sneered at Monet's *Impression, soleil levant*: "I knew it must be something like that. As I'm impressed, there must be some impression somewhere." The barbed comment backfired and the new art movement, characterized by fresh light, visible brushstrokes, and unconventional subject matter, and influenced by the open air and the emerging art of photography, became known as Impressionism.

Artists like Edward Degas and Monet had been captivated by the work of Japanese artists. Monet collected Japanese woodcuts to learn from their compositions, and at the second Impressionist exhibition he showed *La Japonaise*. It was a portrait of his wife, dressed in an outrageous red gown embroidered with a fierce samurai warrior, and surrounded with round paper and bamboo fans. Although he would later dismiss the work as rubbish, it made Monet a very acceptable 2,000 francs.

NATURAL SCAFFOLDING
As well as providing a decorative finish, bamboo is also used in construction, including for scaffolding.

VERSATILE BAMBOO

✦

The list of uses to which bamboo has been put is extraordinary: it includes windmills, zithers, arrows, baskets, fuel, and chopsticks (of course), but also scaffolding for skyscrapers, needles for record players, and, in the form of bamboo ash, as a jewelry polish and a material used in the manufacture of batteries. Bamboo was made into delicate scales, electric light filaments, coffins, bicycles, paper, food, mats, used as an exterior cladding for airplanes and as a poison. It was a medicine for asthmatics, a salve for the hair and skin, used for chairs, stools, and beds, as nail protectors, toys, yurts, waxes, beehives, guttering, beer, acupuncture needles, umbrellas, houses, pavilions, and as an aphrodisiac. In wartime, it was bamboo, not steel, that provided the reinforcing agent in concrete, the canes adding three to four times the carrying capacity.

Wild Cabbage
Brassica oleracea

Native range: Mediterranean and Adriatic coasts; elsewhere as an escape

Type: Biennial or perennial with woody stem and large leaves

Height: 3 feet (90 cm)

+ *EDIBLE*
+ MEDICINAL
+ COMMERCIAL
+ *PRACTICAL*

Where would any gardener be without their cabbage patch? Introduced by Celtic gardeners 2,500 years ago, the cabbage spawned generations of vegetable growers from the Roman emperor Diocletian to U.S. First Ladies Eleanor Roosevelt and Michelle Obama. It also inspired the greatest revolution in food preservation the world has ever known.

FROZEN FRESH

In the frozen wastes of Labrador, northern Canada, in the early 1900s, a fur trapper was breaking the ice in some barrels of salt water to take out a frozen cabbage. Clarence Birdseye, or Bob, as he preferred to be called, had developed the peculiar practice of freezing food in a bid to please his wife, Eleanor, who in their frozen isolation, desperately missed her fresh vegetables. Bob Birdseye, as we shall see, was to make a fortune out of his idea.

His cabbages had traveled a long way through history to reach Labrador. The wild ancestor of this bundle of crunchy green leaves had evolved in middle Europe and the Mediterranean among Celtic people. The Greeks knew their *karambai* and the Romans had two names for it: *caulis* and *brassica*. Perhaps the Roman Empire might have lasted longer than it did, had Emperor Diocletian remained at his post in Rome instead of taking early retirement to grow cabbages at his palace at Spoleto (now Split) on the Dalmatian coast. "Could you but see the vegetables I have raised!" he enthused to a friend as the Empire descended into civil war.

It was the Romans who gave us the word "vegetable," from *vegere*, which means to grow, to animate, or to enliven. But why was cabbage so popular? Simply because, from a handful of insignificant-looking black seeds, edible giants could be grown. In 2000, Barb Everingham of Wasilla, Alaska, grew a record-breaking 105-pound (47.9 kg) cabbage. It was not too far off the sheep-sized, world-record-breaking 124-pound (56.24 kg) cabbage grown by Bernard Lavery at Llanharry in South Wales in 1989.

The package of Vandergaw Cabbage you sent me did much better than the Large Late Flat Dutch.

Testimonial from a Burpee seed catalog (1888)

DIGGING FOR VICTORY

It was quantity rather than size that prompted the King of England, George V, to have the flowerbeds in front of Buckingham Palace in London dug up and replanted with cabbages and potatoes during World War I. It was all part of the government drive, "Every Man a Gardener." The number of allotments was increased from 600,000 to 1.5 million, while the Church of England gave special dispensation for its congregation to work their cabbage patches on Sundays—up until then it had been fine to fight, but not to work on the Lord's day.

By the end of the war, the nation was growing a startling two million tons of fresh vegetables, and many soldiers returned to nurse their wounds and cultivate cabbage beds of their own. The recuperative value of vegetable gardening helped many deal with the nightmares of their recent experiences at the front.

In America in World War II, the U.S. Agriculture Department campaigned against any move to "plow up the parks and the lawns to grow vegetables." National food surpluses were at an all-time high and fertilizer nitrogen was more profitably turned into explosives than cabbage boosters. But when the Burpee

POLYMORPHS

✦

A polymorphic plant, such as the cabbage, is one that, chameleon-like, can evolve different forms. The wild cabbage produced kales, heading cabbages, kohlrabi, Brussels sprouts, oilseed rape, broccoli, and cauliflower. But leave any of these growing together for long enough and they will revert to their wild cabbage cousin. Each variety became a different regional favorite: Brussels sprouts, for example, were first recorded in Belgium around 1750, while broccoli was always an Italian favorite (in 1724 it was known as "Italian asparagus"), and it was Italian migrants who took their beloved broccoli to America.

Victory Garden Seed Packet went on sale in 1942, the seed trade trebled and around four million Americans joined the grow-your-own-vegetable brigade. In 1943, canned food was rationed and the then First Lady Eleanor Roosevelt had some of the White House lawns dug up and planted with carrots, beans, tomatoes, and cabbages. The vegetable beds disappeared under the sward for the next 60 years until Michelle Obama's husband took up the presidency and ordered the restoration of the vegetable beds.

In the UK too, the government campaigned for people to cultivate their cabbages. "Let Dig For Victory be the matter for everyone with a garden or allotment," declared the Agricultural Minister, as Eleanour Sinclair Rohde, the gardening author largely responsible for promoting the herb garden as we know it today, settled down to write her *Wartime Vegetable Garden* guide. German U-boats were targeting merchant ships bringing food to Britain, prompting civil servant A. J. Simons to tell readers of his *Vegetable Grower's Handbook*: "We shall want every bit of Greenstuff the Country can produce. In 1939 this country imported 8,500,000 tons of food from overseas. In 1942 we imported only 1,300,00 tons. No wonder the Government urges us to grow more food at home."

Helping the war effort were "Chase Continuous Cloches," which promised to "double your Vegetable output without increase of space, save you weeks of growing time, [and] provide fresh food the year round." They also marketed a guidebook, *Cloches v. Hitler*, for sixpence. The Ministry organized Dig for Victory exhibitions, set up demonstration vegetable plots, and encouraged every school in the country to create its own vegetable patch. Out of these cabbage-patch pupils came not only a flow of fresh vegetables, but a new, postwar generation of vegetable gardeners. There was another advantage of such high wartime cabbage consumption, as the writer George Orwell noted at the time: "Most people

HOMEGROWN
A woman works her vegetable field in Pie Town, New Mexico, during World War II. The cabbage proved valuable to the U.S. war effort, just as it was to the British.

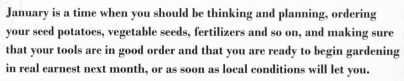

January is a time when you should be thinking and planning, ordering your seed potatoes, vegetable seeds, fertilizers and so on, and making sure that your tools are in good order and that you are ready to begin gardening in real earnest next month, or as soon as local conditions will let you.

"Dig for Victory" leaflet, Ministry of Agriculture, January 1945

are better fed than they used to be. There are less fat people." The nation was in rude health thanks in part to the cabbage.

They were soon to have better access to fresh vegetables than they had ever had before. Back in the early 1900s, Bob and Eleanor Birdseye lived with their son Kellogg in a cabin 250 miles (400 km) away from the nearest store or doctor. They moved there after Bob, born in 1886, had dropped out of his studies at Amherst College, Massachusetts, because his family could not afford the fees. For a brief period he took a job with the U.S. Department of Agriculture, but, always the risk-taker, he persuaded Eleanor that there was a better living to be had from fur trapping.

THE BIG BREAK

Birdseye learned what the native North Canadians already knew: that meat tasted better if it was frozen fast. Fish, rabbit, and duck, naturally frozen outdoors in Arctic temperatures as low as −58°F (−50°C), kept its flavor. Bob decided to experiment with "fresh" cabbage stored in barrels of salt water. As he would say later: "The Eskimos had used [these methods] for centuries. What I accomplished . . . was merely to make packaged frozen food available to the public."

In 1917, the family returned to the United States, where Bob Birdseye went bust trying to "reproduce the Labrador winters" in an old ice-cream factory in New Jersey, with ice blocks, brine, and an electric fan. The family moved to Gloucester, Massachusetts, where they continued experimenting with quick-freezing meat, fish, and vegetables. Bob Birdseye built a mobile freezer, mounting it on a truck and driving it out into the fields so he could freeze the vegetables as they were picked.

By chance, Marjorie Merriweather Post, the daughter of a food-processing company owner, chanced to sample some of Birdseye's frozen goose. Three years later, she bought not only the goose, but the family firm, and in 1930 changed the name to Birds Eye. Curiously, it was not cabbages that became the prime frozen food, but peas.

Tea

Camellia sinensis

Native range: China, Japan, India, and as far north as the Black Sea coasts of Russia

Type: Small tree that can live for more than 50 years

Height: 5 feet (1.5 m) when cultivated

+ **EDIBLE**
+ MEDICINAL
+ **COMMERCIAL**
+ PRACTICAL

While some plants merely tweak the course of history, others grab it by the throat and practically hijack it. *Camellia sinensis*, the tea plant, is such a one. The contents of the teapot almost destroyed Chinese culture, helped bring about America's Bill of Independence, and enslaved hundreds of thousands of people in southeast Asia. Did tea change history? Most certainly.

THE GREAT CALMER

The "char lady," with her offer of a "nice cup of tea," was a dependable figure, dispensing tea to worn-out wardens and exhausted fire-fighters after another night of the London Blitz. On the other side of the world, geisha girls knelt behind their bamboo screens as they prepared ceremonial servings of tea for departing army officers. On board a troop ship in a north Australian harbor, meanwhile, soldiers, apprehensive about the conflict ahead, cupped their hands around tin mugs of chai.

Then as now, there was nothing to match the calming qualities of the concoction produced by steeping the dried leaves of an Asian bush in hot water. The moralist and lexicographer Dr. Samuel Johnson spoke up for tea way back in 1757 in his *Literary Magazine*, describing an acquaintance "who for twenty years diluted his meals with only the infusion of this fascinating plant . . . who with tea amuses the evening, with tea solaces the midnight, and with tea welcomes the morning." Johnson could not have guessed that within 16 years some of his American cousins would create such a storm in a teacup from this "fascinating plant" that it would create a new nation of confirmed coffee drinkers.

Tea has been made from the leaves of a small tree that has grown wild from India to China for over 4,500 years; at least according to legend. The emperor Shen Nung is said to have discovered the potion in 2737 BCE.

Camellia sinensis is a plain plant. The *Camellia* genus, named in honor of a seventeenth-century Jesuit botanist, Camellius, includes some gorgeous garden favorites, but the pale white flowers, touched with a blush of pink, of *C. sinensis* will break no hearts. However, as the Chinese were the first to find, placing the dried green leaves of the plant in hot water produced a strangely satisfying and calming beverage. The Chinese were generous enough to introduce tea to Japan via Korea around 800 CE and to the English in 1657. To encourage plenty of fresh leaf growth, the tea tree was pruned regularly, and shaped into a low bush to make picking easier. Pickers, wearing their wicker picking baskets like rucksacks on their backs, would nip the bud and two terminal leaves from the end of each shoot for premium tea, or, where the plantation manager looked for quantity over quality, the three terminal leaves. This delicate act, nipping thumb and finger together to pluck the growing tip and hold it cushioned in the soft palm of the hand, has stalled efforts to mechanize the tea-picking process almost as much as the low wages paid to tea pickers: tea would be grown in several

FIELDS OF TEA
Thanks largely to the huge amount of land available to it, China has surpassed India as the largest producer of tea in the world.

TASTEFUL RULER
Shennong, the legendary farmer-emperor, tastes herbs to check their quality. He is credited with introducing the principles of agriculture to ancient China.

I view tea drinking as a destroyer of health, an enfeebler of the frame, an engenderer of effeminacy and laziness, a debaucher of youth and a maker of misery for old age.

William Cobbett, Cottage Economy, *1821*

more developed countries around the world, but for the tea pickers' dexterity and their poor pay.

When full, the pickers' baskets were delivered to the on-site processing factory where the green leaves were withered, rolled, fermented, dried, and graded according to the type of tea produced. The traditional favorite in the Far East, green tea, was produced by heating the leaf to arrest the natural blackening that occurred during fermentation. Black tea, which the West preferred, was graded according to quality, ranging from "broken orange pekoe" to "orange pekoe" and "souchong."

CHINA TEA

CEREMONIAL BREW
A nineteenth-century illustration depicting a tea ceremony. In China, offering someone tea serves multiple social functions, including showing respect to an elder, offering an apology, and as a way of giving thanks on a wedding day.

During the eighteenth and nineteenth centuries, Europe turned its collective back on small beers, cheap ale, and well water in order to drink more tea. And the more they drank, the more they wanted, for tea contained small amounts of the stimulant caffeine. William Cobbett railed against it. "It is, in fact, a weaker kind of laudanum, which enlivens for the moment and weakens after." Women, he said, spent the best part of a month per year on the whole "tea-tackle" business, leaving the laborer's

hildren "with dirty linen and holes in the heels of their stockings." Cobbett's objection notwithstanding, tea was flowing freely down the throats of Europeans, rich and poor, by the mid-1700s.

It was then that Britain's East India Company, having secured for itself the vital Indian trading ports of Madras, Bombay, and Calcutta, routed the rival French East India Company in southern India. Having wrested control of

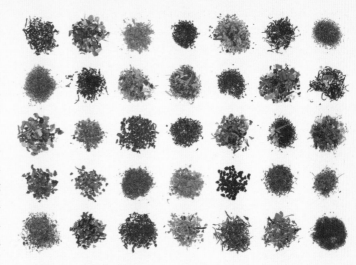

the wealthy northeastern province of India from its Bengali leaders in 1757, the Company became, with strong competition from the French, the leading trader in India for the next century. Along with their cargoes of timber, silk, china, and porcelain, they shipped home China tea.

It was, however, a one-sided business. China was a self-sufficient civilization that barely acknowledged the West and certainly had no need to trade commodities, technologies, or ideas with its remote Western neighbors. Yet the nation was also the largest grower and supplier of the world's tea. With its voracious home market for green tea, China was not interested in exporting the plant, nor in the promise of paper currency, initially offered as payment by the Western tea merchants. China did, however, need valuable metals such as copper, silver, and gold, and the Western tea traders were forced to exchange precious, solid metals when they would much rather have paid in cash. It left them seething with frustration. Trade delegations were regularly dispatched from the West to try to persuade the ruling mandarins to open up their borders. They usually returned empty-handed after being reminded by their hosts that most major technical advances—the seed drill, the metal plow, printing, and dynamite—had been discovered by Chinese engineers several centuries before their "invention" in the West. Only then did someone come up with the bright idea of exchanging tea for opium (see Opium Poppy, p.148).

TEAPOTS

✦

Most nations make tea in a kettle, but the British developed a passion for serving tea from a china pot. The trouble was, in the late 1600s, the quality of local ceramics was not up to the job of holding near-boiling water. The solution arrived with China tea. Porcelain, invented and perfected in China 1,500 years before Europeans mastered the craft, was carried as a ballast load to offset the lightweight cargo of tea. The China teapot and tea service were soon as popular as China tea itself.

THE TEA-JACKERS

In the eighteenth century, the North Americans enjoyed their tea as much as anyone. Yet today Canadians drink almost four times as much tea as their coffee-drinking neighbors in the U.S. In fact, patriotic Americans have consumed less tea than their neighbors for over 200 years, with the historical roots of this story dating back to one December day in 1773, when the tidal reaches of the Charles River in Boston, Massachusetts, suddenly darkened with the spreading stain of tea leaves. It seemed that a group of Mohawk Indians had clambered aboard three tea ships moored in the dock, systematically slit open the entire cargo of tea, and dumped it in the river.

The tea-jackers were not Indians, but white protesters in costume. They were protesting at plans by their self-styled rulers, the British, to impose a tax on goods exported to America, specifically tea. Britain had dropped tea taxes at home in an attempt to put the lucrative tea smuggling trade, which was costing them dear, out of business. Thus it was that they tried to increase their own revenue at the expense of the American colonists. With the British King George III and his Parliament telling their American subjects what they could and could not do, the rallying cry went up: "No taxation without representation." To show Britain what it could do with its tea, the protesters turned Boston harbor

REBELLION

The Destruction of Tea at Boston Harbor (1846) by Nathaniel Currier. Despite the American preference for coffee, tea remains a popular drink. The tea industry is worth billions of dollars each year in the U.S.

into a slime of tea. King George, as obsessed with holding on to his American colonies as he was with keeping his son from the throne, refused to budge on the tea tax proposals. Boston's Tea Party was followed by similar protests in New York, Philadelphia, Annapolis, Savannah, and Charleston, and while loyal American ladies declined tea at their afternoon parties, Britain shut the port of Boston down. The British Crown's mistakes would not be forgotten: when, on July 4, 1776, the Declaration of Independence was adopted by Congress, it not only proclaimed America's separation from Britain, but also reminded Congressmen of King George's "tyrannical acts."

THE RACE FOR TEA

Until the 1850s, the long-haul merchant seamen rode in heavy, lumbering craft, built from up to 1,000 tons of solid, seasoned timber, ships that doggedly plowed their way across the oceans to foreign ports. The collapse of the East India Company's monopoly in 1833 opened up international competition for the tea trade and quickened the pulse of the traders' hearts. The British and the Americans invested in sleeker, faster ships: clippers (because they "clipped" across the oceans) with an aerodynamic profile, sharp bows that could cleave through the waves, and raked-back masts that carried plenty of sail. When the wind blew fair, the clippers sped home with their valuable cargoes (their holds sometimes carried illegal shipments of slaves). They flew through the China Seas, the Indian Ocean, round the Cape of Good Hope, and through the Atlantic to reach New York, London, Liverpool, and Belfast in half the time taken by the old ships.

The tea-clipper captains raced one another home and the press fed on stories of these heroic battles with the elements to bring back the tea. Like the race to bring Beaujolais Nouveau to Paris or London, the tea traders made capital out of their delivery times without dwelling too much on the actual benefits to the tea-drinking public: fresh tea tastes no different from tea that has stood twelve months in a warehouse. As new tea speed records were made and broken, the names on the ships' bows,

ADULTERERS

✦

The rising popularity of tea led to some curious additives being used to bulk out the contents of the tinfoil-lined tea chests, including elderberry flowers, ash leaves (boiled up with sheep dung to achieve the right color), iron filings, and black lead. Green tea was sometimes adulterated with China clay, turmeric, Prussian blue, and sulfate of lime. It was not the fault of the Chinese exporters, according to *Cassell's Family Magazine* of 1897. "Tea . . . is notoriously subject to these adulterations; and it seems that this arises entirely from our own fancy, and not from any desire on the part of the Chinese to pursue such a practice." Tea drinkers were advised to wash tea in cold water and strain it through muslin before drinking it.

HIGH SPEED
A nineteenth-century
lithograph of the clipper
ship *Thermopylae*. The
multiple masts and square
rig enabled clippers to travel
between ports much more
quickly than had previously
been possible.

like *Thermopylae* and *Cutty Sark* (the latter still preserved in the Port of London), added prestige to the tea they carried. Cups of "Cutty Sark" tea were soon on the market.

It did not last. The ships that would eventually render the rival tea clippers redundant, the steamers, were chugging across the oceans. They were slowed by the need to make regular fuel stops, but in 1869 a major new engineering feat gave them a big advantage over the sail-driven tea clippers: the Suez Canal. The Canal, 106 miles (171 km) long, sliced in half the journey time from China to Europe, but only for steam ships. The clippers could not rely on the vagaries of the Red Sea winds and had to continue to make their three-month journey via the Cape of Good Hope. By the end of the nineteenth century, the age of the tea clipper was over.

CEYLON TEA

✦

Sri Lanka is famous for its high-quality tea, yet the country is a relative newcomer in the 4,500-year history of the beverage. Its tea trade only developed after a succession of agricultural accidents. Ceylon, as Sri Lanka was known before its independence from Britain in 1948, had been cleared in part by British planters convinced that the high hills were the perfect place to grow coffee. But the crops fell victim to the coffee rust fungus, *Hemileia vastatrix*, and the coffee rat. The planters turned to cinchona instead, but they could not compete with their Dutch rivals in Malaysia. In desperation, the planters switched to *Camellia sinensis*. Finally they were able to turn a profit.

PLANTATION CROP

In 2009, the United Nations (UN) expressed a concern over "land grabbing," the practice of wealthier nations buying farmland in poorer countries. Nations such as the U.S., India, Libya, the United Arab Emirates, China, South Korea, and Japan were buying or leasing land to grow food as a substitute for fossil fuels: biofuels. The size of the land grab was estimated at around half the area of Europe's farmland. The UN predicted that outsourcing food production and using intensive farming methods to grow it would create food shortages and environmental problems in the host countries. When the South Korean car manufacturer, Daewoo, took out a 99-year lease on 3.2 million acres (1.3 million ha) of Madagascan farmland, it led to civil unrest and the eventual ousting of the president of Madagascar Marc Ravalomanana.

The plantation problem was a classic case of history repeating itself. In the nineteenth century, tea growers expropriated the land in their respective empire territoies, clearing the land of everything else in order to establish plantations of *Camellia sinensis*. The crop displaced local communities, destroyed local ecosystems, and, worse still, was harvested on the cheap using laborers shipped in from other countries, especially India—people who would one day demand self-determination and civil rights. The trade in tea had helped change history at home and at sea, but above all it shifted the social equilibrium in every country where it was grown.

HANDPICKED
Tea pickers photographed in Ceylon (now Sri Lanka) at the close of the nineteenth century. Sri Lanka is one of the largest tea exporters in the world, accounting for almost a third of the total global trade.

Hemp
Cannabis sativa

Native range: Central Asia

Type: Fast-growing annual

Height: 13 feet (4 m)

✦ Edible
✦ **MEDICINAL**
✦ **COMMERCIAL**
✦ **PRACTICAL**

Cannabis, hemp, or marijuana: call it what you will, this plant has a bad name. Variously condemned by soundbite politicians, law enforcement officers, and the parents of college students in the West, it has been ranked as the world's most widely consumed recreational drug. Yet this was among the earliest cultivated plants; it was an important crop to at least two American presidents, the American Declaration of Independence was printed on it, and it promises still to be a savior "green" crop. Just what went wrong with *Cannabis sativa*?

THE VERSATILE NARCOTIC

The 1970s saw some strange scenes enacted in city gardens and vegetable plots: bemused cabbage and carrot growers looked on as uniformed police from the city drug squad seized sizable fern-like plants and marched the grizzled hippies who had grown them off to jail. It is relatively rare for the authorities to legislate against an individual cultivating an everyday plant in private, but *C. sativa* is no ordinary plant. Some 80 years or so after its prohibition, some wondered if, by banning *C. sativa*, the baby had been thrown out with the bath water. The petrochemical's plastics industry is polluting and unsustainable: hemp is its natural substitute. It grows naturally, and fast, without fertilizers, herbicides, or pesticides. When the climate is warm it can reach full height in three months and produce a crop of fibers four times as strong as cotton. This sustainable, quick -turnaround crop can then be processed into just about anything from house insulation and car body panels to "breathable" clothing (thanks to the hollow core of the hemp fiber).

The downside is that cannabis contains varying levels of the scarcely pronounceable delta-9-tetrahydrocannabinol. Shortened to THC, this is the active ingredient that persuaded the Scythians, a nomadic people who occupied the Black Sea region, to engage in some strange practices, according to the Greek author Herodotus. He reported in his *Histories* having seen "the Scyths" crouching in draftproof booths made of sticks and woolen felt, over a dish of hemp seed placed on a bed of

red-hot stones. "Immediately it smokes, and gives out such a vapor as no Grecian vapor-bath can exceed." It was said the effects caused the Scyths to shout for joy.

History has a habit of repeating itself: "The smoke has to be deeply inhaled and held for a few seconds, which is unpleasant for non-smokers. Herbal or menthol cigarette tobacco is milder, but the easiest way on the throat is to add 6 ground cloves to the joint. In the small quantities normally taken, it produces a pleasant hazy relaxed feeling. The French Impressionists used to take large amounts when the effect was something like acid," wrote Nicholas Saunders in *Alternative England and Wales* (1975).

It was THC that contributed to hemp's medicinal properties. Cannabis has been used by physicians for thousands of years both as a pain reliever and to treat a range of ailments from cancer and depression to Alzheimer's disease. Hemp's importance as either a medicine or a narcotic, however, was outweighed by its usefulness as a fiber-plant.

Most authorities agree that *C. sativa* has a long and confusing history. Herodotus reported that "Hemp grows in Scythia. The Thracians make garments of it which closely resemble linen; so much so indeed that if a person has never seen hemp he is sure to think they are linen." But its use as a fabric predated the Scythians: it was probably being processed in China 4,500 years ago (it was mentioned 2,500 years ago). The Chinese continued to cultivate hemp until, by the new millennium, they were the world's biggest producers. China was followed by the eastern European countries, Romania, Ukraine, and Hungary, and by Spain, Chile, and France. Hemp probably originated in southeast Russia, and in the seventeenth and eighteenth centuries, when ships' chandlers had grown to rely on hemp, Russia controlled the bulk of the hemp production used by shipping. A frigate such as the USS *Constitution*, fondly known as "Old Ironsides" after its successes against the British Navy during the War of 1812, required some 60 tons of hemp for its ropes and sails. (At the time, the British Navy was blockading American ports to prevent the import of goods such as Russian hemp.)

HEMP FOR THE HANGMAN

✦

Somehow hemp has come to be associated with textiles, and marijuana with narcotics. Why? The word "marijuana" has Mexican-Spanish derivation, while "hemp" has Anglo-Saxon connotations— *hennep, hamp,* or the old Icelandic word, *hampr*. What is called "ditchweed" in the States (this is feral hemp) was *cannabis* in Latin or *kannabis* in Greek. "Derivation unknown," states one dictionary from the 1930s while reminding its readers of its uses: "sail-cloth, ropes, and the hangman's rope."

CANNABIS PROFITS

Two Americans, among many, profited hugely from hemp: Ben Franklin, the co-author of the American constitution, and a San Francisco shopkeeper called Löb Strauss. Franklin had many claims to fame: he imported the first tin bath from England, invented the lightning (or Franklin's) rod, bifocal glasses, and an efficient household stove. The tenth son of a pious Boston couple, Josiah Franklin from Ecton, Northamptonshire, and his second wife, Abiah, Benjamin Franklin was apprenticed to his half-brother James, a printer who had started up one of America's earliest newspapers, the *New England Courant*. Franklin became a regular contributor to the *Courant*, but when the relationship between James and himself soured, Franklin slipped away to Philadelphia, arriving there with a single Dutch dollar to his name. He was 17. By the age of 42, he would retire from the profitable printing business he had set up and devote himself to public office, diplomacy, science, and also vegetarianism.

THE DECLARATION OF INDEPENDENCE.
JULY 4, 1776.

During the 30 years before the American Revolution, unrest, triggered by Britain's trade restrictions, was building

REVOLUTIONARY FIBER
The most famous document in U.S. history was most likely printed on hemp paper produced at the paper mill of Benjamin Franklin. Today, hemp paper accounts for a fraction of total paper pulp production each year.

between the two countries. Among other commodities, America was forced to rely on British pulp for its paper supplies. This dependency was irksome and Franklin found a way to feed his printing mill with hemp instead. (Both George Washington and Thomas Jefferson ran hemp plantations of their own.) When the Declaration of Independence was drafted it was almost certainly done so on hemp paper from Franklin's mill.

Almost a century after the Declaration was approved, a Nevada tailor, Jacob Davis, and his business partner, Löb Strauss, patented their process for reinforcing twilled cloth, or *jean* (a corruption of Genoa) workmen's pants with copper rivets. Löb, who changed his name to Levi, was a Bavarian migrant who had moved from New York to San Francisco to take advantage of the California Gold Rush in 1853. He switched from selling hemp cloth or "duck" for wagon roofs and tents and turned them into pants for the gold miners. (Although the first Levi jeans were made from hemp, Levi later used *serge de Nîmes*, a cloth imported from Nîmes, France, after workmen complained that the hemp chafed.)

Advocates of hemp have campaigned for it to be brought back into use, claiming that the material makes a more environmentally friendly paper—typical paper requires more chemicals to render it into wood pulp and causes more environmental disruption through logging. They also claim hemp is environmentally superior to cotton, which demands high concentrations of herbicides and pesticides (see Upland Cotton, p.88).

In almost every article of defense we abound. Hemp flourishes even to rankness, so that we need not want cordage.

Thomas Paine, Common Sense, *1776*

In the West, however, hemp remains stubbornly equated in people's minds with dangerous drugs, despite the fact that the hemp grown for cloth or paper has almost undetectable levels of the THC. The war on hemp was initially waged in America during the Prohibition debates of the 1920s and 1930s, which saw booze banned. The nineteenth-century followers of the Temperance Movement had campaigned for prohibition. Yet, despite raids, arrests, and convictions, the business of booze, brewed in bootlegging operations and sold in speakeasies, carried on much as it had before Prohibition, except that corruption among police and politicians rose to new heights. Hemp, or cannabis, was regarded as yet another pernicious intoxicant. That "the weed" was favored by low-lifers, Mexican migrants, and black musicians did not help. When men such as Harry J. Anslinger, commissioner in the Federal Bureau of Narcotics, and newspaper proprietor William Randolph Hearst, condemned it, the die was cast. Hearst's critics pointed out that the newspaper magnate's empire included timber forests for paper pulp and a changeover to hemp newsprint might have impacted on Hearst's profits. But Hearst could have diversified into hemp production itself. A more likely explanation is that Hearst simply believed the rhetoric of Anslinger, a vociferous opponent of cannabis inclined to publish exaggerated or unsubstantiated reports on its negative effects.

The 1937 United States' Marijuana Tax Act signaled the start of a cannabis ban across the Western world. Yet the consumption of cannabis is predicted to rise by around 10% in the next decade.

OLDEST AND LOVELIEST

+

Cannabis sativa caused a greater stir than its blue-flowered sister *Linum usitatissimum*, or flax. Yet the use of flax as the basis for the fabric, linen, is older by far than that of hemp. Neolithic tribes in Switzerland used flax to make linen and the ancient Egyptians used flax linen to wrap up their mummies.

Many an aristocrat, however, banned the business of drying flax because of the rank smell it caused. Just as linen is one of the loveliest fabrics, so flax is the oldest fiber plant in cultivation.

THE ORIGINAL HEMP
Flax (*Linum usitatissimum*) was an early predecessor to hemp as a source of fiber.

Chili Pepper
Capsicum frutescens

Native range: Central and Southern America and the West Indies. Also cultivated in other subtropical climates

Type: Perennial plant, usually grown as an annual

Height: Varies across the different species

♦ EDIBLE
♦ MEDICINAL
♦ COMMERCIAL
♦ PRACTICAL

When overland supplies to Europe of that king of spices, black pepper, were halted with the fall of Constantinople in 1453, it sent a shock wave through the continent. The loss of pepper, *Piper nigrum*, was a serious blow to the economies of the Mediterranean nation states. They were quick to dispatch maritime explorers to scour the known and the unknown world for a suitable replacement. In 1490 they found what they were looking for: chili "peppers."

HOT FUSS

The Dutch housewife who stepped into an Amsterdam grocer's shop in the 1400s and offered a groot for a peck of peppers would have received a handful of hardened black seeds, *Piper nigrum*; a spice that had been carried across the continents from India to reach her. A similar request for peppers in a modern-day Amsterdam supermarket would produce a

pack of that fulsome, fleshy vegetable, *Capsicum annuum*, grown to perfection in Dutch glasshouses just out of town. The confusion—as to what exactly a pepper is—began when Columbus's sailors arrived in the Caribbean in 1492 and sampled some hot-tasting members of the capsicum family.

The native home of the wild-growing capsicums may have been the Guianas: many of its native names suggest a Caribbean root. The capsicums were certainly being cultivated, and valued for their medical and culinary attributes, by the Aztecs, who introduced the plant to the Spanish invaders. Some, although not all, of them, were so eye-wateringly hot they left the white men gasping for beer to slake the raging fire the capsicums produced. When the

If Peter Piper picked a peck of pickled peppers
Where's the peck of pickled peppers Peter Piper picked?

Nineteenth-century tongue twister

sailors reported back to ship they could only describe the taste
as just like that familiar old Asian spice, black pepper. So it came to
be dubbed *pimiento*, the Spanish word for pepper. The source of all
this herbal heat was capsaicin, a compound that is concentrated
in the seed-bearing placenta of the fruit. Capsaicin in its
raw state may have eye-watering, tongue-scalding qualities, but, as the Aztecs discovered, it also possesses important medicinal qualities in that it can reduce blood pressure and relax the
arteries. In modern medicine, capsaicin, used in a cream, can relieve the
agony of arthritis, shingles, diabetes, and neuralgia as well as alleviate
the pain of those who have undergone surgery. In Mexico, the chili is a
traditional treatment for toothache.

Capsicum peppers are now grown commercially
throughout the tropical and subtropical world, in
America, the Far East, and East and West Africa. The
capsicum with which most shoppers are familiar is that
all-year-round salad vegetable, *C. annuum*, the bell or
bull-nose pepper. The bell pepper is a short, bushy
annual with dark green leaves and white flowers that
develops into a bulbous pepper that turns from an electric green to a blush-red, orange, or yellow as they
ripen. The *capsicum* species has many varieties. Only
five species have been domesticated, and only three are
widely used: *C. annuum* (whose varieties include the
bell pepper, paprika, pimiento, jalapeño,
cascabel, and cayenne), *C. frutescens*, and
C. chinense (whose varieties include the
habanero and Scotch bonnet). Taking

CHILI DEFENSE
In parts of Africa, chili
peppers are used to protect
crops. By laying them out
along fences, the strong smell
deters elephants from
moving too close.

TOO HOT TO HANDLE

+

Wilbur Scoville devised a test for
rating the heat in a pepper in 1912
when he was working for an
American pharmaceutical company.
The Scoville Organoleptic Test relied
on the taste buds of a group of
volunteers who sampled a solution
of the peppers diluted in sugar
syrup. Gradually the quantity of
syrup was increased until the heat
of the peppers disappeared.
Scoville's pepper tasters, working on
a scale of zero to over 350,000,
gave sweet and bell peppers, for
example, a score of between zero
and 100, while Scotch bonnets and
habaneros scored 100,000–
300,000. One of the world's hottest
peppers is believed to be the nago
jolokia from Assam, Bangladesh,
and Sri Lanka.

account of others such as the spur pepper, bush pepper, and garden ginger (and those perhaps lurking in the South American forest awaiting discovery), there could be more than 3,000 different pepper varieties worldwide.

HOT SAUCE

Capsicum frutescens is the "pepper" that, for a period, took the place of true pepper. The word *chili* came from the Mexican Nahuatl Indians and refers to the long cayenne or "pod" pepper, the source of such heatwave foods as cayenne pepper. To make cayenne pepper, the chili seed pods are dried, ground, mixed with flour, baked into a hard biscuit, and then ground down into fine red powder. Unscrupulous manufacturers were said to have bulked out the pepper with poisonous red lead. Some forms of paprika will make grown men weep. The hottest paprika comes not from South America, but Spain and Hungary, introduced by Turkish growers in the seventeenth century is and one of the few varieties that can rival the Mexican peppers. The paprikas range from hot to cool, the latter being made from pods where the stalk, stem, and hot seed center are taken out before grinding. The fiery bite of Tabasco sauce comes from the natural capsaicin of South American peppers.

So it was that the Spanish traders who, having conquered most of South America in a short space of time with a relatively small force, returned to Europe bearing their gold and their vegetable treasures, including pineapples, peanuts, potatoes, and the newly christened pepper. The plant spread quickly across Europe and into the tropical regions. It reached India as early as the 1540s, and 400 years later, India—once the biggest exporter of real pepper—was one of the largest exporters of capsicum peppers.

Soon the pepper was taking the place of other hot spices in Asian and European kitchens. The fiery new chili peppers found a place in most kitchen gardens and the brightly colored fruits were strung up on whitewashed house walls like vegetable necklaces to dry in the fall sun. Over winter, the farmer's wife would shred the wrinkled fruit into her stews and potages to pepper up the dishes.

MORE CONFUSION

✦

The pimento tree thrives in Jamaica (and the West Indies, Mexico, and South America), producing Jamaica pepper or allspice (*Pimenta officinalis*). The berries are collected green, sun-dried, then packed and sold. Allspice is used to flavor food, the tree bark to scent cosmetics, and an oil, eugenol (the same as that found in cloves), is extracted for culinary purposes.

The advent of the chili pepper intrigued Europeans. Nicholas Culpeper was "the man that first ranged the woods and climbed the mountains in search of medicinal and salutary herbs," declared Dr. Johnson. He had undoubtedly merited the gratitude of posterity." When Culpeper came to describe the chili, which he called the Guinea, cayenne, or bird pepper, he devoted several column inches of his *Complete Herbal* (1653) to its "virtues" while issuing a preliminary warning about the "immoderate use of these violent plants and fruits."

The Guinea pepper, he wrote, came under the influence of the planet Mars. "The vapours that rise from the husks or pods . . . will so pierce the brain by flying up into the head through the nostrils, as to produce violent sneezings . . . and provoke sharp coughing, and cause violent vomiting." Cast into a fire, it raised "grievous strong and noisome vapours," while eating the pepper could even "prove dangerous to life." Nevertheless, "when corrected of their evil qualities, they are of considerable service," said Culpeper, who recorded such benefits as expelling kidney stones, helping the dropsy, easing birth pains, removing spots and freckles, softening skin, healing the bite of a venomous beast, curing halitosis, toothache, and "hysteric and other female diseases." The chili, in short, was a miracle cure and a satisfyingly red-hot substitute for real pepper.

MEDICINAL SPICE
Chili pepper extracts are used in medicines known as counter-irritants, which help alleviate the symptoms of rheumatism, nerve pain, and other problems affecting the muscles and joints.

Cinchona

Cinchona spp.

Native range: Northern Bolivia and Peru

Type: Evergreen tree or shrub

Height: 15–50 feet (5–15 m)

+ EDIBLE
+ ***MEDICINAL***
+ ***COMMERCIAL***
+ PRACTICAL

It cured kings, queens, and revolutionaries. It made fantastic fortunes for those who mastered its mysteries and ruined many who sought but failed to unravel its secrets. It propped up empires, especially that of the British Queen Victoria, and it facilitated the shipment of as many as 20 million people into virtual slave labor creating social discontent that still reverberates around the globe today.

SWAMP FEVER

"They told me I was everything; 'tis a lie, I am not ague-proof," declares King Lear in William Shakespeare's play of the same name. The "ague" killed off many respectable historical celebrities, Alexander the Great and Oliver Cromwell among them. The British royalty might never have returned to power had not Cromwell succumbed to the fatal bite of an Irish mosquito. It has been estimated that half the world's population remains under the threat of the ague, or malaria as it is better known (from the Italian *mala aria* or "bad air"), a disease that has killed more people than all the world's wars and plagues put together. Until the late 1930s there was but one remedy for the ague: a remedy made from the bark of the cinchona tree. The story of its seventeenth-century passage to Europe, involving as it did love, deceit, corruption, and inter-governmental conspiracy, rivals any work of fiction.

The tale begins along the banks of every festering, mosquito-ridden swamp in Europe, Asia, and West Africa, and on the hillsides of South America. In the former lay the curse of malaria, and in the latter, its cure.

We tend to think of malaria as a tropical disease. Yet until the arrival of foreign ships bearing the malarial mosquito larvae in shallow pools of bilge water, the Caribbean, most of Africa and Malaysia, Sri Lanka, and Burma were malaria-free. Malaria may have been absent even from South America until the arrival of the Western explorers and Conquistadors.

Malaria is a debilitating disease. It contributed to the defeat of the Confederate army by the Union side in the American Civil War in 1865. The Japanese might have established a new empire in southeast Asia, occupying Burma, India, and China in the Second World War, were it not for Allied supplies of the anti-malarial drug, atabrine. In the aftermath of the Vietnam War, an estimated 20,000 Americans were affected by malaria. The sickness, once known as "swamp fever," is characterized by a succession of cold–dry, hot–dry, and hot–wet fevers—a sickness that so weakens the patient that they eventually die from exhaustion. Some victims, however, experience a single attack that gives them life-long immunity to the disease. Some suffer sudden recurrences throughout their life, and yet it is thought that others with particular blood groups are completely immune to its ravages. Malaria is still a mysterious malady.

MOSQUITOES

The source of malaria is not a mosquito, but the presence of a person carrying malaria in their blood. Their condition is passed to others by the bite of the mosquito. Around 13% of the 400 or so different species of mosquito can carry the disease, and the female of the species is more deadly than the male. Lacking his partner's blood lust, the male *Anopheles* mosquito lives on nectar and fruit while the Dracula-like female feeds on blood. In doing so, she passes on the malarial infection. Having sucked blood, the female will seek out stagnant water on which to lay her eggs. Her human prey can reduce the risk of malaria by destroying these breeding grounds, draining the marshes or spraying them with oil, which weakens the surface tension of the water, preventing the female from landing. Other anti-malarial practices involve sleeping beneath mosquito-proof nets or living in homes built on stilts (the mosquitoes' range does not extend more than 20 feet [6 m] above ground). If communities fail to protect themselves, they must, as civilizations have discovered, risk being wiped out by malaria.

South of the Spanish capital Madrid lies Chinchón, a town with a population of 5,000. In the 1630s, long before the place was sacked by Emperor Napoleon during

TINY TERROR
Of the 460 species of the mosquito genus *Anopheles*, a quarter are known to transmit malaria to humans, with 40 of these most commonly associated with the spread of the disease in endemic areas.

the Peninsular War, it formed part of the country estate of the fourth Count of Chinchón, the impresively named Don Luis Gerónimo Fernández de Cabrera e Bobadilla Cerda y Mendoza. In 1629, however, Don Luis was attending not to estate matters but to his sick wife in Lima, Peru. Appointed the Spanish Viceroy to what the Spaniard, Pizarro, had called the City of Kings, Don Luis had resigned himself to paying the price of such privilege: his beautiful wife was in the final stages of malaria. As a last resort, according to an Italian, Sebastiano Bado, his physician suggested that they administer the folk medicine used by Andean peasants, known as *quina quina*. Don Luis reluctantly agreed. His wife recovered and the medicine was brought back to the family estate at Chinchón. Administered to the peons who worked the estate, *quina quina* kept malaria at bay in Chinchón and increased Don Luis' profits.

The Quechua Indians had mastered the medicinal use of the bark of the tree they called *quina*, or "bark," long before they were conquered by Spain. A member of the madder family, Rubiaceae, the quina was a native tree with many different species, some yielding several healing alkaloids, others producing none. The tree they called the "bark of barks," quina quina, delivered 30 separate alkaloids including quinine and quinidine, still used in the treatment of various ailments including heart disease. The Indian folk pharmacists were generous with their knowledge of quina quina, even with the Spaniards, who had introduced terrible new diseases such as measles, and probably malaria, into their midst. The Indians also shared their secret with the missionaries, the religious Catholic guard known as the Jesuits, who had come to save their pagan souls for Christ. The naïve Indians had no idea that the outside world was thirsting for a malarial cure and that, within a century, their stock of quina quina would be plundered almost to extinction.

For almost a decade, from 1650, the Jesuits held a monopoly on supplies of "Peruvian bark" or "Jesuit powder," but it made little impact on European pharmacology: Jesuit powder was regarded as a quack treatment, inferior to conventional procedures such as bleeding the patient with leeches. One eminent English doctor who dismissed Jesuit powder as a charlatan's cure was Sir Robert Talbot. Talbot was a man of influence. He had earned a knighthood and a considerable fortune from

COPPICING AND MOSSING

✦

The bark of the cinchona tree is harvested when the sapling is around 12 years old. In some cases the trees are coppiced; that is, cut to the base and allowed to regenerate from the root. Another way to harvest Peruvian bark without killing the tree involved "mossing"; stripping away the bark lengthways, then binding the wound with moss, a natural antiseptic, and leaving the bark to grow back. During the 1860s "gold rush" for cinchona, however, the South American trees were simply axed, stripped of their precious bark, and junked.

PRECIOUS GIFT
(Opposite) In this seventeenth-century engraving, Peru, symbolized as a young child, offers a branch of the cinchona tree to the figure of Science.

his own cure for malaria. His successes included the King of Englan[d] Charles II, the King of France Louis XIV, and the Queen of Spain. Whe[n] he died in 1681, he was believed to have taken the secret ingredient of h[is] malarial potion with him to the grave. Then Louis XIV revealed th[e] Talbot cure to an astonished world: quinine, or the very Jesuits' powd[er]

> **Peruvian Bark: It somewhat resembles our cherry tree, grows promiscuously in forests, particular in the hilly part of Quito in Peru, and is spontaneously propagated from its seeds.**
>
> *Nicholas Culpeper*, Complete Herbal, *1653*

Talbot had so roundly condemne[d] By the end of the sixteen[th] century, fleets of Spanish ship[s] were transporting the malari[a] cure back to Europe, and Sout[h] American forests were being ruth[-] lessly logged out of the little tree that had been named cinchona afte[r] Don Luis' home town. For a century or so, while Dutch and British hort[i] culturalists battled to bring the plant home for themselves, this Iberian[-] Andean partnership dominated the international market in cinchona.

The medieval art of alchemy focused on the holy grail of turning bas[e] metal into gold. Instead, the alchemists stumbled on a host of incident[al] discoveries. For alchemy's child, chemistry, the quest for synthetic subst[i] tutes for natural products like quinine was equally random. When th[e] young Englishman William Henry Perkin set up a laboratory to searc[h] for a synthetic version of quinine in 1856 using coal tars, he discovere[d] instead a synthetic dye that he called "mauveine," or aniline purple[.] Then only 19, he sold the fruits of his research to Germany and retired [a] very rich man. Until a substitute for quinine could be found, Holland[,] Britain, and Spain sought to control supplies of the real thing.

NATURAL TONIC
By the mid-nineteenth century, the use of quinine to treat malaria was firmly established. Although it was successfully synthesized during World War II, the cinchona tree remains the most economical source of quinine.

CITRATE
OF
IRON AND QUININE
FERRI ET QUININÆ CITRAS, P.B.
Ilford
LONDON.

In 1859, a plant hunter calle[d] Clements Markham found som[e] cinchona plants in the Andes. H[e] sent some to London's Ke[w] Gardens and took the remainde[r] to Calcutta's Botanical Garden[s] and the British governmen[t] gardens in India at Ootacamun[d] in the Nilgiri Hills, where the[y] were successfully established. Th[e] famous Dutch horticulturalist D[r] Johan de Vrij, meanwhile, wa[s] establishing his own cinchon[a] plantation in Java.

BARKING UP THE RIGHT TREE

In 1865, two British brothers emerged on the scene. Charles Ledger, who lived and traded by the banks of Lake Titicaca in Bolivia, sent some cinchona seeds to his brother in England, writing that they came from a plant with a high quinine content—between 10 and 13%—and that his brother should secure a good price for the seeds from the British government. The British spurned the offer and so threw away the potential profits of monopolizing the quinine trade. Instead, De Vrij and the Dutch growers stole a march on the British with their Indonesian plantations.

Seedlings of *Cinchona ledgeriana*—as it was named in Charles' honor—were prone to disease and slow-growing. However, the Dutch growers' centuries-old nursery skills won through. Grafting *C. ledgeriana* onto a hardier rootstock produced a winning plant; by 1884, the Dutch coolie gangs were harvesting enough bark to challenge, and finally overtake, the South American trade. Britain did develop and hold on to the quinine trade in its Indian colonies, but Holland became the quinine king for the next 60 years, processing the bark in Amsterdam from where it was sold around the world.

It all came to a traumatic end in 1942 with the fall of Singapore to the Japanese. During World War II, Britain and its allies were preoccupied with the war raging in Western Europe. Japan, seizing the opportunity to acquire new territories, mounted a pre-emptive air attack on Pearl Harbor in a bid to cripple the U.S. Navy fleet. Having invaded Malaysia and taken Singapore, their land forces then occupied Indonesia, ending Dutch colonial rule and depriving the Allies of the precious cinchona plantations. Meanwhile, another Japanese force moved north through Burma toward the Indian border. Fierce resistance by, among others, the Indian army, was backed not only by Allied guns, but by successful new drugs. Before the Japanese could capitalize on their quinine acquisitions, scientists came up with the elusive quinine substitute and introduced malaria-beating drugs such as atabrine, chloroquine, and primaquine. The Allies, armed with a daily dose of the malaria-busting drug, held out against the Japanese: even before the guns were finally silenced by the dropping of the first atomic bomb on Hiroshima, the Japanese advance had been repulsed.

PLAGUE OF PLAGUES

✦

A collective shudder passed through the world health community in 2009 with news of a strain of malaria that was resistant to the synthetic substitutes for quinine. Medicines routinely taken by travelers to keep malaria at bay had worked well enough, although with certain side effects absent from quinine, for nearly 80 years. But as often happens, the disease appeared to be mutating to outwit synthetic versions of the natural medicine. These days, quinine is used in a range of commercial products from tonic water to mouthwashes, but perhaps it still has a role to play in combating malaria.

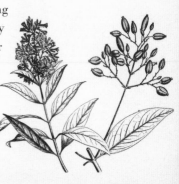

CINCHONA FLOWERS
The cinchona tree produces flowers in small clusters called panicles.

Sweet Orange
Citrus sinensis

Native range: China and southeast Asia

Type: Small tree

Height: Up to 25 feet (7.62 m)

+ *EDIBLE*
+ *MEDICINAL*
+ *COMMERCIAL*
+ *PRACTICAL*

A glass of fresh orange juice is not only a refreshing and tasty way to kick off the morning, it is also a nutritious drink that tops up our personal store of vitamin C. The beneficial qualities of citrus fruits have been known for centuries but shared by few. When Captain James Cook set sail for the Pacific, maritime history was made and the English forever dubbed "limeys"—all thanks to the citrus fruit.

SEA SICKNESS

In 1769, Maori fishermen were working their canoes in Raukawa, the rich waters that sluiced between Te Ika a Maui and Te Waka a Maui (later named North and South Islands), when they spied a strange sight bearing down from the horizon. It was a 105-foot-long, three-masted sailing ship, an ex-merchant collier now armed with cannons and flying the flag of the British Royal Navy. The ship powered through the straits revealing, as it passed, the name painted along the bow: HM *Bark Endeavour*.

The ship carried Captain James Cook (Raukawa Strait would be renamed after him) together with 94 passengers and crew. Unusually for the time, all but two of them were in the best of health.

Captain Cook, a Yorkshireman of humble origins, was an able sailor, a strict disciplinarian, and a genius navigator. He had already made a reputation for himself by charting parts of Canada when, in 1768, he sailed right around South America to Tahiti, New Zealand, and the east coast of Australia, charting the new waters in a voyage that lasted for just under three years. His pioneering route (he would land his little ship on

M.E.Eaton

almost every major island group in the South Pacific) successfully disproved the theory that Terra Australis was one vast continent. Cook also disproved the notion that life on board ship inevitably meant falling ill with the "explorer's sickness," scurvy. Cook made two more

MARITIME ICON
HM *Bark Endeavour*, pictured here off the coast of New Zealand, is an icon of British maritime history.

historic voyages in the best of health until he was killed in a sudden skirmish with the local people on Hawaii. Life aboard HM *Bark Endeavour* was not as hellish as portrayed in popular fiction. (In the opinion of Dr. Samuel Johnson, a sailor would be better off in jail, where he could enjoy more room, better food, and "commonly better company" without the risk of drowning.) But it was an ordered regime. Working in the waist of the ship were the "waisters" or "landmen," some of whom had been pressed into service; above deck were the sailing elite, the "topmen" who fixed the rigging. On the first journey they were joined by two celebrated researchers: the botanists Dr. David Solander and Dr. Joseph Banks. Cook bound them all to a strict regime of hygiene and regular meals (including, wherever he could harvest it, a type of coastal cabbage, *Lepidium oleraceum*, later dubbed "Cook's scurvy grass").

Cook fed his men citrus and sauerkraut (pickled cabbage), as instructed by the British Navy's James Lind. Although not everyone returned (56 men finally disembarked at Plymouth in 1771, all three of Dr. Banks's resident artists having died at sea), it was this expedient that saved most of the crew from the ravages of scurvy.

Scurvy had proved more of a curse for the seventeenth-century merchant mariners than did pirates or poor weather. Symptoms started with blotches of dark skin, loose teeth, and hemorrhaging. It was the fatal signal that the sailor's collagen was breaking down and with it the connective tissues that held the cells together. Generally a painful death followed in days.

The sickness was not confined to the sailing fraternity, jammed on board their boats and subsisting on a diet of salt beef and biscuits for months or years.

INDOOR ORANGES

✦

At the resplendent seventeenth-century court of the Sun King, Louis XIV, a *citronnière* was constructed at Versailles. More than 500 feet (150 m) long and 45 feet (13.5 m) high, it housed 1,200 orange trees and signaled the craze for heated orangeries (see Pineapple, p.14) among Europe's aristocracy, where the sweet-scented orange could blossom. The mercury thermometer had yet to be invented, and in its absence regulating the temperature was a matter of personal judgment. "If the water in the greenhouse is frozen," advised a Dutch gardener, Van Oosten, in 1703, "then you must gently warm the trees . . . with burning lamps." The crop afforded the estate owners (and the quick-fingered gardener) an exotic and healthy addition to their diet.

Hippocrates, the Greek physician, made notes on the mysterious ailment. During the Crusades, the "holy war" conducted against the Muslims by the Catholic Church from 1096, scurvy was another of the ailments borne by the Christians who finally failed to defeat the Kurdish-born leader, Saladin.

But at sea scurvy was holding up serious exploration. The Portuguese explorer Vasco da Gama's voyage to India in 1497 almost ended prematurely when the whole crew succumbed to scurvy. "Many of our men fell ill here," he wrote in his log before managing to land on the east coast of Africa and trade in supplies of fresh oranges. "It pleased God in his mercy that . . . all our sick recovered their health for the air of the place is good." His claims for clean air aside, da Gama was well aware of the antiscorbutic value of citrus fruits. The next time his men fell ill, "the Captain Major sent a man on shore to bring off a supply of oranges which were much desired by our sick." Da Gama lost over half his crew to scurvy, yet, having learned of the cure, he seems to have kept the information to himself; in 1593, the English Captain Richard Hawkins appealed for "some learned man (to) write of it [scurvy] for it is a plague of the sea, and a spoyle of mariners." An Edinburgh gentleman, boarding his first ship as surgeon's mate in 1739, proved to be the man for the job.

James Lind survived his first tour of duty sailing to the Mediterranean and on to the West Indies. By the time he had risen to the rank of surgeon aboard HMS *Salisbury* in 1747, he was testing various cures for scurvy. Selecting 12 sick sailors to act as guinea pigs, he doused them with garlic, mushroom, horseradish, cider, seawater, oranges, and lemons. Those who received the citrus treatment recovered almost overnight, providing Mr. Lind with material to pen his *Treatise of the Scurvy* in 1753. His citrus suggestions took time to filter through to the naval hierarchy, possibly because he had also blamed the illness on poor ventilation, too much salt, and "blocked perspiration" due to cold climates.

A few years after Cook's unfortunate demise at the hands of the Hawaiians, children were singing the lilting rhyme "Oranges and lemons," which is well known to this day:

> **The tree bears fruit all the year round,
> and is adorned with blossom, ripe fruit
> and unripe, all at the same time.**
>
> *Theophrastus c. 371–c. 287 BCE*

Oranges and lemons say the
  Bells of St. Clements,

You owe me five farthings say the
  Bells of St. Martins.

When will you pay me? say the
  Bells of Old Bailey

When I grow rich say the
  Bells of Shoreditch.

The playground rhyme, which ended with the mock beheading of the last in line, was a macabre reference to London's public hangings. Oranges, in reality, came from the East (*sinensis* meaning "from China"); lemons, it is thought, from northwestern India. The citrus fruits were and are one of the most important groups of fruit in the tropical and subtropical regions. They range from the Seville or bitter orange (*C. aurantium*) and the sweet orange (*C. sinensis*) to lemons (*C. limonium*), the mandarin orange (*C. reticulata*), grapefruit (*C. paradisi*), and lime (*C. aurantifolia*). The source of the disparaging expression "limeys" is a reference to the British naval ratings who, after Cook, never set sail without them. The acidic lime juice played havoc with their teeth, but the lime kept longer than oranges and naturally kept scurvy at bay.

ACID TEST
The acidity of citrus fruit varies between species. The lemon and bitter orange are among the most acidic.

*Lemon (*C. limonium*)*

*Bitter orange (*C. aurantium*)*

Coconut
Cocos nucifera

Native range: Indo-Pacific region

Type: Single trunked palm

Height: 100 feet (30.5 m)

✦ **EDIBLE**

✦ MEDICINAL

✦ **COMMERCIAL**

✦ **PRACTICAL**

What goes up brown and comes down white? runs one Hawaiian riddle. The coconut palm is key to our picture of the tropical paradise. It is doubtful whether, as has been claimed, the big nut, falling from the sky, kills more than 100 people a year, but there is no doubt that the coconut rivals bamboo in terms of its usefulness and remarkable versatility.

MONKEY FACE

In 1890, New Yorkers were intrigued by the sight of foreign starlings, recently released in Central Park by Eugene Schieffelin as part of his mad plan to introduce to the U.S. all the birds mentioned in William Shakespeare's plays. The industrialists of the time, however, were focused on another exotic import, the most economically important member of the palm family: the coconut.

In the pre-plastics age, it proved a boon to manufacturers hungry for cheap, third-world materials that could serve a multitude of purposes from paint, carpets, and baskets, to food and drink. The coconut (what the Portuguese called the "monkey face" and *côcos*—the latter a slang word for "head' and "hobgoblin") fitted the bill. With the same ignorance that prompted the Victorians to dismiss the Irishman's "lazy beds" (see Potato, p.176), the coconut harvest was dubbed the "lazy man's crop." Natives were said to slumber beneath its leafy umbrella until the soft thud of a nut falling on the sand woke them. Opening the nut with a machete, they downed the "milk" and shared a little of the white "meat" with the hens before resuming their siesta in the shade.

The reality was a little different. In Indonesia and the Pacific Islands, the coconut farmer rose early to harvest a crop that was shipped worldwide. There was not a cell in the coconut palm that lacked a use. Whole nuts were bought by showmen for their coconut shies (from an old English word for "throw");

What is a man with three eyes and yet can cry out of only one?

Hawaiian riddle

coconut fibers were processed into matting; and dried kernels, or *copra*, went to the soap and margarine makers. According to one Indonesian proverb, a coconut had a different use for every day of the year. Dried fronds went on the fire; the kernels were fed to babies, hens, and pigs. Sweets and chutneys were made from the ripe kernels; baskets and mats from the woven leaves; and brooms from bound-together stalks. Squeezing the grated kernel created a cooking cream that lightened floury rice dishes and spiced up fish and banana dishes.

TOUGH NUT
A closeup of coir rope being made in a market in Goa, India. Coir is a coarse fiber extracted from the fibrous outer shell of a coconut.

Lifting the lid on the coconut exposed a thin water-like liquid inside. It was an elixir. Perfectly sterile, it was safe to drink in the aftermath of any tsunami that soured the water wells. It was even used as a sterile, intravenous drip for the wounded during World War II. Collected in a woven plait of coconut leaves, the liquid could be fermented into a drink, toddy, which, in its freshly fermented state served as a yeast-like concoction in bread-making. Distilled, toddy turned into the brain-swimming spirit arrack. First aid could be administered to any injuries incurred on the road home after a night on the arrack by washing the wounds in sterile coconut water while applying the chewed young leaves to stanch any bleeding.

Mankind was quick to export coconut across the globe. Missionaries took it to Guiana, the Portuguese to Guinea and, in the sixteenth century, it was planted across the east coast of tropical America. But coconuts can float, and this method of seed dispersal had already spread the palm with the help of the Pacific currents. But what were its true origins? The oldest names for the coconut are in Sanskrit, pointing to India as the source. However, the discovery of the fossilized remains of a tiny proto-coconut on New Zealand's North Island suggests it might have been first taken into service here 5,000 years ago.

WASHING PROBLEM

◆

Once made from animal fats, or tallow, soaps now contain the oils of the coconut and the African oil palm (*Elaeis guineensis*), originally from western tropical Africa. But demand for the African oil palm has been causing problems. Since it accounts for almost half the world's trade in edible oils, palm oil plantations have taken over vast areas of native forest in Malaysia, Indonesia, and Papua New Guinea, and threaten native lands in Thailand, Cambodia, India, the Philippines, and Latin America. One solution could be to restrict production of palm oil to plantations that have not replaced tropical forests.

Coffee
Coffea arabica

Native range: Ethiopia
(formerly Abyssinia)

Type: Evergreen tree

Height: Up to 32 feet (10 m)

+ *EDIBLE*
+ MEDICINAL
+ *COMMERCIAL*
+ PRACTICAL

Coffee has had a transforming effect on history. Without coffee there would have been no cafés. Without cafés there might have been no Boston Tea Party, no Harry Potter books, and no latte life. And then where would the world have been?

SONG OF PRAISE

"How sweet coffee tastes!" wrote the composer Johann Sebastian Bach "Lovelier than a thousand kisses, sweeter than Muscatel wine." It was the 1730s and the middle-aged Bach had recently completed his *Coffee Cantata* (*Schweigt stille, plaudert nicht* or "Be still, stop chattering") ready for its premiere at Zimmerman's Coffee House, where fellow composer Georg Philipp Telemann had set up Bach's Collegium Musicum.

The *Coffee Cantata* was but one of the artistic and fiscal fruits of the new trade in that seductive beverage. In 1650, students with literary aspirations popped round to one of England's first coffee houses in Oxford. Within the decade, the English diarist Samuel Pepys was patronizing London's coffee houses along with friends such as the poet John Dryden. In the early part of the twentieth century, Jean-Paul Sartre spent many creative hours in La Coupole in Paris; by the middle part of the century, the beat poet Allen Ginsberg was working away at his poem "Howl" at Caffe Mediterraneum or the Med in Berkeley, California (which was credited with the invention of latte—similarly, Auckland's DKD coffee house is credited, by some, with the invention of the New Zealand "flat white"). By the mid-1990s, a single mother on welfare benefits, Joanne Murray, was busy working on the manuscript of *Harry Potter and the Philosopher's Stone* at The Elephant House, a café in Edinburgh, Scotland.

BLACK GOLD

Perhaps the first fiction surrounding coffee rose out of the native home of the coffee bean, Ethiopia. Coffee is Ethiopia's black gold. One of the first homes of *Homo sapiens* and a nation that still operates on a pre-Gregorian calendar, placing it seven to eight years behind the rest of the world, Ethiopia is our oldest country. In the twentieth century, partly because of the coffee trade, it became one of the world's poorest. Coffee accounts for over 60% of Ethiopia's overseas earnings; the slightest fluctuation in demand and the effect this has on its sale price can spark an economic crisis.

Home to Africa's oldest Muslim settlement, as well as being the first Christian country, it was the monks of Ethiopia who, if legend has any basis in truth, gave us the drink. The story goes that Kaldi, a goat herd, was searching for his lost flock when he found them feeding avidly on the red "cherries" of what Linnaeus, in 1753, categorized as *Coffea arabica*. He danced with delight when he tasted the cherries, sharing his new-found pleasure with a passerby. He in turn was so invigorated by the caffeine punch of the plush red cherries that he took them to his monastic friends, who cultivated the tree and brewed the drink that kept them wide awake during their prayers.

Coffea arabica is, economically, the top variety of coffee. It accounts for over 70% of world production. While liberica (*C. liberica*) and excelsa (*C. dewevrei*) trail behind, its closest rival is robusta (*C. canephora*). Other varieties, which include the fabled Jamaican Blue Mountain, Brazil's Mundo Novo, and the dwarf San Ramón, all share the common characteristics of a fruit or "cherry" surrounding a pair of oval seeds (in some cases a single "peaberry" develops instead). One other characteristic is that the bean is rendered infertile when stripped of its outer flesh.

The Arab world made the most of this feature when, zealously guarding their treasure, they traded coffee beans from neighboring Sudan into Yemen and out of the port of Mocha. Marco Polo (see box) was credited with bringing coffee back to his native Venice, and by 1615 the Venetians were

INTREPID EXPLORER
This miniature painting was featured in the book *The Travels of Marco Polo*, which was originally published during Polo's lifetime. It is said that the explorer was the first man to bring coffee into Venice.

Once coffee hits your system ideas quick-march into motion like the battalions of a great army.

Honoré de Balzac, "The Pleasures and Pains of Coffee," 1830s

introducing the "Old World" to the new caffeine-based beverage that would rival Spanish chocolate from the Americas and China tea. The first people to bring away a coffee tree were the Dutch, which explains why that country still finds it hard to operate without a daily dose of *koffie*. By 1616, resourceful Dutch gardeners were cultivating and propagating the trees under their new glasshouses (a heated *ambulacrum* was already in operation at the Leiden Botanical Gardens in 1599). Through the seventeenth century, they shipped the saplings east to Malabar in India and Batavia in Java. Java, in what is now Indonesia, would become one of the world's main coffee exporters and make the Dutch masters of the coffee trade.

The French gained a grip on the crop when, in 1720, a French naval officer, Gabriel Mathieu de Clieu, set out for Martinique with a single coffee tree. He husbanded the precious plant through storms, the threat of piracy, and a mad passenger who attacked it. Becalmed, and enduring a water shortage, he shared his meager rations with the little tree. It survived and was planted reverentially behind a protective thorn hedge, its progeny forming the basis for Martinique's coffee industry. The coffee tree had escaped and was soon spreading to the West Indies, Central and South America, and Sri Lanka.

BREAKFAST PLEASURE
By the seventeenth century, coffee was enjoyed by bourgeois families across France—as depicted in this 1739 painting, *Le Déjeuner*, by François Boucher.

The burgeoning fashion for coffee houses drove coffee's expansion. "The first of these," reported the helpful historian Thomas Macaulay (he

described the coffee houses as an "important political institution") had been "set up by a Turkey merchant, who had acquired among the Mahometans a taste for their favorite beverage." In 1683, a coffee house opened in Venice, followed in 1720 by the famous Caffè Florian in St. Mark's Square, patronized by Casanova (it being the only café at the time that admitted women) and, two centuries later, still serving the traditional slug of *caffè corretto*.

If the coffee house was a place of artistic creativity (although one London commentator condemned them for their "stink of tobacco, worse than the hell of brimstone"), it was also the place to do business. In 1688, Edward Lloyd's coffee house in Lombard Street became a haunt for ship owners and the starting place for the shipping insurance company, Lloyd's of London.

the London Stock Exchange sprang out of Jonathan Miles's coffee house, also in Lombard Street. Then there was the little coffee house in Wall Street, New York, where the economist and America's first Secretary of the Treasury, Alexander Hamilton, worked up his plans for a national bank. He should have stuck to coffee: in 1804, he died in a duel with Vice President Aaron Burr amid claims that Hamilton had fired to miss, but Burr had shot to kill. Plans for the 1773 Boston Tea Party (see Tea, p.26) were laid in the city's Green Dragon coffee house, while the Declaration of Independence was first pronounced in public at Philadelphia's Merchant's Coffee House. Drinking coffee, as opposed to "English" tea, became a patriotic matter.

Since then, coffee consumption has risen inexorably, creating third-world economies that were subservient to the vagaries of the trade (the 2000 slump in coffee prices put thousands out of business). Coffee grew in almost every country between the Tropics of Cancer and Capricorn. Along the equatorial zone, however, the tree was capable of carrying new blossom side by side with the maturing cherries, like an orange tree, which necessitated the labor-intensive business of hand-picking the ripening cherries. Shipped to the developed countries, coffee made millionaires out of the manufacturers, but paupers of its producers. In the second half of the twentieth century, this led to ethical "trade-not-aid" campaigns from those religious and secular organizations that had developed links with native communities. Dismayed by the disparity between the affluent café set and the estimated 25 million subsistence farmers, they set out to source goods directly from the producers, passing profits back to the grower nations. In the 1990s, campaigners took their crusade to America where, despite claims of a tradewash, Starbucks in 2009 became the world's largest purchaser of fairtrade coffee. It was a milestone for a campaign that had its roots in Holland, the nation that first brought the coffee tree out of Africa.

SOCIAL BOND
Three men chat in a coffee house in Algiers, Algeria, at the end of the nineteenth century. Drinking coffee has become a social activity in cultures across the planet.

FROTHY COFFEE

✦

"Espresso is to Italy what champagne is to France," declared Charles Maurice de Talleyrand, indicating his preference for the coffee concentrate. The cappuccino, an espresso made with hot milk, came later. The fashion for latte, made by passing steaming milk over an espresso, and mocha (the coffee and chocolate drink, rather than the bean), swept through the U.S. and cannoned into Europe in the late twentieth century. Turkish coffee is proverbially best drunk "black as hell, strong as death, and sweet as love" and is a far cry from the beverage offered by one old-fashioned Welsh seaside café: "frothy coffee."

Cilantro
Coriandrum sativum

Native range: From southern Europe and North Africa through to southwestern Asia

Type: Aromatic annual plant

Height: Around 2 feet (60 cm)

✦ **EDIBLE**

✦ **MEDICINAL**

✦ **COMMERCIAL**

✦ PRACTICAL

Where would Indian cookery be without the aromatic, spicy bite of cilantro India was famous as the land of spices—"On India's spicy shores," as the poet William Cowper put it ("Charity," 1782). Yet cilantro was not a native Asia herb, but a Mediterranean one that was exported to Asia. Why? Because this tal slender, aromatic plant—famed for its ability to counter flatulence—was both a her and a spice.

KITCHEN HISTORIES

This tall, waving, wayside weed is as likely to be found growing wil along a Minnesota highway as down some quiet village lane in Cyprus Order up a salad in Egypt and it may contain cilantro leaves, picke young and green, regarded as a delicacy by some, and an abomination b others. Buy a bowl of soup in Peru and there the leaves are again. A street curry vendor in Mumbai will sell an aromatic dish flavored with coriander seeds (while the leaves of *Coriandrum sativum* are known a

"cilantro," the seeds carry the name "cori ander"). Step back into the Middle Ages and you might find a woman, desperate to conceive, binding between 11 and 30 seed (the numbers were mysteriously significant to her inner left thigh—a sure spell fo inducing pregnancy. Why did this wild Medi terranean plant have such an impact on the culinary and medicinal world?

Traded from India like turmeric, one of the great natural purifying foods and one that countered the effects of heat on meat, cilantro is a member of the Umbelliferae family of aromatic seed-bearing plants. Others include caraway (*Carum carvi*), cumin (*Cuminum*

When the children of Israel were returning to their homeland from slavery in Egypt, they ate manna in the wilderness and the manna was as coriander seeds.

Numbers 11, the Bible

cyminum), dill (*Anethum graveolens*), and fennel (*Foeniculum vulgare*). They may not have toppled any heads of state or triggered any wars, yet they each played their part in the world's culinary history.

Caraway seed was traditionally used to spice up Europe's cakes, breads, cheeses, and soups, as well as to impart its distinctive flavor to the German liqueur *kummel*; cumin not only added zest to curry powders, but was also used as a herbal medicine, particularly as a stimulant and a sedative. Dill, an added ingredient in the pickling of cucumbers, was also recommended as a cure for what Culpeper called the "windwhile." Fennel, at first used to flavor soups and fish sauces, was found to contain such useful oils that it was eventually listed in the British Pharmaceutical Codex 1907 and was used in confectionery, condiments, pickles, cordials, and liquors.

Cilantro, however, was something of a mystery. Like caraway, dill, and fennel, its healing properties related to the digestive system. Cultivated for at least 3,000 years, Chinese parsley, as it is sometimes known, was noted by the Chinese as a sure way of promoting longevity. The Greeks, who named it *koriandron* in reference to the bedbug (*koris*) because of the fetid smell of the leaves, admired its medicinal qualities as much as the Romans, who included it in their potions for preserving meat. Cilantro originated in the dry Mediterranean scrubs, and it was thanks to the Roman Empire that cilantro was introduced to northern Europe and included by the French monastic distillers when they laid down their bottles of Chartreuse and Benedictine, drinks with a reputation for promoting good digestion. It was almost certainly Roman merchants, fixing deals with the traders who traveled the silk roads (see White Mulberry, p.130) or sailing their traders across the Indian Ocean, who sold cilantro back down the line to India, where it became an essential culinary ingredient.

SPICE OF LIFE
A mural painting depicting various foods in a burial chamber, c. 1400 BCE. The ancient Egyptians used coriander to add flavor to their bread.

VERSATILE SEED
In India, coriander seeds are boiled in water and drunk as a traditional cure for the common cold.

SPICE OR HERB?

✦

Herbs and spices were once deemed far more important than mere flavorings. They were interpreted as the earthly symbols of supernatural powers, used as much in magic as medicine (the two disciplines were close sisters), and their characters were minutely studied. Culpeper, for example, noted of dill that "Mercury hath dominion of this plant," while of caraway he wrote that "this is also a Mercurial plant." Fennel was "an herb of Mercury, and under Virgo, and therefore bears antipathy to Pisces." Culpeper missed cilantro off his list.

Saffron
Crocus sativus

Native range: Asia Minor

Type: Corm

Height: 6 inches (15 cm)

+ EDIBLE

+ MEDICINAL

+ COMMERCIAL

+ PRACTICAL

Saffron was a luxury without parallel in the medieval world. It was a vital colorant for both the cook and the dyer, but it seems setbacks and disaster were destined to happen wherever it was grown. Is this why it remains the most costly spice in the world?

THE LION HERB

Crocus sativus is an attractive, corm-based plant that throws up a spear of green leaves only after bursting into a perfectly symmetrical flower. It plays a special role in a range of human activities from traditional Chinese medicine to dyeing fabric and rice. Its most important physical attribute, as far as mankind is concerned, is minute, as Nicholas Culpeper explained succinctly in his *Complete Herbal* of 1653. "The flowers . . . made up of six long, but roundish pointed, purple leaves, enclosing in their middle three stamina, of a fiery, yellow, red colour; which being gathered, and carefully dried in a saffron-kiln, and made into square cakes, is the saffron of the shops."

A plant in flower is a plant preparing to reproduce. Equipped with both male and female parts, the flower is designed to attract its own particular pollinator, an insect or bird, which transports the pollen from the anther of the stamen (the male part) of one plant to fertilize the female part—the pistil, which is made up of the stigma, the style (stalk), and the ovary—of another plant. In harvesting saffron from *C. sativus*, that process is arrested as the orange-red stigmas, the plant's powerhouse, are plucked out by hand, dried, and then sold whole or as saffron powder. Since there are only three stigmas to each flower it takes a lot to make a little: 150,000 saffron blooms might make a kilo of saffron.

"It is an herb of the sun, and of the Lion, and therefore you need not demand a reason why it strengthens the heart so exceedingly," declared Culpeper, who advocated that no more than ten grains be given as a medicine at any one time. Some physicians, he revealed, prescribed dangerous doses from "a scruple to a scruple and a half."

The saffron-flowers blow in September; but the leaves come not forth till the spring.
Nicholas Culpeper, Complete Herbal, *1653*

scruple was not only a moral servation, but also an apothe-ry's measure equal to 20 grains, 1.296 grams). Physicians such these, he warned, risked a ffron overdose signaled by "an moderate, convulsive laugh, hich ended in death."

Used sensibly, the bittersweet d pungent saffron could aid gestion, reduce high blood ressure, and stimulate both enstruation and circulation. Saffron appeared, sparingly, in national shes such as Spanish *paella* and *zarzuela* (a fish stew), Italian *risotto*, d French *bouillabaisse*. It flavored cakes and liquors and was used as a rewing herb to clear the air in Roman times. Wherever it appeared, it emed to bring brief riches, followed by disaster. Alexander the Great ok saffron baths to ease his wounds, but then caught malaria and died. was a lucrative crop for the Greek islanders of Thera ow Santorini) until the terrible volcanic eruption of 1630 BCE, which buried beneath the ash beautiful osaics picturing the crocus harvest. The burghers of asel, Switzerland, profited from saffron in the 1100s ntil their crop suddenly failed. Much the same fate efell the crocus growers of Nuremberg in Germany, stern England, and Pennsylvania. The latter were appily exporting saffron with a price tag equivalent to s weight in gold until the British blockade during the Var of 1812. "It grows plentifully in Cambridgeshire, nd between Saffron Walden and Cambridge," reported ulpeper, who omitted to mention that Saffron Walden ad actually changed its name in gratitude to the spice. But here too the market was short-lived, as farmers hose to concentrate on the new crops such as corn and otatoes coming out of America.

Around 3,500 years after it was first cultivated, the vorld's most expensive spice was growing in Kashmir, pain, and Afghanistan, where, it has been said, it ffers farmers a realistic alternative to growing the pium poppy.

POPULAR CURES

✦

One popular seventeenth-century medicine, hermodactyl, was described by Culpeper as "nothing else but the roots of saffron dried." Several people were prosecuted for administering it in England including, in 1619, the "puritan and religious fanatic" William Blancke. According to the investigating committee, the "Dutch-born medical and surgeon barber . . . made the usual ref. to JC. (Jesus Christ)" during his examination and confessed to administering "pills of hermodactyls, (which) Coll called 'absurd'." Blancke retorted that he could "show absurder prescriptions of theirs" but under cross-examina-tion admitted that he "didn't know the causes of dropsy & ague."

Papyrus

Cyperus papyrus

Native range: Egypt, Ethiopia, and tropical Africa

Type: Wetland sedge

Height: 5–9 feet (2–3 m) but can reach 15 feet (4.5 m)

+ EDIBLE
+ MEDICINAL
+ COMMERCIAL
+ **PRACTICAL**

Papyrus was used to record history itself when it was first dredged from the muddy banks of the Nile Delta around 3000 BCE. It gave us paper and, although its use died out a thousand years ago, this ancient Egyptian plant may yet have a future in the twenty-first century.

Pause in your reading. Forget the words, the font, and the images, and ru your fingers down the page. Feel the paper. What you feel are trees, shippe across the world then chipped, pulped, bleached, layered, and delivere ink-ready to the printer. These fine, smooth sheets represent 5,000 yea of development since *Cyperus papyrus* was first turned into paper.

The papyrus was a plant that originated in the river basins of Eth opia, and grew in the Nile Delta until it was badly affected by drought the eleventh century. The Egyptians began writing on papyrus abou 4,000 years ago, marking our transition from prehistoric to historic.

A WIDENING PAPER TRAIL

Although papyrus was usurped by parchment—animal skins that ha been flayed, dried, and pressed flat—it was valued for its lightness an flexibility. By around 800 CE, its use had largely ceased, although scribe at the Vatican continued using papyrus for the papal bulls for a whil after. By then, China's papermaking technology was well established. C Lun was credited with the invention of the process where fine-meshe bamboo frames were dipped into vats of wet paper pulp, withdrawn, an then pressed flat to dry. He developed his methods around 105 CE, an by 751 CE the technique had reached the Arab world. They refined th process using rags as the raw material, an carried the paper trade into Spain as the conquered the country in the eleventh centur

PRACTICAL USES
Until relatively recently, *Cyperus papyrus* was abundant in the Nile Delta, Egypt, where it was used to produce a wide range of practical items, including boats, sandals, and baskets.

We must consider the distinctive characters and the general nature of plants from the point of view of their morphology, their behavior under external conditions, their mode of generation, and the whole course of their life.

Theophrastus, c. 371–c. 287 BCE

the same year that the Arabs were
finally driven back to North Africa,
Columbus left for the Americas only to
find that Mexican Aztecs and Toltecs had
been producing their own papers from tree
bark. (Bark paper was still being made in
the state of Puebla in 2000.) As with
papyrus, the key ingredient in the wet

paper mix was cellulose. Found in plant cell walls, cellulose is the rigid
material that gives plants both strength and pliancy, and Cai Lun's invention may have been inspired by observing how wasps chewed out plant
cellulose to create their lantern-like paper nests. French scientist, René
de Réaumur, certainly acknowledged the contribution of *le guêpier*, the
wasp nest, when in 1719 he worked out that wood could be substituted
for rags if laborers, like the wasps, could devise a method of grinding it
down. Eventually, in 1843, one Saxon Keller came up with the means of
making groundwood pulp, and 12 years later Mellier Watt patented
chemical pulp.

PAPYRUS PULP
Papyrus "paper" was made
from the pulp of the papyrus
plant. Long strips of pulp
were laid out side by side,
with another series of strips
laid on top. These two layers
were pressed tightly together
until they formed a single
sheet, which was then
polished smooth.

In the 1960s, feature writers committed such histories as these to
print by banging away at their manual typewriters on reams of paper.
Turned into solid slugs of type, their words of wisdom were locked into
a page frame, hauled onto inky presses, and printed out on great
rolls of newsprint. Around 50 years on, trickling computer characters
and digital downloads have transformed the industry, presenting newspapers, magazines, and perhaps even the book in your hands, with an
uncertain future.

Even so, the advent of emails has contributed to a
40% increase in paper use in some countries. In paper
terms, the average American prints out the equivalent
of nine mature pines a year. Indonesia, which possesses
the world's second richest biodiversity, has seen 75% of
its forest cover logged away, mainly to make paper. Two
solutions could resolve the problem: the first would be
to improve paper recycling. The second would be to
source local materials to make "local" paper. Blending
recycled paper with tree-free materials could produce
sustainable paper supplies and take the pressure off
the world's forests. Almost any fibrous plant can
contribute to papermaking, from bamboo, hemp, and
bagasse (the waste left during sugarcane processing), to
corn and rice straw—and, perhaps, papyrus too.

SCHOOL OF THOUGHT

✦

Theophrastus lived at Eressos on
the Greek island of Lesbos between
c. 371 and c. 287 BCE. A Greek
philosopher, he was a prolific
writer, although only very few of his
books have survived. Two that still
exist are *Enquiry into Plants* and
On the Causes of Plants; works
that earned him the title
of Father of Botany. He died in c.
287 BCE. "We die just when we are
beginning to live," he wrote.

Foxglove
Digitalis purpurea

Native range: Western Europe

Type: Biennial with purple or white flowers

Height: Up to 6.5 feet (2 m)

+ EDIBLE
+ **MEDICINAL**
+ COMMERCIAL
+ PRACTICAL

The discovery by an eighteenth-century medic that the foxglove was an imp[ortant] medicinal plant gave the world one of its most valuable cardiac dru[gs]. The secret healing properties of the poisonous plant had been part of folklore [for] centuries, but in an age of witchcraft, it was unwise to admit it.

FOXES GLOFA

A curious memorial hangs on the walls of a church in Birmingha[m], England. It records the demise of a local doctor, Will Withering, aged [58] and is decorated with a stone carving of what used to be called *fo[xes] glofa*. Withering, born in 1741, had battled with two diseases, dropsy a[nd] tuberculosis, for almost 40 years. He beat the first by "inventing" [the] foxglove, but was defeated by the second, which killed him in 1799. [Of] course, Will Withering did not actually "invent" the foxglove, althou[gh] he did bridge the gap between medicine and herbalism when he me[t a] patient who had been cured of dropsy with a herbalist's mixture. Wh[en] rooting around in the medicine purse, he found foxglove. For ten yea[rs] he pursued thorough clinical trials on its constituent drug, digita[lis] establishing that it was a cure for dropsy.

The doctor had been appointed to Birmingham General Hospital [by] Erasmus Darwin—grandfather of the great Charles—in the days wh[en] dropsy, or hydrops (an old medical term for edema), was like a plag[ue] on the world's nation states. The illness had the grotesque effect [of] swelling the body to such a degree that victims sometimes drowned [in] their own bodily fluids, the lungs becoming so waterlogged that th[ey] were asphyxiated. Physicians tried purging the victim, drawing [off] gallons of fluid. Sometimes it succeeded; the Earl of Oxford was sa[id] to have been "purg'd 2 or 3 Times" and followed a diet of "Cana[ry] and Water, thickened with the Yolk of a new-laid Egg" and "[his] Victuals . . . cook'd with abundance of Garlick; and Horse-radis[h]" a treatment that was "blest with intire Success." Just as ofte[n] however, sufferers died.

The Fox-gloves in that they are bitter, are hot and dry, with a certaine kinde of clensing qualitie joyned therewith; yet they are of no use, neither have they any place amongst medicines.
John Gerard, Herbal, 1597

WITCHING FLOWER

Before Will Withering's time, no right-minded physician would have contemplated bringing in the wild foxglove to effect a cure. The herbalist John Gerard had dismissed "what some call in French, *Gantes nostre dame* [Our Lady's gloves]." The nation's many herbalists might have taken issue with him had they not been fearful of being accused of witchery. While doctors took a holistic approach to their patients' ills, advocating good air, exercise, rest, and a modicum of strong emotions such as pleasure or anxiety, the country housewife relied on hand-me-down knowledge to care for the sick. She knew her hedgerow cures, treating worms with vermicidal plants such as mugwort or wormwood, or prescribing salads, pottages, and tisanes (infusions of dried herbs) for a particular condition. Until the 1400s, she could only update that knowledge from hearsay, since, because the *lingua medica*, the language of medicine, was Latin, her gender kept her in a state of illiteracy.

As these Latin texts were translated and pirated copies came into circulation, she learned, for example, that wild parsnip in a decoction helped the bowels to move and the urine to flow. From Thomas Hill's *Gardeners Labyrinth* (1577) she discovered even greater benefits: "Parsnep moveth the venereal act, procureth Urine, and asswageth the Cholerick, sendeth down the Termes in Women; it profiteth the Melancholicke, increaseth good blood, helpeth the straightnese of making water, amendeth stitches of the sides or purisies, the bite of venemous beast, it amendeth the eating of Ulcers, the bearing of this root is profitable." Despite Gerard's protestation, she knew "doctor foxglove" to be a potent and powerful plant, as capable of killing as curing the patient. Small doses of digitalis could improve a condition, but if the ailment was a malfunction of the kidneys, the drug, no longer excreted by the body, gradually built up into a lethal dose.

Maude Grieve, in her *Modern Herbal* (published in 1931), described the foxglove as useful for heart and kidney conditions, as well as internal hemorrhages, inflammatory disease, delirium tremens, epilepsy, acute mania, and other diseases. She might have added some handy hints for the gardener: the foxglove seemed to protect other plants grown nearby from disease, improved the storage of potatoes and tomatoes, and, as a cut flower, prolonged the life of other blooms in the vase.

WILL WITHERING
An engraving of the English botanist, based on a painting by the Swedish artist Carl Frederik von Breda. Withering first learned of the use of digitalis from a herbalist in Shropshire, England.

FLORAL MITTENS

✦

What are the origins of the name "foxglove"? *Fox* may be a corruption of "folk," a reference to the knowledge of its medicinal use in folklore. Other names include the little folks' glove, witches' bell, the fox's gliew (the Norwegian gliew was a bell-like instrument), floppy dock, and, in German, *Fingerhut* (thimble). In his *Dictionary of English Plant Names*, 1973, Geoffrey Grigson suggested that, since foxgloves often grow in the disturbed ground by a fox's earth, the association of fox and glove was a natural one.

Yam

Dioscorea spp.

Native range: Southeast Asia, the Pacific Islands, Africa, and South America

Type: Tropical climbing perennial vine

Weight: Various. *D. elephantipes* can weigh in at up to 700 pounds (318 kg)

+ **EDIBLE**
+ **MEDICINAL**
+ **COMMERCIAL**
+ PRACTICAL

There are about 600 species of yam growing in the Pacific Islands, Africa, A. and America, and the edible root has long been the staple food in many p of the world. But its growing popularity as a food source, especially in Africa, n have contributed to a significant decline in the growing and consumption of o indigenous foods. Some species of yam are so toxic that they are used to poison tips of arrows: but perhaps even Africa's traditional edible yam, *Dioscorea sat* should come with a health warning.

MIXED BLESSING

The yam has been a staple food crop for more than a 100 million peo in the humid and subhumid tropics. Somewhat starchy and bland taste, yams are rich in carbohydrates and various minerals and vitami although they contain very little protein. In addition, they also cont the toxic substance dioscorine, which is destroyed when yams are boil baked, roasted, or fried. In West Africa, yams are peeled, boiled, a pounded into the nutritious dough *foo foo*; in the Philippines, they made into candies and jellies; in Guyana they are made into the b *kala*. Even the toxic varieties *D. hispida* and *D. dumertorum* are son times eaten when food is short. (Since the yams must be left for a week least before poison levels drop to an edible level, the hapless househ hen usually serves as the test taster.) Some roots are used to make ins ticides, and *D. piscatorum* has long been used in Malaya as a poisone fish bait and for poison arrows. Thanks to their medicinal properties, plants were named in honor of Dioscorides, author of *De Materia Medi* written in the first century CE. Today, yams produce the plant steroi sapogenins, and different species are used in the production of bir control pills, cortisone, and for the tre ment of asthma and arthritis.

The yam alone did not change the cou of dietary history in regions such as Afri but along with the import of refined foods and t distribution of protein-rich food like corn a soybeans, it figured in a problem that Africa is o now starting to address: food poverty. The "developi world," as opposed to the "developed world," (something o contradiction given the current levels of obesity and diet-rela health problems in the West), is hungry. This is, in part, because the developed world has used land in other countries as its own vegetable and flower garden: the labor is cheap, the climate is good, and the land costs little. But plantation crops, bound for America, Europe, and Asia, can exhaust local soils, cause pollu-

tion, and deplete water supplies. The labor and land needed for the foreign crops takes families away from raising and eating indigenous foods, such as the versatile cow pea, calabash (gourd), and Malabar "spinach." Although foods like these have been mocked as "poor woman's work, poor man's food," they can provide better-tasting, nutritionally rich meals that are packed with micronutrients.

There are around 7,000 species of edible plants in the world, yet many African families have come to subsist on two plants at most: a single cereal such as millet, and a root vegetable like the yam. Such foods should come with a health warning. While the life expectancy of the average Swiss citizen in 2007 was 80 years and rising, life expectancy in Nigeria had dropped to 47 according to UNICEF, less than it had been half a century before. There are plenty of other reasons to be factored in, from political instability and endemic corruption to civil wars, but the loss of traditional seed supplies and the kitchen knowledge that went into cultivating and cooking the old foods has not helped. The new carbohydrate-rich, protein-poor diet has been blamed for a rise in diseases such as arthritis and diabetes, and the loss of natural immunity to the devastating effects of the parasite *Giardia lamblia*.

At some time or another mankind has used at least 3,000 plant species for food: these days only about 20 plant species feed most of the people in the world.

Tony Winch, Growing Food: A Guide to Food Production, *2006*

ALL IN THE NAME

+

In India it is *aloo*, from the Sanskrit *âlu*, a word for any edible and nutritious root. Yet it was the European word "yam" that encircled the world. Why? One story relates how some African slaves in Spain were seen digging up tubers for their evening meal. Upon being asked what they were eating, they mistakenly replied that they were eating, using the Guinean word *nyami*, meaning "to eat." In Spanish, this has evolved into *ñame*, in Portuguese it has become *inhame*, and in French it has become *igname*. A further corrupted version, "yam," has come to mean just about any root the "natives" were prepared to dig up and eat. Just to compound the confusion, the yam in America also refers to the unrelated sweet potato (*Ipomoea batatas*).

Cardamom
Elettaria cardamomum

Native range: India

Type: Perennial, cane-like with spear-shaped leaves

Height: 2 feet (60 cm)

+ **EDIBLE**
+ **MEDICINAL**
+ COMMERCIAL
+ PRACTICAL

It may be an essential item in Indian cuisine, but cardamom these days is often regarded as an afterthought for the kitchen spice rack. Yet it is one of the most aromatic and exotic herbs, and was once known as the Queen of Spices to distinguish it from the Spice King, black pepper.

FOOD FOR THOUGHT

In his hymn, quoted opposite, the Victorian Bishop of Calcutta hints at a paradise tainted only by the hand of civilization. In fact, this was a diatribe against the icon-worshiping native: "In vain with lavish kindness / The gifts of God are strown; / The heathen in his blindness / Bows down to wood and stone." Nevertheless, the good bishop doubtless enjoyed one of the great Indian and Ceylonese spices, the cardamom. A common ingredient in Indian pickles, curries, and desserts, it has found its way into Finnish pulla bread, the coffee consumed by drinkers in the Middle East (cardamom is thought to detoxify coffee), and perfumes concocted by the Greeks and Romans. Hardly the stuff of history, and yet it was crowned the Queen of Spices. The description arose in its country of origin, India. Here, growing wild in the eponymous Cardamom Hills, the monsoon forests of the Western Ghats in Kerala, cardamom was critical to the economics of this part of southern India. The small or "true" cardamom was *chotta elaichi* (as opposed to the larger *bara elaichi*).

Great care was exercised in picking the fruits from the plant, which was a member of the same family as ginger (Zingiberaceae). In cultivation, the plants were grown from seed or divided from the parent plant, and by the second or third year were yielding little capsules

GRAINS OF PARADISE
✦

Elettaria cardamomum, also known as the Malabar Cardamom, is regarded by some as superior to other types of cardamom. Another close relative is *Afromomum melegueta*. Grown on the west coast of Africa, the pungent-tasting seeds range in color from red to orange. They were traded across Africa and Europe from the 1200s and were commonly used to fortify beer and add a spicy tang to wine.

What though the spicy breezes
Blow soft o'er Ceylon's isle;
Though every prospect pleases,
And only man is vile.

Reginald Herber, Bishop of Calcutta,
"Greenland's Icy Mountains," 1819

packed with seed. Since the spicy essence of cardamom lasted better the longer the seeds remained in the capsules, the seed cases were carefully cut before they ripened and then slow-dried to preserve the aroma. The best of the crop went to the royal courts: it was customary to present guests with the gift of cardamoms, stored in tiny, handcrafted silver or golden barrels and offered in the palm of the hand to the guest, who accepted the gift with a pinch of finger and thumb. Once the nicotine habit reached India, the silversmiths would prepare for their nawabs green cardamoms covered in silver leaves that had been dipped in rose water laced with tobacco. The cardamom was a key ingredient in India's ancient Ayurvedic medicinal tradition, where it was used to treat bronchial ailments and poor digestion, especially that caused by an intolerance to dairy products. When cardamoms reached the Mediterranean, the Greeks and Romans used the spice to sweeten their breath, their perfumes, and, perhaps, their love lives (the herb was rumored to have aphrodisiac qualities).

The first record of cardamoms occurring in Chinese medicine goes back 1,300 years. By 1000 CE, the spice was being transported—by Arab merchants—overland from China. Later, in the 1500s, it was being shipped by sea. The Portuguese traveler Duarte Barbosa, brother-in-law of the explorer Ferdinand Magellan, whose ship the *Vittoria* became the first to circumnavigate the world, described the plant in 1524. The Europeans enjoyed its soothing, calming qualities, and with its hint of eucalyptus it was regarded as a first port of call for the apothecary dealing with a digestive problem or a nursing mother with a colicky baby. Cardamom was an essential item in the medieval pharmacy.

Until the 1800s, when British farmers started planting cardamom as a second crop in their overseas coffee plantations, the only source of cardamom was from India and Ceylon. Recognizing its virtues, Western scientists struggled to classify it. For a while it carried the Latin name *Matonia*, so named by Sir James Smith, founder of the Linnaean Society in London, after Dr. William Maton, who had assiduously studied it. In 1811, it was reclassified as *Elettaria cardamomum*.

NATURAL MEDICINE
Cardamom pods are employed throughout southern Asia to treat an array of ailments, including respiratory infections and indigestion.

CARDAMOM FRUIT
The yellow-green fruit of *Elettaria cardamomum* can be up to an inch (2.5 cm) long and contains black seeds.

Coca

Erythroxylum coca

Native range: The Andes

Type: Shrub growing in partial shade

Height: Up to 6 feet (1.8 m) when cultivated

+ **EDIBLE**
+ **MEDICINAL**
+ **COMMERCIAL**
+ PRACTICAL

U sed without ill effect for thousands of years in South America, the leaves *Erythroxylum coca* caused no great problems until they were used against Indians. When the world learned how to extract cocaine from the leaves, nothi was quite the same again for celebrities, world-renowned psychiatrists, and ev the world's biggest drinks company.

FEEL-GOOD FACTOR

The light green leaves of the coca shrubs that grow in the Andes of Sou America have been picked with the care of the connoisseur for at lea 2,000 years. The reason is that, unlike its neighboring trees, the leaves *E. coca* represent one of the world's most valuable cash crops. The pro ucts of the leaves are largely illegal in the Western world, but the pla has provided sustenance and an income to the people who live in t place where they grow.

Erythroxylum coca leaves have an extraordinary effect on the peop who chew them. After about ten minutes they feel good. They feel ene gized, and ready and capable of doing just abo anything. Filled with a sense of wellbeing, the chewe feel their inhibitions falling away. They are almo intoxicated with pleasure. The intoxication is re enough, for the leaves of *E. coca* contain alkaloids th raise the concentrations of dopamine in the brain wh ingested (see box). The effect was first noted in t 1500s by Spanish conquistadors when they encounter the soon-to-be-subjugated South American India who revered the leaf. Its effects were further noted the Viennese psychiatrist Sigmund Freud—he on stopped using it himself when a colleague, and fello doctor, overdosed and died in a bout of depressio Slave masters fed the leaves to their workers in order cut costs and increase production, and the corpule World War II commander of the Luftwaffe, Hermann Goering, used it unsuccessfully to keep his weight down. The man who came up with a

SELECTIVE ADDICTION

+

Drugs like cocaine and heroin produce a rush because they release dopamine in the brain. Dopamine, which is also released by food and sex, produces feelings of pleasure for a short time. Even the anticipation of taking a drug such as cocaine can release dopamine, which, in someone who is addicted, is experienced as a craving so strong that the user is willing to take all kinds of risks to receive another hit. But this "dopamine theory of addiction" has yet to explain why some people become addicted while others do not.

COCA COLOR
When dried, the leaves of the coca plant are dark green on top and dark gray on the underside.

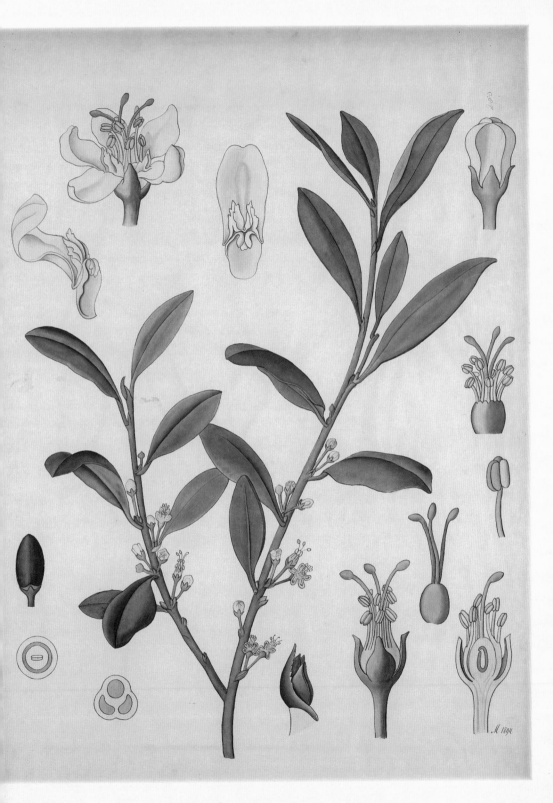

drink he called Coca Cola employed it in his early recipe while research into New York murder victims in the early 1990s found that 31% had traces of cocaine in their bodies.

What is it about these curious leaves? For the Incas the coca leaves were the superdrug of their time. The nation was centered on Cuzco, a city built at over 12,000 feet (3,600 m) above sea level. Here, chewing the coca leaves had a similar effect to using an oxygen supply in the mountains: it enabled the *chasquis* (see box), who habitually carried their precious vicuna wool pouch or *churpa* of coca leaves around with them, to work at altitudes that would leave anyone else breathless. The use of coca leaves, however, was mostly reserved for religious ceremonies or medical purposes (coca, for example, was a strong anesthetic). That was until the Spanish invasion and the subsequent arrival of missionaries. By the late 1500s, the Catholic Church had placed a parish priest in almost every enslaved settlement in the Andes and the missionaries, with the zeal of their religious convictions, rid their flocks of this devilish coca habit. But their mission was frustrated by another group of Spaniards: the slavers. Latin America was the only serious source of new silver bullion in the 1600s, and the Spanish ruthlessly exploited the indigenous Indians to work silver mines such as the one in Potosí, Bolivia. The working conditions would have shamed even the nineteenth-century abolitionists (some of whom thought sending child sweeps up congested chimneys was an acceptable occupation for the poor). The men, women, and children worked on in the mines partly because the Spanish fed them on coca leaves. The Indian working people, aside from the chasquis, had rarely used the leaf before; now they were being enslaved to it. While by the 1620s well over half a million miners are estimated to have died at the mine, production nevertheless rose, in some years by as much as 50%.

CHASQUIS

◆

The key to managing an empire is efficient communications. The Inca Empire did so through its *chasquis,* couriers who could carry urgent messages from one place to another quickly and efficiently. The Inca chasquis relied on their coca leaves so much that distances in the Andes came to be measured not in miles, but in *cocadas,* the quantity of coca leaves required to complete the journey. Coca leaves allowed men to carry packs equivalent to their own body weight for over 20 miles (32 km) in the steep Andean terrain on little more than a breakfast bowl of porridge.

INCA MESSENGER
The *chasquis* traversed northwestern South America carrying messages for their Inca rulers. Inside the *qipi* on their back they would often store coca leaves for the journey.

GETTING HOOKED

Not surprisingly, in the nineteenth century, the slave owners of the southern states of the U.S. took to adding coca leaves to the inadequate meals they gave their own workforce. The coca leaf, meanwhile, was making new inroads into everyday life, especially among both genuine and quack physicians. Coca leaves were, and still are, used in medicine. The work of two scientists led to their use as an anesthetic in optical, dental, and other forms of surgery: the German Friedrich Gaedcke first isolated the active alkaloid in 1855, and three years later Albert Niemann published his improved process for what he called "cocaine." It was soon found to have an extraordinary effect on those who ingested it.

By the twentieth century, cocaine (variously known as "coke," "blow," "nose candy," "snowball," "tornado," and "wicky stick") had become the recreational drug of hundreds of thousands of fast-living and wealthy "cokeheads." One of the most celebrated was a young Viennese neurologist, Sigmund Freud. When Freud learned of an experiment with cocaine in the Bavarian military (soldiers who used the drug ate less food while still performing their normal tasks), he took it regularly for three years. He was said to have prescribed it to some patients and only gave it up himself after the death of a colleague. It is possible that his experiments spurred on the production of several medicines whose most active ingredient was cocaine.

In the 1960s, at least one cough medicine manufacturer noticed unexpected sales during the summer instead of during winter when people were more prone to colds. It turned out that their concoctions contained legal amounts of opium-based ingredients and were being taken at summer rock festivals by young people looking for new ways to get out of their heads. In the early 1900s, a similar trend was noted when a number of "doctor's specials"—medications mostly designed as catarrh cures although some were marketed as aphrodisiacs)—were flying off pharmacy shelves. The specials were heady stuff, containing as they did a combination of quinine (see Cinchona, p.42) and cocaine. It was around then that an Atlanta pharmacist, John Pemberton, was trying to replicate the extraordinarily popular drink, Vin Mariani, which contained a marinade of coca leaf. Invented by the Corsican Angelo Mariani, the drink was produced by steeping coca leaves in a good red wine for six months. The resulting brew was popular and prompted Pemberton to come up with his own "French Wine Cola." When the city of Atlanta

NATURAL NARCOTIC
Coca plantations, such as this one in Bolivia, do not just supply the cocaine factories. The leaves of *Erythroxylum coca* are used to make the popular tea, *mate de coca*, which is widely drunk in South America.

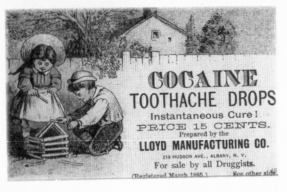

banned alcohol, Pemberton responded with a non-alcoholic substitute based on a number of ingredients including essence of coca leaves and caffeine from the kola nut (see box opposite).

His recipe for what he called Coca Cola (rather than Coca Kola) was more successful than his marketing methods and it was left to another businessman, Asa Candler, to take over the beverage and the name to found what was to become the world's biggest drinks company, and one of the world's most famous brands. After selling the company, Candler died in 1929, a very wealthy man. The soft drink, the first to be consumed in space, now sells in over 200 countries without the opiate that once helped launch it. It does contain one ingredient that has proved even more irresistible: sugar (see Sugarcane, p.166).

WARTIME HIGH

The concentration of any plant-derived drug inevitably creates problems: look at tobacco, heroin, and alcohol. By the early part of the twentieth century, cocaine was being sniffed and snorted by more and more people as street prices fell. The authorities tended to link cocaine, controversially, with heroin. Although both drugs were opiates, evidence suggested that cocaine did not have the same addiction rates as heroin (see Opium Poppy, p.148). Nevertheless, up until World War II, regular users tended toward discretion. This was especially the case in Berlin, where prewar cocaine consumption and the nightclub circuit were inseparable; during the war, as the Nazi regime cracked down on such decadence, high officials like Goering, who used cocaine, kept their skeletons well hidden. Amphetamines, freely distributed during wartime, also helped to damp down the cocaine market.

The end of the wartime supply of amphetamines, social change, and above all, air travel, which made smuggling so much easier, touched off the cocaine market once again. It was not long before criminal cartels had begun to organize themselves around production and supply. The border between the United States and Mexico proved to be particularly vulnerable to this. Until then, the traditional method of taking the drug was to sniff a line of powdered cocaine into the nose through a straw or a rolled-up dollar bill

We must try to better understand the confusion and disillusion and despair that bring people, particularly young people, to the use of narcotics and dangerous drugs.

From U.S. President Richard Nixon's speech on drug abuse, 1971

hile the euro or ten-pound note were just as effective, the advent of
ystallized cocaine, which could be smoked, suddenly extended the
tential market to those who had just spent their last dollar (or euro) on
me coke. Crack opened a new and more sinister chapter in the history
cocaine. Crack, or rock cocaine ("crack" referred to the sound of the
ystal as it burned in a pipe) was cheap and readily available. It helped
e drug achieve the dubious reputation of being the second most
mmonly used drug, behind cannabis, in the whole
America.

Solutions to the problem seemed simple enough:
al with the misuse of the drug at home and destroy
source abroad, but just as the South American
dians had paid the price for Spain's greed for silver,
ey were once again to pay the price for a richer
tion's mistakes. The street price of refined cocaine,
ld by the gram, fluctuated. In 1985, Henry Hobhouse,
his book, *Seeds of Change*, estimated that a hectare
coca shrubs would yield around 33 pounds (15 kg) of
re cocaine with a street value of $2.5m. No Peru-
an, carrying out the traditional picking cycle of three
mes a year, expected to receive more than a fraction
this for their labors, but coca at least provided a
ving and chewing the coca made working on a poor
et possible. Nevertheless, in the early days of the
venty-first century, as part of a U.S. aid package to
olombia, "illicit" crops of coca and opium poppies in
e Putumayo region of rural Colombia were sprayed
ith glyphosate and granular herbicides. Even before the sprays
escribed by one advocate as no more harmful than table salt) began to
ll, voices were raised in protest. One claimed that using herbicides on
e precious rainforests was as irresponsible as the spraying of Asian
inforests with the defoliant Agent Orange (a U.S. plan to deprive the
emy of food and shelter) during the Vietnam War. Another claimed it
as tantamount to "dynamiting the Taj Mahal" for the potential damage
could wreak on the rainforests. Even more alarmingly, the "fumiga-
on" of the forests was said to be not only destroying perfectly legal
ops, but also the rich biodiversity of the Amazon itself. Afterwards,
searchers claimed no ill effects had occurred from the aerial spraying.
ut still there seems to be no end of problems associated with the little
aves of *Erythroxylum coca*.

A CUP OF KOLA

✦

The African kola nut has been
chewed for centuries across West
Africa and was incorporated into
the religious ceremonies of the
Nigerian Yoruba. Though native to
Africa, two species especially—*Cola
acuminata* and *C. nitida*—are
grown commercially in tropical
regions worldwide. Why? Because
the kola nut contains around 2%
caffeine and other alkaloids
including theobromine and the
heart stimulant, kolanin. Kola once
had the potential to rival tea and
coffee as a more popular non-
alcoholic drink.

Eucalyptus

Eucalyptus spp.

Native range: Mostly Australia

Type: From a low shrub to a tall tree

Height: 30–180 feet (10–60 m)

+ EDIBLE
+ **MEDICINAL**
+ **COMMERCIAL**
+ **PRACTICAL**

Nineteenth-century railroaders and ornamental gardeners loved Australia's national tree, the eucalyptus; as the tree flourished in its trackside plantation it yielded plentiful supplies of cheap fuel to power the steam trains. As an ornamental garden tree it was a great conversation piece, especially in California. The tree was even rumored to cure swamp fever. No wonder it became the world's most widely planted hardwood. So why were protesters hacking down eucalyptus plantations in places as far apart as Thailand and Spain a century later?

UP A GUM TREE

More than 700 different species of native gums, or eucalypts, were growing around the maritime edges of the world's smallest continent when Australia's first settlers arrived. For a century or so, the new settlers struggled to fell and burn as many as they could in order to lay their hands on the valuable grazing ground beneath for their sheep and cattle. But for Joseph Banks, one of the plant collectors aboard Captain James Cook's ship HM *Bark Endeavour*, the eucalypt was a delight. On May 1770, while Cook was charting Australia's east coast, Banks and the Swedish botanist Daniel Carlsson Solander (who had studied under Linnaeus at Uppsala University) landed in an area that Cook later called "Botany Bay."

Banks went ashore and gazed up in admiration at the tall, graceful trees with their strange peeling silvered bark and lance-shaped leaves whispering in the breeze. But it was French plantsman Charles Louis L'Héritier de Brutelle (1746–1800), not Linnaeus, who named the species *Eucalyptus obliqua* (dubbed "messmate" or "stringybark" by the locals). L'Héritier named the eucalyptus meaning "well covered"—a references to the way the tree protects its flowers.

We rowed we rowed o'er the water so blue
Like a feather we would float along
In a gum tree canoe.

Traditional Australian folk song

Banks, Solander, and L'Héritier were equally excited about the tree. It was an exotic; it grew faster and taller than any tree they had ever encountered before, and the leaves, when rubbed, exuded a curiously medicinal smell. They would not have been surprised to discover that just over two centuries later those first few plants, collected from Australia, had so spread that they accounted for almost 40% of all the tropical forest plantations worldwide, covering just over 100 million acres (42 million ha). They could be forgiven for believing they had stumbled across the world's most wonderful tree.

GREEN GOLD

The eucalypts are among the tallest broadleaved trees in the world, and the mountain ash (*E. regnans*) of South Victoria and Tasmania is the tallest of all. There are few of these leviathans—some measure over 450 feet (140 m)—remaining, as many were logged out during the nineteenth century. "The cork-oak, fir, red cedar, and other trees are there being planted under government direction, in room of the destroyed trees, many of which were useless in commerce, or for building purposes," explained "The Gatherer" in *Cassell's Family Magazine* of the 1890s. It was an ill-conceived idea that was swiftly discredited as the eucalyptus proved itself extraordinarily useful.

The resins in the bark produce kino-tannic acids used in mouthwashes and throat syrups, while the leaves produce oils employed in antiseptics, balms, diuretics, and disinfectants. The volatile or essential oils are put into vitamin supplements—they help the body absorb vitamin C—and into perfumes, providing a tangy lemon scent. The flowers provide scented pastures for bees (eucalyptus honey is world-renowned), and its oils have even been used to flavor menthol cigarettes. When it was discovered how to extract eucalyptus cellulose (by chopping the timber into chips, then emulsifying these into pulp by boiling them in

FIRE TREE

✦

The darling of Australian wildlife, the koala bear relies on the eucalyptus, quietly consuming up to 2 pounds (1 kg) of eucalyptus leaves each night. The bear has learned to live with such a volatile food source—the trees frequently fall victim to bush fires, but will regenerate afterward thanks to harvester ants that feed on the seeds of several species. During a fire, the tree drops extra seeds, which are taken by the ants into underground stores and that germinate in the fresh, ashy earth. Other types of eucalyptus, the mallees, survive forest fires through special underground root systems that sprout with fresh growth after the fire.

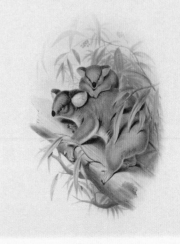

chemicals to release the wood fibers), eucalyptus began to be used everything from underpants to fire-resistant uniforms and from toi paper to cardboard. It was even used for newsprint when the May 1956 edition of the Brazilian newspaper *O Estado de São Paulo* w printed entirely on eucalyptus fiber.

THE PRINCE OF THE EUCALYPTS

The most prized of the eucalyptus was, according the botanist Baron Sir Ferdinand von Müller, the bl gum (*E. globulus*), the floral emblem of Tasmania. was unrivaled in its usefulness and the quality of oils, von Müller declared in the *Descriptive Atlas of Eucalypts of Australia – Eucalyptographia* in 18 Half a century after Australia's first governor, Arth Phillip, had dispatched a bottle of the essential oils Joseph Banks, von Müller began actively promoti the potential benefits brought by the eucalyptus tre Müller (he acquired the "von" after the King of Wü temberg conferred upon him the title Baron for l studies of the eucalypts; the British gave him l knighthood) was, arguably, the trees' greatest adv cate. It was Müller who persuaded the Englishm Joseph Bosisto to patent his process for extracting of eucalyptus. Bosisto went on to market the throughout Europe and America, and Bosisto's Euc lyptus Oil became a household name.

Müller also sent eucalyptus seeds around the worl to France, India, South Africa, Latin America, and the U.S. federal botanist William Saunders, but his g of seeds to the Melbourne archbishop J. A. Gould 1869 had phenomenal consequences—or so it seeme You see, eucalyptus was thought to "cure" malari Gould had sent his seeds on to a group of French Tra pist monks who had been battling with malaria— "swamp fever"—at Tre Fontane in Rome. Again an again the monks had tried to establish the malari busting eucalyptus, clearing scrub and draining swam to establish the seedlings. When at last they succeed and the eucalyptus were firmly established, the fo fevers were finally banished. Only later did anyo conclude that it was the loss of the swamps and not th rival of the eucalyptus trees that defeated the disease. (The Trappists turned the tree to their advantage by making and selling the eucalyptus-flavored liqueur Eucalittino.) Meanwhile, numerous claims regarding the benefits of the Australian gum tree were put forth. Eucalyptus timber could be made into houses, carts, and bridges. It was said to give temporary relief to the patient dying of gangrene or veneral disease. It could allegedly purify polluted air.

These claims, some more valid than others, led to the treescape in parts of America being transformed by the Australian gum, as investors, confident of quick profits, arranged the planting of thousands of eucalyptus from seed. In South America and particularly Brazil, the gum trees grew and grew. It was thanks to the efforts of agronomist Edmundo Navarro de Andrade, who died in 1941, that great forest farms of eucalyptus were planted alongside railroad tracks. Even in the mid-twentieth century, when more than 13 million acres (5.5 million ha) of the country was reforested, over half the trees planted were eucalypts. In India too (see box opposite), with much of the country on the same latitude as Brazil, eucalyptus plantations were spreading across the land to the detriment of the indigenous trees. It triggered increasing unease about the inexorable march of the eucalyptus. The sterile plantations, said its detractors, provided poor cover for wildlife compared to the native forests; eucalypts were blamed for causing dangerous soil erosion, and so prodigious was their arboreal thirst that they were accused of depleting local water supplies. The loss of biodiversity, and the encroaching cash economy of eucalyptus plantations, which undermined traditional bartering economies, turned discontent into direct action. By the 1990s, farmers as far afield as Bangkok, India, and Spain were ripping up gum-tree saplings in protest at this forest monoculture.

Having made as great an impact on the landscape as it had on the history of timber growing, it looked as though the eucalypts were reaching the end of the line, but the tree may yet have a contribution to make in the future. Haiti became one of the world's poorest nations when its tree cover was removed; the Ethiopian economy has suffered since it lost over 95% of its original forests; and there are serious environmental concerns for Thailand, which has seen half its trees felled in the last 20 years. The eucalyptus may be used to aid rapid reforestation of countries such as these.

NATURAL CANVAS
The bark of the rainbow eucalyptus (*Eucalyptus deglupta*) is shed in patches throughout the year, exposing a bright green surface underneath. As this young bark matures its color evolves, through blues and oranges to dark maroon.

Ferns

Phylum: Filicinophyta

Native range: The lost supercontinent of Pangaea

Type: Fern

Height: Up to 30 feet (9 m)

+ EDIBLE
+ MEDICINAL
+ **COMMERCIAL**
+ PRACTICAL

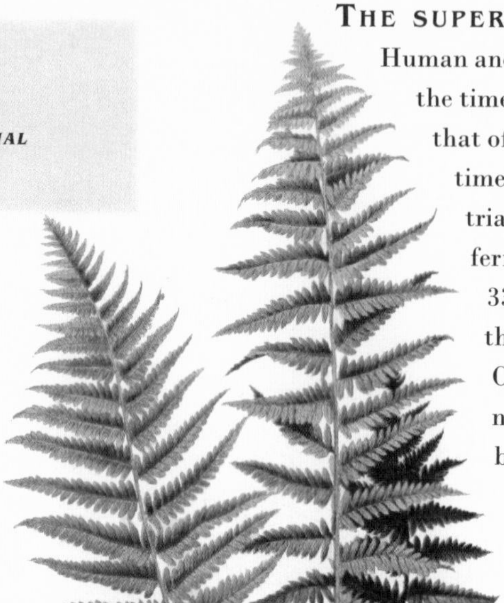

They are among the oldest plants in the world, and when they died their remains were transformed into the source of power that drove the Industrial Revolution, turning America from a wilderness into a superstate. They are now doing the same for the world's largest nation, China. This same energy source is also one of the prime causes of what is almost certainly the greatest catastrophe facing the world today: climate change.

THE SUPERPLANTS

Human ancestry goes back around four million years, to the time when human evolution branched away from that of the other primates. If that seems like a long time, consider the evolutionary span of the terrestrial and epiphytic (growing on rocks and trees) ferns. Ferns were born an almost inconceivable 335 million years ago. They appeared during the Carboniferous period, which succeeded the Cambrian, Ordovician, Silurian, and Devonian periods, and lasted 60 million years. Long before dinosaurs roamed the surface of the planet, the landmass consisted of one super-continent, Pangaea (Greek for "all lands") with the equator running through what is now Greenland, Newfoundland, and northern England. Pangaea was flat, swampy, and subject to great inundations as the glaciers of the southern hemisphere melted and froze. Toward the end of the period, gigantism ruled, and the swamps were colonized by mud-seeking amphibians that labored to draw their 15-foot (4.6-m) carcasses through the ooze. Their belly marks and footprints would be discovered 290 million years later. Dragonflies spread 18-inch (46-cm) wings to soar over the heads of 6-foot (1.8-m) millipedes crawling around beneath monstrous trees, such as *Lepidodendron*, *Sigillaria*, and

e ancestors of the horsetail (*Equisetum*), which stood over 60 feet
8 m) tall. Although they soared up to 30 feet (9 m) high, the
ants that would be instantly recognizable to people today
ere the ferns.

Their feathery leaves and fronds fed on the sun's
ys, locking in the solar power until they fell
d turned to compost or were eaten. Increas-
gly, they were buried under muddy swamp
diment. Initially, these turned into a
ongy layer of peat until, over the
urse of many millennia, they were
mpressed into a carbon-rich strata
cked with pent-up, black energy: coal.

Mankind was slow, at first, to make use of the
ergy that the ferns and other plants had stored in the earth: people
ere more accustomed to exploiting the planet's surface than rummaging
ound beneath it and, although one Bronze Age Welsh tribe learned to
e their funeral pyres with coal, there was little serious mining until
oman times.

Once established in northern Europe, the Romans used coal, among
her fuels, to heat their hot baths and hypocausts. There was a pause of
most 11 centuries between the collapse of Rome and the start of a medi-
al, monastic coal trade in County Durham, northeast
ngland. By the 1700s, the trade in "black gold" was
ecoming big business.

In 1724, Daniel Defoe published the opening
olume of his *A tour thro' the whole island of Great
ritain*, wondering at Newcastle's "prodigious heaps,
may say mountains of coals which are dug at every
tt and how many of these pitts there are." As the
al industry expanded in Britain, Germany, Poland,
nd Belgium, rural migrants were recruited to work
e mines. (In Scotland during the 1600s and early
700s, families were legally enslaved into mining,
though this was eventually outlawed.) In their
range new communities, mining families, accustomed
living with the daily risk of death from fire, flood,
r asphyxiation, were treated as social outcasts. They
ecame a race apart, bound together by their resilience
nd pride in the face of terrible working conditions.
he mining disasters they faced were so commonplace

DIRTY FUEL
As the world slowly faces
up to the reality of climate
change, calls have been
made for the use of
coal-fired power stations
to be stopped entirely.

LOCAL ACTION

✦

As world powers began holding
climate-change conferences to
try to hammer out a political and
practical solution, different
countries began to try to reverse
the trend. The small German
town of Freidburg, for example,
installed more solar (photovoltaic) roofs than there were in
the whole of the UK. China,
meanwhile, was installing more
low-energy systems than any
other country in the world,
despite building yet more
coal-fired power stations.

that in 1767, according to Barbara Freese in *Coal: A Human History*, the British newspaper *Newcastle Journal* stopped reporting them. "We have been requested to take no particular notice of these things," reported their correspondent, no doubt to the satisfaction of the mine owners.

FULL STEAM AHEAD

By the middle of the second millennium CE, the ferny remains were beginning to make people both rich and famou There was James Watt, notable for his improvements to the steam engi during the 1780s, and George Stephenson, who constructed some of t first steam locomotives. Coal also created some minor celebrities, none curious as Count Rumford. Born in 1753 into a family of British loyalis in Woburn, Massachusetts, Benjamin Thompson (as he was known the married a wealthy woman nearly 20 years his senior when he was 1 abandoning her four years later when he fled, in the wake of the Declar tion of Independence, to England. It transpired that he had been a s for the British and had been actively involved in the forming a commanding of local militias. In Britain he earned himself a knighthoc for his scientific work (with the help of some influential political conne tions), before moving to Bavaria, where, having reformed the militar and introduced workhouses for the poor, he was honored with the title Count. (He was almost certainly still working as a British spy in t Bavarian court.) He adopted the name Rumford after the New Ham shire town where he had abandoned his wife, and returned to Londc with a mission: to cure the world of the smoking chimney.

"The plague of a smoking chimney is prove bial," he wrote, warning that "those cold a chilling draughts of air on one side of the bod while the other side is scorched by a chimney fi . . . cannot but be highly detrimental to health He was convinced that the effect on those of weak constitution could be fatal: "I have not doubt in my own mind that thousands die in th country every year of consumptions occasione solely by this cause." Count Rumford developed special, smoke-free fireplace, which was still the market more than a century after his death 1814. Although President Franklin Roosev

hailed him as one of the greatest minds America had ever produced, for the most part he became the forgotten hero of the modern home whose achievements remain largely unrecognized.

LONDON PARTICULAR

London in Victorian times was totally dependent on coal, and in winter the city lay under a sulfurous cloud of thick smoke, which Charles Dickens in *Bleak House* (1852) called "a London particular." London, and other capital cities like Paris and New York, eventually cleared the skies with clean air legislation, but the problem had not gone away. In 1969, people were amazed to see images of planet Earth photographed from space. It looked brilliantly clean, and blue, although such beauty masked a hidden problem that was growing more serious with each passing year. The combined effect of burning fossil fuels and releasing methane gases was destroying the stratospheric ozone layer, which protects planet Earth from the Sun's harmful ultraviolet radiation. By 2000, two million years' worth of fossilized ferns and trees were being consumed every year. One environmentalist, Herbert Girardet, described it as "an orgy of consumerism that was wrecking the planet." People who, a century before, would have manned the barricades for the right to have coal-fired heating in their homes, were now adding their voices to the chorus of protest against destroying the fossilized ferns. There were calls for nations across the globe to end their "linear" exploitation of planet Earth: instead of taking coal from nature, burning it, and then pumping it out as waste, we should be reverting to the cyclical nature of nature itself and turning all outputs into inputs for future generations (see box).

Coal is a portable climate. It carries the heat of the tropics to Labrador and the polar circle; and it is the means of transporting itself whithersoever it is wanted. Watt and Stephenson whispered in the ear of mankind their secret, that a half-ounce of coal will draw two tons a mile, and coal carries coal, by rail and by boat, to make Canada as warm as Calcutta, and with its comfort brings its industrial power.

Ralph Waldo Emerson, The Conduct of Life, 1860

SEVEN GENERATIONS

✦

Sustainable development, according to the United Nations' Brundtland Report (1987), is "development that meets the needs of the present without compromising the ability of future generations to meet their own needs." But which future generation? Our grandchildren? Or our grandchildren's grandchildren? The figure proposed by Herbert Girardet (see left), looking at previous civilizations that had considered the problem of planning ahead, was seven generations.

Soybean
Glycine max

Native range: Southwest Asia, but first cultivated in Greece

Type: Annual bushy oilseed plant

Height: Up to 6.5 feet (2 m)

+ **EDIBLE**
+ MEDICINAL
+ **COMMERCIAL**
+ PRACTICAL

From a village vegetable in ancient China and Japan to a major source of protein for the world's vegetarians, the soybean took around three millennia to become one of the most important food crops on the planet. For Argentina, the second largest country in South America, the genetically modified variety promised to be the miracle crop that would rescue its economy; but maybe there are still lessons to be learned from the old bean.

HOLY CROP

"Child of the White Crane," "Large Jewel," and "Flowery Eyebrow": some of the names given to the indigenous Chinese soybean are positively poetic. Beans, however, have a certain digestive reputation and another of its soubriquets, the "White Spirit of the Wind," betrays the bean as the bearer of fierce "belly winds." Nevertheless, the protein- and calcium-rich soybean or *dadou* (meaning "the great bean") has been cultivated in China and Japan at least since the days of China's Western Chou dynasty, which came to an end in 770 BCE. A bean of great antiquity, its origins can be traced back more than 3,000 years. The soybean, which is one of the five holy crops of the East, along with rice, wheat, barley, and millet, has served the people as a meat and milk substitute ever since (see box opposite).

The plants, which can grow up to 6 feet 6 inches (2 m) high, produce clusters of bean pods that, like the leaves and stems, are covered in a coat of fine hairs. The beans themselves, depending on the variety (there are more than a thousand varieties), come in a rainbow of colors from white, yellow, gray, and brown to black and red.

In the kitchen, the versatile vegetable became one of the most important foods for Chinese, Japanese, Korean, and Malaysian cooks. The beans could be used fresh, sprouted, fermented, or dried. They could be eaten whole, pods and all, as the Japanese dish *edamame*. Crushing the bean and mixing it with chalk-free water produced a dairy-free "milk"; roasting and toasting the bean and, having removed the outer skin, grinding it down to a powder, produced baking flour and a product that could be used to bulk out products such as ice cream; sprouting the beans produced

hat the aristocracy dismissed as "coolie
ood," but what others enjoyed as a
ealthy, vitamin-rich salad.

Beans like the "Large Jewel" and
Flowery Eyebrow" were oiling the
heels of industry long before horticul-
uralists classed it as an oilseed rather
han a pulse. Soy oil has found its useful
ay into a whole range of items,
ncluding paints, plastics, and cosmetics.
uddhists were creating alternatives to
eat with curds of soybean more than a

housand years ago. The Japanese, meanwhile, grew soybeans for their
oyu—made from steamed soybeans and roasted wheat, fermented and
ressed—and their dairy-free cheese, *daizu* or *tofu*, and that Asian version
f Vegemite, *miso*.

DEMON BEANS
This Japanese print from
the eighteenth century
shows soybeans being
thrown to ward off evil
spirits. The practice was a
feature of Japan's annual
bean throwing festival.

MISTAKEN MISSIONARIES

When Dutch missionaries reached Japan in the 1700s,
hey discovered for themselves the attractions of *shoyu*,
ut mistook its name for that of the bountiful bean
self. When they sent samples home to Europe, they
escribed them as "shoyu" or "soya." The Western
ame stuck, and it was in the West that the soybean
romised to turn into a little miracle. With any food
lant that can be transformed into a "commodity,"
here are profits to be made. The soybean, unable to
olerate frosts, made little impact on the farmlands of
orthern Europe, but when it reached America it
hrived. Soybeans yielded around 20% oil and 40%
roteins, and from the 1920s a stream of soy started to
nd its way into every conceivable processed food from
read and burgers to dog and baby food. More signifi-
antly, it turned farm animals into meat machines; the
nsatiable hunger of the industrialized world for meat
as largely met by growing soybeans for beef cattle
nd battery hen feed.

In the 1950s, agricultural scientists began cracking
he genetic code of various plants. Each plant cell
ontains genes that determine how that plant will grow
nd harvest. Having mastered these genetic codes,

BEAN FEASTS
+

As nutritious as wheat, beans are
among the world's most important
crops. They include the Mediterranean carob used in Spanish
chocolate, which also served
goldsmiths as the original "carat"
weight. There is the American jack
bean, the tropical *lablab*, the
prehistoric broad bean, and the
kidney, stick, and "French" haricot
beans, which all originated in South
America. Beans have acquired a
tangle of myth and traditions
including the bean feast, a
celebration for the farm hands held
on Twelfth Night. During the
ceremony, the person who found
the single bean buried in the
Twelfth Night cake would be
crowned the Bean King.

What shall I learn of beans or beans of me?
I cherish them, I hoe them, early and late I have
an eye to them and this is my days work.

Henry David Thoreau, Walden, *1854*

scientists could then modify the plant
genetic makeup. Genetic modification, or GM
allowed the scientist to transfer genes from
one plant to another. GM plants were being
bred by the 1980s, and they promised to solve
world starvation, according to the geneticists. Their detractors condemned
GM as "Frankenstein's food," describing the practice as "agro-chemistry
gone mad." Nevertheless, the first commercial GM crop, tomatoes, was
harvested in 1994. By 2005, GM crops such as corn, cotton, canola,
squash, papaya, and soybeans were being grown in 21 countries around
the world, although mostly concentrated in four places: the United
States, Brazil, Canada, and Argentina.

ENVIRONMENTAL IMPACT
The growing number of
soybean plantations in South
America is causing concern
among environmental
scientists, particularly
because of the impact this is
having on the Amazonian
rainforests.

GENE BEAN

Argentina hit world headlines in 1982 when it landed a military force on
the tiny Malvinas—or Falklands—Islands in an attempt to reassert its
claim to the islands' sovereignty. The disastrous campaign (it cost the
lives of 649 Argentinians) was not the country's first calamity. North of

the cold, sheep-grazing pastures of Patagonia
lies a vast region of temperate grassland
known as the *pampas* (Quechua Indian for
"plain"), which is some of the richest farm
land found anywhere in the world. In the nineteenth century, the pampas was changed
forever by the world's growing appetite for
beef and grain. As migrant laborers flooded in,
steam railways tracked across the pampas,
hauling huge refrigeration units filled with
Argentine meat destined for export. The country's population rose from a little over a million
in the 1850s to eight million by 1914. Then the
postwar Great Depression saw meat exports
plunge. The military leaders who seized power
were themselves replaced by the "people's
president," Juan Domingo Perón (husband of
Eva Perón, or Evita), in 1946, but it wasn't
enough to arrest the economic decline caused
by the meat crisis. By the end of the twentieth
century, the Argentinian economy was in crisis,
facing near-bankruptcy and a dramatic deval-
uation of its currency.

M soy was the cash crop that promised
to save the country. From 1997, almost
half the pampas, 27 million acres (11
million ha), was devoted to growing GM
soybeans. An immediate benefit was the
halting of soil erosion caused by plowing:
the beans could be drilled direct into the
soil. Yet, even as production rose (there
was an estimated 75% increase in the
five years leading up to 2002), problems
emerged. Rural unemployment rose with
the loss of small farmers, driven out by
the soy-based agribusiness. Meanwhile, the soy crop, genetically
programmed to resist the herbicides sprayed to control its rivals, gave
rise to superweeds resistant to the conventional herbicides, and to rogue
soy plants. These had to be sprayed with a different herbicide. In neighboring Brazil, which had been producing higher yields of non-GM soy,
farmers resisted the "gene bean," but they were overruled in 2002. (There
were suggestions that some of Brazil's soy was already spiked with GM
seed brought over the borders with Argentina.) As world demand for soy
showed no sign of slowing, environmentalists have been concerned about
its expansion through rainforest regions and the *cerrado*
landscape of interior Brazil.

Some, meanwhile, have started to look back East,
to the first home of the soybean, and the life's work of
a small-time Japanese farmer, Masanobu Fukuoka. A
soil scientist who spent half a lifetime breeding fungi
under laboratory conditions, Fukuoka had become
convinced that in order to take care of the earth,
farmers needed to take better care of the soil, and the
only way to do so was to help it take care of itself
through a regime of no cultivation—this meant no
compost or chemical fertilizers; no weeding with hoes
or herbicides; and no dependence on chemicals.
Fukuoka put his theories into practice when he returned
to work the little family farm on the island of Shikoku,
convinced that by following this rigorous program, the
soybean would one day return to its status as one of
the five holy crops.

GM CROP

In the U.S., as much as 85%
of the total annual soybean
crop is from genetically
modified seed. Since the first
GM crop was cultivated, the
soybean has been adapted to
provide benefits such as a
higher nutritional content.

FEEDING FRENZY

✦

A global food crisis looms. Rising
incomes in Asia have fueled a rising
demand for meat, just as they did
during the industrialization of
Europe and America. One kilo of
beef requires seven kilos of cereals;
one kilo of poultry meat requires
three kilos of cereal, and the land
needed to grow the cereals is
simply running out. But there is
deep disagreement over how this
food crisis can be averted. While
one side favors supersized farms
and GM crops such as soy, the
other side sees the solution in small
farms, great biodiversity, and the
lessons of men like Fukuoka.

Upland Cotton

Gossypium hirsutum

Native range: China, India, Pakistan, Africa, and North America

Type: Short-stemmed annual

Height: 44–50 inches (1.12–1.27 m)

+ EDIBLE
+ MEDICINAL
+ **COMMERCIAL**
+ **PRACTICAL**

Unraveling the way that cotton changed history is like trying to tease apart the constituent parts of a blue cotton dress. Once the dye, thread, fiber, seed, and boll have been separated out, King Cotton is revealed as having been a mainstay of the slave trade, the first domino to fall in America's Civil War, and the catalyst for the Industrial Revolution.

GUM TO DYNAMITE

Compared to its main rivals, wool and linen, cotton is cool, elegant, and chic, the material of choice before the arrival of upstart nylon, but the cotton harvest cost more in terms of human misery than any of its competitors. Home stylists may argue over plain versus stripes, period as opposed to modern, paint over paper, but usually they agree on one thing: cotton fabrics have a distinctly contemporary feel. Strange, then, that this material first saw the light of the weaving loom more than 3,000 years ago. Cotton in the wild grows as a leggy perennial. Because it is easier to machine-harvest, commercial cotton is cultivated as a short-stemmed annual. There are 39 different cotton species under the genus *Gossypium*, and it was *G. hirsutum*, or what came to be known as "upland" cotton, that eventually dominated the world of commercial cotton. *G. hirsutum* now makes up 90% of the world's crop.

Cotton is one of the most important non-food crops in the world. Cotton thread is used in just about every cloth-based product from bandages and diapers to muslin and paper. The seed goes into soap, margarine, and cooking oil. The linter fibers find their way into cosmetics, sausage skins, dynamite, and plastics. Ice cream, the propellant in some fireworks, and that scourge of the sidewalk, chewing gum, all contain cellulose from the cotton plant. Long before the cotton barons found industrial uses for it, however, cotton meant one thing only: cloth.

You gotta jump down, turn around, pick a bale of cotton
Jump down, turn around, pick a bale a day.

Traditional slave song

REPARATION

[tu]rning any plant into a fabric [in]volves first reducing the plant [in]to thin, long sections that can [be] plaited or woven together. [Fr]om constructing a roof of [ba]mboo leaves or making a carpet [ou]t of sisal, the same principle [ap]plies. In the case of silk (see [W]hite Mulberry, p.130) the [co]coon of the silk moth was pried [ap]art and teased out into a [th]read; when it came to flax, the

COMMERCIAL COTTON
Gossypium hirsutum has been cultivated to produce a number of varieties. Those with longer fibers —known as "long staple upland"—are favored for commercial production.

[p]lant was pulled rather than cut, dried and then "retted," or steeped in [w]ater until the plant material had rotted away, leaving the fiber exposed, [a] seriously smelly process. After scutching (separating), combing, [tw]isting, and bleaching the fibers in the sun, the flax was wetted and [sp]un, or spun dry, to produce a heavier, hard-wearing yarn. It was rela[ti]vely easy to turn wool into a weavable thread: the sheep was shorn, the [fl]eece washed, and the wool carded and spun by the spinner, or "spin[st]er," into reels of woolen thread. The process for making cotton thread [w]as much the same: it just took twice as long.

The yellow, cream, or rose-colored flowers of the [c]otton plant are close relatives of the dreamy hibiscus [a]nd the cottage hollyhock. Nevertheless, it is hard to [r]econcile the vision of cotton drapes billowing in the [s]ea breeze through a cottage window, with the raw, [h]ard, human graft involved in the manufacture of [m]aking cotton. Transforming a sweltering field of [c]otton bolls into a bolt of curtain cloth was back[b]reaking business.

Cotton started out with the cotton head, the [d]istinctive white, fluffy boll that was formed from [t]he flowerhead when it was ready to shed seed. The [b]olls had to be plucked from the plant and piled into [s]houlder bags: the American artist Winslow Homer [r]ecorded the process in 1876, painting two beautiful, [c]olored black slaves wading through a sea of cotton to [fi]ll bag and basket in *The Cotton Pickers*. The bolls [w]ere then ginned—pulled across a nailed board to [s]eparate the hairs that formed the lint (which would become the thread) from the seed. After any debris was removed, the li▮ was carded (combed) to straighten out the fibers ready for spinning in▮ yarn. The yarn could then be woven into cloth.

When the Old World of Europe met the New World of America, whe▮ Portuguese and Spanish mariners mastered the trade winds swirlir▮ around the Atlantic Ocean and beached their boats in the Americas, t▮ exchange of plants that happened as a result changed history in man▮ ways. Cotton, however, was already being converted into cloth on bot▮ sides of the Atlantic. Cotton was being made from wild plants in plac▮ as far apart as Peru and Pakistan. Cotton-making is believed to hav▮ spread east from Pakistan into China, Japan, and Korea, and west int▮ Europe, reaching Spain in the 900s. Six centuries later, when the Spa▮ iard Hernando Cortés arrived in Mexico, he found the local Aztecs ha▮ long ago developed their own cottage cotton industry. Cortés wa▮ presented with a gold-encrusted ceremonial cotton robe by the Yucatá▮ Indians, shortly before his soldiers started murdering them.

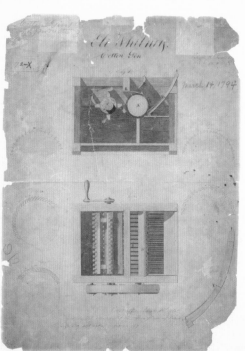

SATANIC MILLS

Cotton remained relatively expensive for the next two centuries. In th▮ eighteenth century, fashionable European ladies of leisure might hav▮ craved one of the dreamy cotton indienne gowns that were then bein▮ brought, at great expense, from India. Few could afford the luxury. Ye▮ within a century, cotton prices were plummetin▮ and the production of cotton goods was powerin▮ up: the cotton-weaving cottage industry was bein▮ industrialized. Mass-production started up in wha▮ the poet William Blake dubbed "the dark satani▮ mills" as Britain became a major cotton-cloth maker, processing thousands of bales of the whit▮ stuff imported from India, Surinam, and Guyana▮ Industrialization was not universally welcomed. ▮ pugnacious industrialist with a reputation fo▮ stealing other people's ideas, Richard Arkwrigh▮ built several of the early mills, each one hailed as ▮ technological breakthrough. Cotton mills wer▮ vulnerable to fire, but many blazes were blamed o▮ arson. Each new mill promised to drive anothe▮ batch of cottage cotton weavers into factor▮ work—or into the workhouse. One young appren▮ tice from Nottingham, in England's East Midlands▮ Ned Ludd, led organized revolts against men lik▮

COTTON COUNTRY
A watercolor painting of the
McConnel & Company
cotton mill in Manchester,
England in 1913. Manchester
acquired the name
"cottonopolis" thanks to the
concentration of cotton
mills in the area.

rkwright, firing mills, giving his name to the Luddites, and generally
clogging up the works" (literally dropping wooden clogs into the maw
' a working machine, with dramatically damaging consequences).

It was to no avail. In the 1760s, another Englishman, James
argreaves, introduced an ingenious spinning frame that could be oper-
ed by one person, yet spin several threads at once. Before the decade
as out, Arkwright had brought out his Improved Water-Frame Spin-
ing Jenny. Within another decade, Samuel Crompton's Improved Spin-
ing Mule was unveiled: this could spin a thousand
reads simultaneously. In America meanwhile, Ely
Vhitney patented a cotton gin (*gin* being short for
engine") that substantially reduced the manual labor
quired to extract the cotton seeds. The profits that
oured forth from cotton farming stoked the Industrial
evolution and prompted the London Stock Exchange
be founded on the back of King Cotton's wealth.

Meanwhile, cotton fields had started up in
amestown, Virginia, in the U.S., and also in Barbados
nd Exuma, in the Bahamas. As cotton demand grew,
nd as cotton processors invented ever more efficient
nachines for extracting the cotton from its seed, the
otton fields spread. American cotton growers had
nded a single bale of cotton—their first—in Liver-
ool, England, in 1784. It rotted in the Mersey rain
hile the port authorities argued over its legitimacy.
3y 1861, America was shipping over four million bales
year. Cotton, meanwhile, was killing the soil. With
he topsoil in Georgia seriously damaged by intensive

THE SOUND OF COTTON

✦

Wind the bobbin up,
Wind the bobbin up;
Pull, pull,
Clap clap clap.

Clapping rhymes like these are
sung still to pre-school children in
the post-industrial age, a reminder
of the far-off days when the
industrial age descended on Britain.
Songs from the other side of the
Atlantic had a far more pervasive
effect on the popular music of the
twentieth and twenty-first centuries
with the advent of jazz and blues
songs like "The Boll Weevil."

growing, cotton growers spread west, into Louisiana, Arkansas, Texas,
and, in the 1880s, north up the Mississippi River. The land belonged to
the local Indians, but the Native Americans had no hope of holding their
ground against the economics of King Cotton. Their land was expropriated and they were evicted in forced migrations that turned them into
another tragic statistic in cotton's history.

THE RISE AND FALL OF THE SLAVE TRADE

As cotton became America's biggest export, slave ownership soared.
By 1855, almost every other person in the American South was a
black African slave. There were an estimated 3.2 million of them working
the cotton, tobacco, and sugar crops, forming an underclass at the base
of an unstable economic pyramid. Above them were the plantation
managers and owners; above them were the investors and shareholders in
the North American and British banks that loaned money to buy more
land and more slaves. When the crash came, only those at the summit
escaped unscathed.

Public sentiment was fueled by an emerging media, which, when it
finally found its voice, spoke out against slavery, and precipitated the
crash. In 1855, the South baled almost 2 billion pounds (0.9 billion kg) of
cotton (50 years earlier they managed a mere 104 million pounds, or 47
million kg). The industrial North, instead of shipping all the raw material to Britain, had started to process more and more of the material at
home. The boundary between North and South had become a boundary
between making stuff—industry and manufacturing—and farming stuff

th slaves. "Cotton is king," was how e South Carolina senator, James enry Hammond, put it when he oked at the economy; but if cotton as king, his subjects, the slaves, were ing on their feet.

In April 1861, Confederate soldiers om the South, opposed to Abraham Lincoln's antislavery stance, fired Union forces. It was the opening round in the War of Rebellion, or as e South called it, the "War Between the States." Lincoln, who would assassinated four years later by an actor sympathetic to the South, lled for volunteers. As the seven States of the Confed-acy were joined by another four from the South, the age was set for a very bloody and very public war. merica had systematically documented its history om its founding—no other nation was young enough have kept such detailed records of its past—and hen it came to its own Civil War, America's press rps systematically documented the fate of the 0,000 people destined to die in battle.

Despite early victories by Southerners such as tonewall" Jackson, the industrialized North had the perior firepower and technology. Following a blockade the Southern ports, which choked off cotton sales, e North emerged as the victor. When Confederate mmander Robert E. Lee surrendered in April 1865, it as but a short step for Congress to proclaim the eedom of all slaves. But it was a poor victory. Cotton roduction shifted to other parts of the world, to China d West Africa, where cotton had been first cultivated the nineteenth century. (West Africa would rise to come the fourth biggest cotton exporter.) The uthern economy had been devastated—even though e former slaves were now free to farm the little land ey were given, they were too poor to do so. Slave-free echanization and chemical pesticides would eventu-ly save America's cotton industry from ruin, but the npact of the black slave trade will never go away.

When a new hand, one accustomed to [picking cotton], is sent for the first time into the field, he is whipped up smartly, and made for that day to pick as fast as he can possibly. [. . .] they are not permitted to be a moment idle until it is too dark to see.

Solomon Northup, Twelve Years a Slave, *1853*

BOLL WEEVIL

✦

Cotton is a natural fabric, yet more chemicals are sprayed on cotton than on any other crop. Today, cotton accounts for less than 3% of the world's farmed land, but it consumes about a quarter of the world's pesticides. The pesticides keep one of the world's most expensive pests, the boll weevil, under control. The beetle reached America's cotton fields from Mexico in the 1890s. Within 30 years it had become endemic, costing an estimated $300 million a year, most of the money being spent on aggressive pesticides.

Sunflower
Helianthus annuus

Native range: Southwest U.S. and Central America

Type: Annual

Height: 8–15 feet (2.4–4.6 m)

It started cultivated life among the North American Indians, was taken to Europe and hybridized in Russia, and then found its way back to the States in the seed sacks of Mennonite farmers escaping Soviet pogroms. As the sunflower set off become one of the most important sources of cholesterol-free oil in the world, obscure artist in a French asylum was preparing a series of sunflower paintings the would change the art world forever.

STALIN'S GOLDEN GIFT

+ **EDIBLE**

+ MEDICINAL

+ **COMMERCIAL**

+ **PRACTICAL**

We have the First Nation peoples of the Americas to thank for first cultivating the sunflower. The seeds were one of the vital seasonal foods of the West American Indians who, two or three thousand years ago, were grinding up the seed kernels to make a flour and treating the fleshy plant head that held the seeds as a vegetable. The Hopi Indians, famous for their brilliantly colored body paints, fabrics, and pottery, had learned to extract the blue, black, purple, and red dyes from sunflower seeds. They used the fibrous leaf and stem parts to weave into textiles and basket

and it was Indian medicine men who discovered its medicinal properties, using it as a healing cream for cuts and wounds, even for treating snake and insect bites. No wonder the sunflower became an object of worship for the Aztecs.

In 1510, American sunflower seeds were brought to Spain and in the late 1600s to Russia. Peter the Great, emperor of Russia from 1682 to 1725 and architect of the then-emerging Russian state, toured Germany, Holland, England, and Vienna when he was 25 years old, collecting information and ideas on everything from boat building to farming. He is credited with adding the seeds of the sunflower to the groaning wagon loads of samples he sent home to Moscow. It was not long before the Russian peasant was cracking his teeth on its toasted, salted seeds and pounding the plant to extract the vegetable oil. It took a little longer—another 80 years—before the Russians appreciated the full commercial

tential of this golden little gift. By the
00s, fields of the heliotropic (see box)
wer heads were punching yellow holes in
e expansive wheat prairies. How the little
nflower had grown: from the 1930s the
viet leader Joseph Stalin was pouring
search into improving the plant, and within
) years the Russians were successfully
eeding giant flower heads over 1 foot (30
n) in diameter, and had also boosted the
nflower's oily yields to 50%. Although
ertaken by Argentina at the end of the
ventieth century, the former Russian states
ntinued to dominate world production,
ongside China and America.

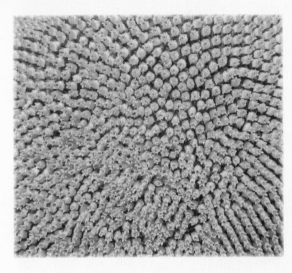

HIDDEN TREASURE
The large head of the
sunflower is densely packed
with thousands of ray florets.
Beneath these reside the
seed-bearing disk florets.

The sunflower head is composed of two minute flower types: the outer
ellow (sometimes red) ray florets, and the dense inner black disk florets
at develop into a pincushion of rich, low-saturated fatty seeds. The
esence of these tiny flowers places the 50 or so species of *Helianthus* in
e Compositae/Asteraceae, or daisy, family, which itself runs to some-
here in the region of 23,000–32,000 different species. While the rod-like
em and ovate leaves have their uses (from bird seeds
baking products), it is the flower head that feeds on
e sun and delivers the oil. Sunflower oil can be turned
to margarine, salad dressings, cooking oils, and even
aps and varnishes.

The residual oilcake, along with the plants' stems
d leaves, helps fatten up farm animals, and the
brous materials can also be pounded into paper. One
terprising inventor, who found that the stem pith
ad a lower specific gravity than cork, used it to manu-
cture lifebelts and buoyancy aids. The fortunate few
ho escaped with their lives when the *Titanic* sank in
e Atlantic in 1912 could thank not only their lucky
ars, but the sunflower too.

ENIUS AND TRAGEDY

wenty-four years earlier, while the sunflower
ntinued to be exploited for its commercial possibili-
es, an artist, battling with his life-long history of
epression, was confronting a vase of sunflowers. He

HELIOTROPIC CONFUSION

✦

The Italian name for the sunflower,
girasole (Old Italian: *tornasole*;
French: *tournesol*) refers to the
heliotropic action of the sunflower:
it turns its head to bask "full-face"
in the sun. The name *girasole* may
have been the root cause of
confusion over another member
of the family, the Jerusalem
artichoke (*Helianthus tuberosus*),
which is neither from the Middle
East, nor an artichoke. Settlers
learned how to dig up and cook
the pungent roots, which tasted like
the artichoke, in its native America.
"Jerusalem" may be a corruption
of *girasole*.

You may know that the peony is Jeannin's, the hollyhock belongs to Quost, but the sunflower is mine.

Vincent van Gogh, in a letter from 1889

MODERN ART
Van Gogh's *Vase with Fifteen Sunflowers* (1888) was just one of a series of *Sunflower* canvases painted by the artist.

wrote to his brother, Theo: "I am hard at it, painti[ng] with the enthusiasm of a Marseillais eating bou[il]labaisse, which won't surprise you when you kno[w] that what I'm at is the painting of some sunflowers[.]" He planned to produce a dozen panels in blue an[d] yellow and hang them in the Yellow House at Ar[les] in southern France—the home of his friend, Pa[ul] Gauguin. Vincent van Gogh worked on these pain[t]ings with thick brushstrokes, in the impasto sty[le] that gave the flower heads a three-dimension[al] textured finish. The flowers seemed to burst out [of] the canvas. "I am working at it every morning fro[m] sunrise on, for the flowers fade so quickly," complained Van Gogh, as [he] struggled with a series of paintings that were destined to become som[e] of the most famous in the world. Van Gogh had a history of depressio[n.] Shortly before he killed himself, he had quarreled with his old frien[d] Gauguin, and, armed with a razorblade, rushed at him in the stree[t.] Gauguin held his ground and stared him down, whereupon Van Gog[h] ran off, only to mutilate himself with the razor, cutting off part of h[is] left ear. (An alternative version suggests that the two men actuall[y] fought, injuring Van Gogh in the process.)

The artist was born in 1853 at Groot-Zundert in Holland. His fath[er] was a minister in the Dutch Reformed Church and Vincent was as serio[us] a Northern Protestant as it was possible to be. For a while, Van Gog[h] wondered about running an art gallery, as his uncle had done. He eve[n] found himself working behind the counter of the Galerie Goupil in Th[e] Hague in 1869, transferring to London in 1873, then Paris, but he lo[st] the job in 1876. He lost another job as an assistant teacher in Englan[d] and yet another as a clerk in Dordrecht, in the Netherlands. Only whe[n] he began to mix with a group of Parisian artists, including Henri d[e] Toulouse-Lautrec, did he detect the light ahead: he woul[d] devote himself to painting. In 1885, Van Gogh cam[e] across some Japanese etchings. This taste of Japanaiser[ie] excited him and prompted him, like Monet (see Bamboo[,] p.18) to re-evaluate his work and abandon all thos[e] "brown tones . . . bitumen and bistre," as he put it [in]

other letter to brother Theo. Three years later he set
f for the south of France, to Arles: "About this
aying on in the South, even if it is more expensive,
nsider: we like Japanese painting, we have felt its
fluence, all the impressionists have that in common;
en why not go to Japan, that is to say to the equiva-
nt of Japan, the South?" he asked Theo. The move to
e sunny south lifted his depression in those final
mmers as he sought to capture the essence of his
eloved sunflowers. "I am now on the fourth picture of
nflowers. The fourth one is a bunch of 14 flowers—it
ves a singular effect." But during the winters every-
ing seemed to go wrong again. "I always have the
pression of being a traveler going somewhere. And
the end of my career I will be in the wrong: I will
en find that not only the fine arts, but even the rest
ere nothing but dreams," he wrote in one of his last
tters to Theo.

On July 27, Van Gogh shot himself in the chest. He
awled home to his lodgings, where he died two days
ter beside a stack of sunflower canvases. A little over
century later, his *Vase with Fifteen Sunflowers* was
ld by Sotheby's in London for a world-record sum.
he price tag was just under $40m, and it tumbled into
significance any previous figure paid for a work by a
odern artist.

COMMERCIAL CROP
Sunflower oil is now the
world's fourth most popular
oil (after soy, palm, and
rapeseed), with Argentina,
Russia, and Ukraine the
three largest producers.

Rubber
Hevea brasiliensis

Native range: South America

Type: Rainfall forest tree

Height: Up to 140 feet (42 m)

+ EDIBLE
+ MEDICINAL
+ **COMMERCIAL**
+ **PRACTICAL**

I n the 1970s, stories of a terrible illness began to emerge. AIDS would claim th lives of an estimated 20 million people between 1981 and 2003 (and orpho another 12 million children) in sub-Saharan Africa. During 2008, AIDS would clai another 1.4 million. In a bid to combat AIDS, health professionals turned to a mat rial that had been used by Mayan and Aztec cultures: cahuchu. The worldwide us of cahuchu—or rubber—condoms for health protection and contraception ros rapidly in the years that followed.

BALL GAMES

There were no cahuchu condoms in the ancient South American civiliza tions, but the "weeping wood" as it was known, was widely used. Peop painted the soles of their feet with the sticky compound to keep the dry and protect the skin from fungal infections. Mayans collected th milky sap-like fluid material and, shaping it into a large, tight spher developed a game with the object of bumping, heading, or shoulderin the sphere through a carved stone ring. No one knows how far back th American Indians discovered cahuchu, but they were cutting the bar of the wild cahuchu and collecting the milky sa in the shell of dried-out gourds when the Spanis arrived in the early 1500s. The Indians used ball of soft clay, fixed around the end of a stic which they thrust into the latex pool. The sa collected on the clay, which was gently heate until the latex had hardened. The clay mold wa then simply washed away, leaving a hollow ba of raw rubber.

The word "cahuchu" formed the basis of mos other cultures' names for the latex—for exampl the French *caoutchouc*. The word "rubber" cam from another source altogether—the learne Dr. Joseph Priestley, who discovered the grea

I have seen a substance excellently adapted to the purpose of wiping from paper the marks of a black lead pencil.

Dr. Joseph Priestley (1733–1804)

job these little balls of latex did in erasing pencil marks from paper. He found that the carbon pencil marks lifted magically with a little gentle "rubbing," and his description stuck. From around 1770, little cubes of "India rubber" were being sold as erasers. Not long after, sheets of the rubber began to be marketed as a waterproof cloth. But there was a drawback: India-rubber cloth grew soft and unpleasantly clammy as it warmed. As such, it was condemned by stagecoach drivers and postilions until a Scottish clerk, Charles Macintosh, created a clever sandwich of cloth and rubber. Macintosh died in 1843 having patented his process, conferred his name on the waterproof coat, and created a generation of grateful and dry hackney-cab drivers.

MR. MERRIMAN'S RUBBER DRESS

The history of the non-edible *Hevea brasiliensis*, or Pará rubber tree, is studded with curious characters like Macintosh. There was the Frenchman, Charles Marie de la Condamine, who wrote the first scientific paper on rubber in 1775. Condamine had fallen out with his colleagues during an exploration in Peru. Too broke to return to France, he embarked instead on the first scientific journey of the Amazon, noting the use of cinchona to combat malaria, the practice of killing fish with poisoned arrows, and the use of the rubber, before he returned to France with news of his findings.

Then there were the two Americans, Thomas Hancock and Charles Goodyear, who stumbled on the idea of treating raw rubber with sulfur, lead oxide, and heat. Like any plant, rubber decays as it ages, but Goodyear and Hancock discovered how to transform it into a more flexible, longer-lasting material. The process was dubbed *vulcanization* after Vulcan, the Roman god who beat hot iron into shape on his anvil under the shadow of Sicily's Mount Etna. Vulcanization led to a rush of new applications for rubber. As with plastics a century later, factories, laboratories, and back-street workshops sprang up as industrialists strove to found their fortunes on rubber. *Cassell's Family Magazine*, first published in 1874, reported on one such effort, an all-over inflatable rubber dress invented by a Mr. Merriman of America. This "life-saving aid for those who sail the seas . . . was demonstrated in Britain by Captain Paul Boyton. [It was] manufactured chiefly [of] India-rubber" and came equipped with a small paddle and a towable bag of provisions sufficient

VULCANIZATION
Charles Goodyear (and Thomas Hancock) developed the process through which natural rubber became more flexible and durable.

The sap of the rubber tree is harvested using a process known as "tapping," in which a thin layer of bark is incised along a downward spiral.

to last ten days. They included an ax, "which might serve to protect oneself against any inquisitive or ferocious sea-monsters. We would not like to be shipwrecked anywhere . . . but if the worst must come, we hope we may have been able to rig ourselves out in Mr. Merriman's new dress." It was not a demand for inflatable lifesavers that triggered a gold-rush-style demand for rubber, however, but the convenience and curse of the twentieth century: the automobile. Thousands flocked to Britain's first national motor show at London's Crystal Palace in 1903 to admire the gleaming new cars, each stood on a set of pure rubber tires.

The dash for white gold had begun. Farmers in Brazil abandoned their smallholdings to go and tap the wild cahuchu. The trees that grew along the accessible riversides were worked hard, and the indigenous people were worked even harder. Rubber barons ruled their riverside estates like private fiefdoms, reaping the rewards of an unregulated market. Native Indians were enslaved, expelled, or murdered; women were forced into prostitution, and men routinely mutilated to prevent them fathering children. As rumors of conditions on the estates emerged, the search for new sources of latex developed a humanitarian dimension.

RUBBER COLONIZES THE WORLD

At least 2,000 different plants produce a rubber-like latex. In the Soviet Union, dandelion latex was a sound source of rubber until their scientists developed a substitute, Sovpren. Another source was the Malayan tree, *Ficus elastica*, exploited since the early 1800s, but difficult to harvest.

When demand for rubber grew, collectors simply felled more trees. With natural supplies shrinking, last-minute efforts were launched to rescue the rubber tree—or at least to tame, domesticate, and profit by it. Sir Joseph Hooker, the director of the Royal Botanic Gardens at Kew, England, was asked by Clement

READY TO ROLL

+

Solid tires of rubber were first fixed to a vehicle and rolled out on a public road in 1867. In 1888, a Scottish engineer, John Dunlop, patented the bicycle tire and from here on tires and rubber shared their history. Rubber possessed unique qualities: incredibly strong, it could be flown at high altitudes and exposed to sub-zero temperatures. Rubber aircraft tires could be retreaded up to eight times. The French tire magnate André Michelin and his brother Édouard developed pneumatic tires that could be fitted to rail cars.

arkham to send someone to Brazil to fetch back seeds of
e rubber tree. Markham had earlier arranged for cinchona
d cocoa to be brought back from America. *Hevea*,
wever, proved a reluctant traveler, and successive
nsignments either died on the journey or the seed failed
germinate. Henry Wickham, an English planter living
one of the more notorious Brazilian rubber-trading towns, Manaus,
ade a breakthrough in 1876. Wickham liked to give the impression that
had smuggled the seeds out of Brazil in a clandestine operation that
xed the rubber owners. Since he managed to export 70,000 seeds,
mmissioning a ship to carry them, the deal may have been more
raightforward than he claimed. Although less than 5% of the seeds
rminated, it was sufficient to provide 3,000 *Hevea* seedlings—the first
be grown abroad. The rubber tree had left its homeland.

Kew's seedlings were sent on, dispatched in Wardian cases (see
ineapple, p.14) to the Royal Botanic Gardens at Peradeniya, near
andy, Ceylon (now Sri Lanka), where 2,000 saplings were settled in.
hey were also sent to Holland's Hortus Botanicus Bogoriensis in Java,
idonesia, and to the Botanic Gardens in Singapore. It was here, in
ingapore, that one of Hooker's own men from Kew, Henry James
urton, mastered the horticultural craft of selection and propagation
ithout resorting to seed. His successor, Henry Nicholas Ridley, solved
n annoying problem with the imported *Hevea*—tapping the trees for

SMUGGLED SEEDS
Saplings grown from seeds
smuggled out of Brazil (and
germinated at the Royal
Botanic Gardens at Kew,
England) were used to
establish the first *Hevea*
plantations in Asia.

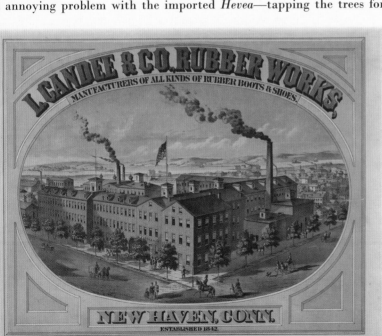

RUBBER PLANTS
As demand for rubber grew
(already by 1910 there were
over 2.5 million car tires on
the road), the industrialization of rubber production
became vital.

latex seemed to send them to a premature grave—b
developing new tapping methods. Meanwhile, Henr
Thwaites, the botanist at Peradeniya who had intro
duced seedlings of cinchona, dispatched seedling
around the region. With Thwaites producing th
trees and Ridley solving the teething problems,
was the turn of the planters to try the new crop.

At the time, no colony planter could imagine, a
he rode around his coffee plantation, that a rubbe
wheeled vehicle would rapidly replace the hors
beneath him. But in 1910, there were some 2.5 millio
tires on the road. Only 80 years later, with three
quarters of the world's rubber devoted to thei
production, there would be 860 million tires. Rubbe
would be used on supersonic aircraft, as a spark
proof floor in firework factories, and for contracep
tion. Rubber was elastic, impermeable to gases, an

not only had a high resistance to electrical currents, but also high frictio
resistance to wet surfaces. It was so important in both world wars tha
those countries that lacked supplies devoted vast resources to creatin
substitutes from coal tars and petrochemicals. While Germany came u
with "Buna" during World War II, the U.S. urged its citizens to donat
their rubber to the war effort: "America Needs Your Scrap Rubber,
declared one poster, pointing out that a single gas mask required 1.1
pounds (0.5 kg) of rubber and a heavy bomber as much as 1,825 pound
(more than 800 kg).

By the turn of the twentieth century, concerns were being raised ove
the world's profligate consumption of crude oil, the main source o
rubber substitutes. Oil shortages
suggested there might be an even
bigger future for real rubber.

In the early days of the twentieth
century, plantation owners in Malaya
and Ceylon were losing heart after a
fungal disease had ravaged the coffee
bushes (see Coffee, p.54). Many
remained reluctant, however, to
commit to a new crop. Henry Nicholas
Ridley sought in vain to persuade the
white plantation owners to convert
their land to farming rubber and

RIDE TOGETHER

WORK TOGETHER

SAVE RUBBER
FOR VICTORY

stead found a convert in a Chinese planter, Tan Chay Yan, who set own 40 acres at Bukit Lintang, near Malacca Town in Malaya (now part f Malaysia), in 1896. At the cost of the loss of the native forests and lant diversity, the new plantations launched Malaya's rubber industry. 'an Chay Yan's lead persuaded other planters to follow suit, and world ubber production eventually moved almost entirely out of Brazil and nto Southeast Asia.

There was yet one more twist in the curious history f rubber. Seeing the success of *Hevea brasiliensis* when t was grown as a plantation crop, Brazilian growers ried establishing their own plantations. Each time, owever, the crop fell victim to a leaf fungus. The isease was endemic to Brazil, but in the wild it never eached the epidemic proportions that it did in artifi- ial plantations.

FORDLANDIA

Rich industrialists have an altruistic habit of setting up new communities designed to benefit the workers, he neighborhood, and ultimately the benefactor's own rofits. John Cadbury did so with Bournville (see Cacao, p.184); the Irish Quaker John Richardson built deal homes for his linen-mill workers at Bessbrook in Northern Ireland; and Titus Salt constructed a village or his workers in northern England, allowing himself he vanity of naming it after himself.

Fordlandia arose less out of a conviction to improve he lot of the rubber workers than a desire to beat the British at their own game. When the U.S. found itself importing almost hree-quarters of its rubber and the Europeans, controlling the Far East rade, dictating the price, the motor magnate Henry Ford agreed to nvest in a new rubber plantation at Boa Vista on the Tapajos River valley. Ford took over 2.5 million acres (1 million ha), renamed the place Fordlandia, and replaced the forest with a U.S.-style town and enough rubber trees to meet the requirements of 2 million autos a year. Between 1928 and 1945, the Ford Company poured $20 million into Fordlandia and a neighboring project, Belterra, 80 miles downstream. Fordlandia's 7,000-strong population, which included 2,000 workers, objected to the American lifestyle imposed on them (including free American meals and square-dancing lessons), but what really defeated Henry Ford's vision was the leaf fungus. Both plantations were eventually abandoned.

DYING FOR RUBBER

✦

In 1988, a 44-year-old Brazilian rubber tapper was murdered, gunned down at his home in Xapuri. This was no ordinary murder, nor was the victim, Chico Mendes, the average sort of rubber tapper. Mendes had fought to save his native forests from loggers and ranching. In the 1960s, the rubber market was depressed and growers were selling out to cattle ranchers, whose animals and fodder crops were deforesting the countryside. Mendes's environmental campaigns in both Brazil and India led to the establishment of at least 20 reserves at home—and ultimately to his murder.

Barley

Hordeum vulgare

Native range: Worldwide

Type: Cereal

Height: 3 feet (1 m)

+ **EDIBLE**
+ **MEDICINAL**
+ **COMMERCIAL**
+ PRACTICAL

Barley has been the farmer's friend for thousands of years. As one of the most important food plants for people and their beasts, barley is a key cereal. But in the guise of good Sir John Barleycorn, barley is also the basic ingredient in the distilling of that fiery spirit, whiskey. In this respect barley has something of a troubled history.

BARLEY RISE

Early farming was a revolution like no other: more dramatic than Neil Armstrong's first step on the moon and more transforming than any technical advance since the wheel. The earliest agriculturalists were concentrated in a region that ran from Turkey down the eastern Mediterranean coast and Mesopotamia (from the Greek *mesos*, "middle" and *potamos*, "river," a reference to the fertile land that lay between the Euphrates and the Tigris) and into Iran and Iraq. This was the true cradle of civilization.

No one knows for sure who these first farmers were, or how they came to raise crops of cereals such as barley. Whatever prompted the move from nomadism, cropping wild wheat and barley, and later, deliberately sowing seed in prepared ground, allowed settled communities to grow, villages to become established, and towns to prosper. Two of the earliest were Çatal Hüyük in Turkey, and Jericho, later to become marooned in the disputed territories of the Middle East. Their stout outer fortifications suggest they were as war-torn then as now. Were they under regular siege because of their one great advantage over any number of passing nomadic tribes—that they were rooted in agriculture, in cropping, grinding, and storing corn for the following year?

Be't whisky-gill, or penny wheep,
Or ony stronger potion,
It never fails, or drinkin' deep,
To kittle up our notion.
Robert Burns, "The Holy Fair," 1785

BARLEY HARVEST
Scenes like this have changed
little in the 9,000 years since
barley was first cultivated in
the Middle East, but the
cultivation of barley itself
has spread across the globe.

he remains of barley grains, dating back to 7000 BCE , have turned up
Jarmo in northern Iraq, and just about every other archaeological site
early farms, for this was an essential cereal—as useful for the pot as it
as for hungry livestock. Naturally, the art of barley husbandry spread
e a sea swell through Europe, Asia, and into North Africa. Barley,
ong with wheat, prolonged people's life span beyond the average of
ound 40 years. It even shaped their faces, as people
veloped the grinding, edge-to-edge bite required by a
real diet. For the Greeks and Romans, barley was
vereign over wheat as a bread flour, which explains
hy the Latin goddess Ceres wears a crown of plaited
rley and not wheat. Because of its low gluten content,
wever, barley could not rise to the occasion of the
rge loaf and was eventually displaced by wheat.
arley has even been found to have medicinal qualities:
common local anesthetic used in dentistry is a
nthetic version of a barley alkaloid.

The importance of Sir John Barleycorn to the malt-
er, however, remains unchallenged to this day. Malting
volves first germinating the grain then drying the
routed seedlings. The resulting "malt," mixed with
ater, brewed with yeast, and barreled with care,
akes beer. It also makes whiskey. "The Highlanders
f Scotland] regale themselves with whisky, a malt
irit, as strong as Genevas, which they swallow in
eat quantities, without any signs of inebriation,"

THE OLDEST PROFESSION

+

The world's first building was either
a temple or a farmhouse. Given the
need for food and warmth before
worship, the farm probably came
first. While farmers may not
officially hold the title of being the
oldest profession, they could lay
justifiable claim to it. Farmers were
cutting their crops and in doing so
shaping the landscape for 5,000
years; yet the word "farm," from the
Latin *firma*, meaning a fixed
payment, rent, or lease, and
referring to a parcel of land let or
farmed out, did not come into
general use until the 1600s.

claimed the Scottish novelist Tobias Smollett in *Humphry Clinker*. He added that it was "an excellent preservative against the winter cold, which must be extreme on the mountains. I am told that it is given with great success to infants." This was in 1771. Just over two centuries later, the Scottish government put a figure on its cost to society, in terms of criminality and health problems, at £1.125 billion ($1.7 billion), or £900 ($1,300) for every adult. What had gone wrong? And was barley to blame?

Of the five essential spirits—brandy, rum, vodka, gin, and whiskey—the latter is more closely associated with its country of origin than any other. Scotch, or Scotch whisky (or whiskey, depending on where you come from), has been made with malted barley, smoky peat fires, and a dripping still since the 1400s. It was primarily a medicinal drink that stayed on the north side of the English border, with gin, or "mother's ruin," being the preferred spirit in England. The distillers' craft had been developed by Muslims; not to produce alcoholic drinks, forbidden under Islam, but for Arabian scents and essences ("alcohol" comes from the Arabic *kohl*, the powder Arab women used as eye makeup). The craft was carried into Europe, and north and west into Scotland and Ireland where the unpronounceable (to the English tongue) *uisce beatha*, or "water of life," was soon flowing. *Uisce* became "whiskey," but the Scots' propensity for brewing did not delight the conquering English. The home stills were outlawed, destroyed, or licensed out of business by the excise men in a flurry of self-righteousness that had more to do with collecting taxes than saving souls.

Thae curst horse-leeches o' th' Excise,
Who mak the whisky stells their prize!
Haud up thy han', De'il! Ance, twice, thrice!
There, seize the blinkers!
An' bake them up in brunstane pies
For poor damn'd drinkers.
For poor damn'd drinkers.

"Scotch Drink," 1785

So wrote Scotland's national poet Robert Burns, who had as little enthusiasm for the revenue men as the distillers themselves who, when the heat was turned up, took to the hills.

In the 1830s there were around 700 arrests for illegal whiskey-making in Scotland; 40 years later there were a mere half-dozen. At the same time, a new method of

distilling, the continuous still, was coming onto the market. The traditional old "pot" still produced a distinctive whiskey, a drink with flavor and character; the continuous still was its automated equivalent. It was capable not only of distilling alcohol from grain, but of doing so continuously. When blended with a traditional malt whiskey, the continuous-still spirit could be passed off as real whiskey. Although a Royal Commission laid down the rules for defining a proper whiskey in 1909 (top of the list came a single malt, that is a whiskey made only from malted [ba]rley, double-distilled, and created only at a single one of Scotland's [di]stilleries), everyone and anyone, with a license and sometimes without, [co]uld make a powerful whiskey (average alcoholic [co]ntent around 40%) from just about any grain.

America had started to give up on its traditional [da]rk rum, made from slave-trade molasses, when British [an]d Irish settlers began distilling and selling their own [w]hiskeys made from malted barley and rye. Then [di]stillers in Bourbon County, Kentucky began producing [pu]re corn whiskeys. Their efforts were particularly [ap]preciated by an influx of disgruntled Pennsylvanians [fle]eing the excises on liquor in their home state.

Rye whiskeys continued to be made, but it was [K]entucky Bourbon, stored in fresh barrels of American [oa]k, their insides charred to improve the flavor (Scotch [di]stillers preferred to use barrels that had been used to [st]ore other spirits), that ruled the day. In neighboring [T]ennessee, they turned out a sour-mash whiskey (using [ye]asts from an earlier brew for fermentation) that was [fir]st filtered through "mellowing" vats before being [po]ured into a cask to mature. (Ironically, the state's [la]ws, which forbade the sale of alcohol, meant that [w]hile the booze could be made there, it could not be [so]ld there.)

OATS AND RYE

✦

The cereal grains oats (*Avena sativa*) and rye (*Secale cereale*), were domesticated later than wheat and barley, but nevertheless played a significant role in the history of civilizations. Like most domesticated plants, oats and rye are both weeds that were tamed and farmed.

Oats, aside from becoming an important cereal crop in colder, wetter parts of the globe (even during a short, wet summer the grain would ripen), also fueled the two beasts that drove forward the agricultural revolution: the horse and the ox. Rye is a younger crop, possibly cultivated less than 2,300 years ago, but still an important source of bread.

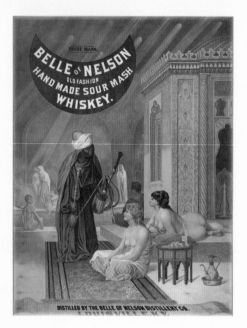

Other countries that adhered to whiskey's barl
basics included Canada, Ireland, and Japan. Japa
opened its first distillery in 1923, modeling its wh
keys on the traditional single-malt Scotch, wi
malted barley dried in peat-fired kilns to give t
barley a distinctive smoky flavor. Canada's whiske
makers, who started up in Ontario in the 1900s
order to make use of the growing quantity of grai
also resorted to barley, although they added rye ar
corn to the mash.

Irish whiskey is at least as old as Scotch whisk
even older according to the Irish, who believe that t
art of distilling was exported from Ireland to oth
nations, including France, by Irish missionaries in t
Dark Ages. The early farmhouse stills allowed distin
tive local spirits to be distilled not only from barl
but from whatever grew close at hand. They we
vernacular drinks, each particular to its own neighborhood, laid dow
with reverence after the fall harvests and, as with the French farmer
eau de vie, served daily with due ceremony and moderation as an eveni
aperitif or a dawn pick-me-up. So it was with the traditional Irish spir
made from the potato, *poteen*. While there existed rough and hasty brew
(often brewed on traveling stills to escape the excise men), most poted
brewers were craftsmen, proud of their product. Like the other region
spirits, including eau de vie and whiskey, poteen was eventual
condemned for its dangerous and corrupting influence. As with the crac
down on small, independent Scottish distilleries in the nineteenth centur
its eventual prohibition probably had more to do with destroying loc
entrepreneurship and raising revenues.

BANNING THE DRINK

Even more reprehensible was the practice of dosing indigenous peop
with cheap spirits. In Canada, America, and Australia, natives wei
poisoned by what the Americans dubbed "firewater." In Canada, a seve
teenth-century priest, Father Chrétien LeClerq, condemned the "lew
ness, adulteries, incest" and other crimes among his flock, resulting fro
"the sad consequence of the trade in brandy." The brandy was inferi
French spirits traded by North American fur trappers with native India
who had no history of distilling strong drink. While both the Canadia
and U.S. governments outlawed the trade, prohibitionists added this
their list of condemnations when they came to campaign for a dr

...nerica in the early 1900s. Whiskey corrupted their ...ys, wasted good grain that could be better fed to the ...ngry, and, worse still, was being brewed by German ...migrants who were no better than they should be, ...imed an alliance of rural and fundamentalist non-...nformist churches, a powerful women's lobby, and ...nerica's medical profession. They forced Congress to ...n booze in 1920.

The repression of small-scale distilling in Europe ...s nothing compared to the social experiment of ...ohibition rolled out across America, but it was an ...periment that went badly wrong. Its repeal in 1933 ...oved Sir John Barleycorn, as the song put it, to be ...e strongest knight.

...tle Sir John in a nut-brown bowl
...oved the strongest knight at last;
... the huntsman he can't hunt,
...r loudly blow his horn,
...d the tinker he can't mend his kettles or his pots
...ithout a little John Barleycorn.

...e champion of malt whiskey was Winston Churchill. He gave strict ...structions to his Ministry of Food: "On no account reduce the barley ...r whiskey. This takes years to mature and is an invaluable ...port and dollar producer."

A glass of whiskey and a moment's reflection played its ...rt in the history of the war when Churchill and President ...anklin Roosevelt prepared for the Allied invasion of Europe. ...ere were tensions and a lack of consensus between the two ...en as final arrangements for the invasion of German-...cupied France began in 1944. The greatest cliffhanger of ...e war saw Allied forces poised to cross the English Channel, ...iting for the order to launch. Had the Germans predicted ...e attack? Would bad weather, which could have swamped ...e landing craft, force a postponement? It seems the two men ...ally reached an agreement on how to proceed at the eleventh ...ur after a reflective glass or two of whiskey. The attack was a ...ccess and the rest, of course, is history.

Hop
Humulus lupulus

Native range: Northern Europe and the Middle East

Type: Climbing perennial plant

Height: Up to 6.5 feet (2 m)

+ *EDIBLE*
+ *MEDICINAL*
+ *COMMERCIAL*
+ *PRACTICAL*

Village brewers have always made good use of pathside plants. Meadowsweet (*Filipendula ulmaria*) and bog myrtle (*Myrica gale*) helped flavor and preserve ale, while the fruits of the wild service tree, still celebrated on British inn signs as "chequers," are said to have provided a passable brew since Roman times. But a better understanding of the virtues of the hop transformed ale into beer and contributed to a universal upsurge in beer drinking.

BREWING UP

For centuries, hops have been used for dyeing and paper- and rope-making and as a source of medicine in the treatment of liver and digestive complaints. Today, however, 98% of the hops that are grown are used to preserve and flavor beer. Closely related to cannabis, *Humulus lupulus* is a climber that, in spring, surges from the earth and races up whatever support it can find. The hop is dioecious (from the Greek meaning "two households"), producing separate male and female plants. It is the female that produces the musk-scented, resinous little flower cones that are harvested and dried before being delivered to the beer brewer.

Wild hops will scale a hedge or smother a shrub to reach the light, but in the hop yard or garden, the plants are set in a mound of rich humus

and trained up wire or jute strings attached to a network of wires overhead. The wires are tethered to tall timber posts—traditionally taken from chestnut groves as chestnut contains strong natural preservatives—turning the yard into something resembling an enormous bird cage. The hops are grown on until the fall. Although the hops are nowadays mostly harvested by machine, until recently they were picked by migrant workers and city families, many from poor, working-class neighborhoods. Relishing the working holiday and a spell in the open air, the pickers camped out on farms, in sheds, tents, or trailers and were paid piecework rates to bring in the crop.

Concerning the hop: as a result of its own bitterness it keeps some putrefaction from drinks to which it may be added so that they may last so much longer.

Abbess Hildegard of Bingen, Physica Sacra, *c. 1150*

HOP DRYING
After harvesting, hops must
be dried in kilns. In some
regions, most notably the
southeast of England, these
kilns take the distinctive
shape of "oast houses."

the menfolk strode along on stilts to reach and cut down the ripe
ants, or bines, their family members below plucked the hops into great
nvas cribs. The hops were then taken away to be dried in kilns (known
"oast houses") before being sent, tightly packed in Hessian sacks or
op pockets," to the fall hop sale. The heady, resinous scent that spread
rough the saleroom and the neighboring streets on hop sale day can
ll be detected in a jug of "real ale"—that is, one that has been brewed
traditional methods and allowed to mature in the barrel. As William
bbett wrote in *Cottage Economy* (1821), "There are two things to be
nsidered in hops: the power of preserving beer, and that of giving it a
easant flavour."

ROM ALE TO BEER

e hoppy flavors arise after the brewer adds hops to
e beer in the final stages of brewing. Hops are also
ed in the initial stages, when the plants' natural
mulones are transformed into isohumulones—chem-
als that sterilize the beer and give it that distinctive,
tter taste. But in order to create the right conditions
r this chemical metamorphosis, the hops must be
iled in the brewer's "wort" (a liquid obtained from
eeping malt) for around one and a half hours. The
entity of the brewer who stumbled on this curious
scovery will never be known, but the revelation
arked the beginning of "beer" and the end of "ale."

ALE AND BEER

✦

In the twenty-first century, a bottle
of ale and a bottle of beer are seen
as one and the same thing, but in
the twelfth century, ale was made
without hops whereas beer was
made with them. The Romans,
however, drank *cervesia*, which,
like the Spanish *cerveza*, may have
originated from a Celtic ale, as in
the Welsh *cwrwf*.

PRESERVATION PLANT
Adding the female flower
clusters of the Common
hop (*Humulus lupulus*)
to the brewing process
turned ale into beer, and
in doing so increased its
shelf life.

Ale, from the Anglo-Saxon *ealu*, was the everyday drink
in northern Europe. It was made with malted barley
(grain that had been sprouted and then dried) and
preserved and seasoned with spices and herbs such as
meadowsweet and bog myrtle. Having been boiled and
then left to ferment, the ale was a relatively bug-free
beverage, far safer to drink than the average
cowhorn of water from the village well. But
ale had one big drawback: a limited shelf life.
In hot weather especially, ale was quick to turn
sour. The hops that would transform unstable ale
into preservable beer originated in Europe and
the Middle East. They were known to possess
preservative qualities and were fermented into
a drink by the Egyptians, who brewed a
beverage called *symthum* from the hop. Yet neither the
Egyptians, Sumerians (who were great ale brewers), the
Greeks, nor the Romans hit on the idea of boiling hops in
their ale for precisely one and a half hours. Or even if they
did, no one thought to leave drinking their ale long enough to
discover that it had gained a new lease of life.

It is not unreasonable to suppose that the unsung hero of beer
brewing wore a plain tunic and hood and worked within the walls of a
monastery somewhere in the Middle Ages of middle Europe. The Christian fathers and mothers were keen brewers, as one of the earliest blue-
prints for a new monastery in Switzerland, drawn up in the early 800s
but never built, shows: the design included three kitchens, each with its
own brewhouse attached. In 736, the first association of hops with beer

THE STRONG STUFF
By the mid-sixteenth
century, dark beer—known
commonly as stout—was
enjoyed throughout England.
Its popularity declined as
breweries began producing
lighter ales.

appears in the written records of
a Benedictine monastery at
Weihenstephan near Munich,
Germany. Three centuries later,
around the time when the first
universities were being established in Paris, France and
Oxford, England, Abbess Hildegard of Bingen wrote of the
beneficial qualities of hopping
beer in her book, the *Physica
Sacra*, written in c. 1150. Hildegard (quoted on p.110) was born

P HARVEST
m its medieval monastic origins, hop farming developed into a
e-scale commercial operation as the taste for hop-conditioned
rs grew to exceed that for traditional ales.

1098 and died in 1179. Helpfully, she added that if
hops were to hand, the brewer might use a handful
ash leaves to preserve the beer.

In Hildegard's time, religious orders had turned
e brewer's craft into a respectable business, a tradi-
n that continued into the twenty-first century with
ews such as the legendary Trappist beers of Belgium
d the Netherlands. In the home, beer-making was
e preserve of the mistress of the house, while the
nastic brewer made the most of mass sales. Trading
th the maltster—the grain dealer who bought the
·mers' barley and then sprouted and dried it ready
· the monastic mash tub—the monks brewed their
ima, *secunda*, and *tertia melior* (literally their "first-
st," "second-best," and "third-best" brews). In
ntral Europe, the popular production of hopped
ers over unhopped ales grew steadily, as did the
mand for hops. Middle Europe, and Germany espe-
lly, became the heartland of the hop field.

CHANCE DISCOVERY
✦

You might feel fuggled after one
too many pints of beer. Fuggles,
like Goldings, Pride of Ring-
wood, and Eroica, is one of the
beer brewer's classic hop
varieties. "The original plant
was a casual seedling which
appeared in the flower-garden
of Mr. George Stace, of
Horsmonden, Kent," explained
agricultural professor John
Percival in the *Brewers'
Journal* of 1902. "The sets
were afterwards introduced to
the public by Mr. Richard
Fuggle, of Brenchley, about the
year 1875." Fuggles went on to
account for 90% of the hops
used to flavor and preserve
British beer.

Down with beer

The monastic network in the Middle Ages was like some forerunner of the internet chatroom. News, knowledge, and gossip were traded by the brethren and their staff as they traveled between monasteries, and word of the new, hop-conditioned beer soon spread north into the neighboring Lowlands—including modern-day Belgium and the Netherlands—and northern France. But *bière*, as the English king Henry VI called it in the 1400s, did not make an easy crossing of the Channel that separated the bière-drinking Europeans from the ale-drinking English. Wild hops may have been native to this island nation, yet there was marked hostility to the notion of spoiling good English ale with "foreign"

**Ale, man, ale's the stuff to drink
For fellows whom it hurts to think.**

A. E. Houseman, A Shropshire Lad, *1896*

hops. But you cannot keep a good beer down: East Anglia and the southern counties of England were busy, wool-weaving regions, and home to many migrant Dutch weavers with a thirst for their home-brewed beer. It was soon being shipped in from abroad and finally being made in England.

Brewers' hops were growing in Kent by the early 1500s although even in William Shakespeare's time, hopped beer was less popular than hopless ale. The conservative ale brewers even persuaded the burghers of several cities, including Coventry, to ban the adulteration of ale with hops. The tide of beer, however, was against them. Armies marched, and navies sailed, on a diet of meat, bread, and beer. On board ship, drinking

HOP HEARTLAND
An advert for Bock Beer, c. 1882. A strong lager often brewed for special occasions, Bocks originated in the northern German city of Einbeck (from which it takes its name) in the fourteenth century.

BOCK BEER

water quickly turned brackish and naval pursers always provisioned their vessels with sufficient ale or beer for the voyage: around a gallon per man per day. But the crew that sailed on a warship carrying barrels of traditional ale, which soured within days, were soon suitably soured themselves. Given the choice (not that many of the press-ganged sailors were), the seamen would opt to join their shipmates who sailed aboard a man o' war with barrels of long-lasting, hopped beer in its hold. Throughout the sixteenth and seventeenth centuries, the battling British seemed to be constantly at war, and the new foreign beer brewers were as generous with their donations, used to fund the arms trade, as the taxman was with the excise duties. So by 1615 Gervase Markham in his *English Huswife* noted that "the general use is by no means to put any hops into ale, making that the difference between it and beere." Nevertheless, he recommended the wise wife to add "to every barrel of the best ale . . . halfe a pound of good hops."

When, in 1620, the "Old Comers" (or the "Pilgrim Fathers," as they were later called) set sail from Plymouth, their ship, the *Mayflower*, was provisioned with beer and hops. By 1635, the settlers were brewing their own beer.

There was to be no looking back. 370 years later, the Czech people were drinking more than 41 gallons (156 l) a year each, with Ireland, Germany, Australia, and Austria following behind. The U.S. was consuming 22 gallons (81.6 l) per person a year, and China 70 gallons (266 l). Beer was a bigger business than Abbess Hildegard could ever have imagined.

HOME COMFORTS
The dimpled shape of the
traditional British pint glass,
topped to the brim with ale,
is a familiar sight in pubs
across the British Isles.

Indigo
Indigofera tinctoria

Native range: Southern Asia

Type: Shrub

Height: 6 feet (2 m)

+ Edible
+ Medicinal
+ **COMMERCIAL**
+ **PRACTICAL**

Indigo, and its competitor woad, provided the prime sources of the color blue until an army of workers wearing blue denim stretched the natural resource to its limits. The arrival of a chemical substitute triggered the move for India's independence from the rule of the British Raj and helped finance the first shots fired in World War I.

A BRILLIANT BLUE

The great Venetian explorer Marco Polo (1254–1324) noted a strange, and smelly, industry taking place in what is now Kollam in Kerala, India, in 1298: indigo production. Still used extensively in West Africa and Asia today, indigo (*nil* in Hindi) was extracted by soaking the leaves of the plant in liquid. Fermenting the leaves of *Indigofera tinctoria* produced the brilliant blue dye, indigotin. Although the stink of fermenting indigo made social outcasts of the dyers (some of the European processes involved the use of urine), it has been a popular dye for over 4,000 years.

The Greeks called it the "blue dye from India" (*indikon*), highlighting the East–West trade that saw packhorses, loaded with bags of indigo traveling the silk roads out of northern India. Why spend months risking bandits and bad weather to bring indigo into Europe? From white weddings to black funerals, color speaks a language of its own. Blue represented wealth, and still does to the nomadic Saharan Tuareg tribesmen, the "blue people," with their indigo-blue robes and turbans. Blue suggested truth; it hinted at human mortality; and, as the calming color of the sky and sea, in some holistic treatments it was used to help lower respiration and blood pressure.

Blue was also perceived to be a working color. Aside from European military uniforms (war was good for the indigo trade), the nineteenth-century industrialization of Europe and America produced a "villa" middle class and a laboring class who wanted tough fabrics to protect them from sparks, dung, barley bristles, and blood—all the things, in fact, that made up a day's work for the average laborer. From the stevedore shifting cotton bales in New York harbor to the Parisian stoker shoveling coal on the Lyon Express, working men and women wanted cheap, strong clothing. The demand for bib-and-brace overalls, boiler suits, dungarees (named after India's Dongri Killa, the fort of Bombay, the source of cheap, undyed calico cloth) and, above all, jeans, mushroomed. The demand for blue jeans—now the must-have pants (the

verage American wardrobe contains at least seven
airs)—was already threatening to overwhelm natural
upplies and driving chemists to search for a synthetic
ource of blue dye 50 years before blue jeans became
he on-board work clothes for American naval ratings
1 1901.

Although it did not match the quality of *Indigo
nctoria*, its closest rival was *Isatis tinctoria*—woad.
The British," observed the conquering Roman, Julius
aesar, "color themselves with glass, which produces a
lue color," a reference to the "painted people" or
'ictish warriors who daubed themselves in woad the
etter to scare the enemy. The craft of turning woad
ito the blue dye used to color working clothes had been
nastered by French dyers, especially in the Pays de
ocagne, or "land of the woad ball," as Languedoc
ame to be known. A chemical dye, Prussian blue, made
rom alum and animal bones, had already been discovered in Germany in
he early 1700s, but in 1856 a young Englishman, William Henry Perkin,
aving set up his laboratory to search for a synthetic version of quinine
sing coal tars, instead discovered the synthetic dye mauveine. This was
ollowed by the synthesis of indigo dye by the German chemist Adolf
on Baeyer in the 1860s, an achievement that earned
im the Nobel Prize in Chemistry in 1905.

When industrial substitutes hit the indigo markets
1 the 1870s, it had a catastrophic effect on the Indian
conomy. In the early 1900s, demand for natural indigo
ell to an all-time low, feeding demands for Indian inde-
endence and bringing the rule of the British Raj to an
nd less than 50 years later. The expansion of the
hemical dye industry continued in Germany, which by
900 had cornered the market. The profits generated
elped fund Germany's entry into World War I.

SYNTHETIC DYES
Despite his commercial
success, Sir William Perkin
chose to retire from
dyemaking at the age of 36
in order to focus on research
into organic acids.

EARTHY COLORS

✦

Indigo's earthy sister, henna, is
made from the leaves of the henna
bush (*Lawsonia inermis*). Dyers
worked with a vast range of other
plants before the nineteenth-
century revolution in chemical
colors. Austrians had *Carthamus
tinctorius* (or bastard saffron), for
scarlet, pink, and rose; Irish women
collected lichens and carrageen
moss, while their Scottish sisters
plucked hillside heathers to make a
clear yellow; and Holland's madder
(*Rubia tinctorum*) men taught
Europe how to grow and process
this source of the deep red dye.

he blue bared its eternal bosom, and the dew
f summer nights collected still to make
he morning precious.

hn Keats, "Sleep and Poetry," 1884

Sweet Pea

Lathyrus odoratus

Native range: Southern Europe

Type: Climbing annual

Height: 8 inches (20 cm)

+ EDIBLE
+ MEDICINAL
+ **COMMERCIAL**
+ **PRACTICAL**

*L*athyrus odoratus is the wild flower that turned a thousand heads and arose one of its most dramatic manifestations at the ancestral home of Diana, Princes of Wales. Although in the 1850s it caused almost as much of a stir as the craze fc the tulip, it did not alter the course of history quite as much as its close cousin, *Pisu sativum*, the edible pea. A Bavarian monk paved the way for modern genetics, ar DNA, with the pea. If only Darwin had known.

WILD ESCAPE

The scented, purple flowers of the original, wild sweet pea are still to k found hedging paths and green lanes in the Mediterranean spring o Malta and Sardinia especially. However, in the 1600s it was from anothe of the neighboring islands, Sicily, that the Franciscan monk Fath Franciscus Cupani noticed a curious variety growing in the garden c

his monastery at Palermo. It was a natural muta tion or "sport," an elegant little bicolored flowe with maroon-purple "standards" and magenta purple "wings." He collected the seed and grew on the following year, discovering that it gre true to its seed. Delighted, Father Cupa collected the seed and saw that the flower gre true once again. Three years after he first foun the flower, he dispatched seeds to a botanist at a Amsterdam medical school, Dr. Caspar Commeli in 1699. Seeds were then passed on to anothe botanist, a schoolmaster called Dr. Robe Uvedale, who lived in Middlesex, England. third sport—this time white—appeared ar then, shortly after, a fourth named the Painte Lady, which was pink and white.

Here are sweat peas, on tip-toe for flight
With wings of gentle flush o'er delicate white,
And taper fingers catching at all things
To bind them all about with tiny rings.

John Keats, "Endymion," 1818

he new "sweet sented pease" were doing
he rounds: "April 15. Planted some yellow
ndian corn in the new hot bed . . . to
pply those that fail in the cups. April 16.
owed in the new garden on the border by
he Brick Walk, Love lies a Bleeding,
ainted Lady Peas, Larkspurs, Yellow
upines & Double Poppies." Here was the
icar of Selborne in Hampshire, Gilbert
Vhite, writing of the Painted Lady in his
itchen-garden diary for 1752.

In 1793, as interest in this Queen of the
nnuals grew, a seedsman from Fleet
treet, London, published the first sweet pea list. It listed five varieties:
he original purple bicolor, the white sport, the pink and white Painted
ady, and a maroon and a red-flowered variety. Growers started to exper-
ment with their own garden collections, looking for new mutations to
row on or experimenting with cross-fertilization: "blossoms are
ollenated [sic] by hand with pollen of another variety, using either a
amel's-hair brush, a rabbit's tail affixed to a stick or forceps holding the
tamens," explained one garden manual. By now, the horticultural
cotsman Henry Eckford had started work on the sweet pea and, eventu-
lly, he produced an additional 115 varieties. The gardener, who had
orked on various great estates (he gained a reputation for mastering the
ultivation of pelargoniums and dahlias for the Earl of
Radnor in Wiltshire), finally gained the horticultural
ccolade of a first-class certificate from the Royal
Horticultural Society in London for his Bronze Prince
weet pea. Eckford left the service of others to run his
wn nurseries at Wem, in Shropshire, England from
here he dispatched his sweet-pea seeds across the
orld. They proved especially popular in America. The
weet pea, however, had one more surprise. Around
900 a grocer, a gardener, and a gentleman separately
iscovered a curious new sport from one of Eckford's
hell-pink sweet peas, the Prima Donna. Its startling
ink color and great, blowsy frilled edges prompted all
hree men to name the new variety, but it was Silas
ole, the gardener at Althorpe Park—the ancestral
ome of the Spencer family and latterly of Princess
iana—whose name stuck: the Countess Spencer.

AN EDIBLE PEA
The sweet pea is inedible,
becoming toxic if eaten in
large quantities, so another
genus within the Fabaceae
family—the edible pea
(*Pisum sativa*)—is cultivated
for consumption.

SEEDS OF LIFE

✦

Seeds represent the most
important development in the
evolution of plants. Packaged up in
their protective coats, they can be
transported across the continents,
on the air, in water, on the hides of
animals, or in the intestines of birds
to spring into life again when
conditions are good. Most important of all, each seed is the parent
plant in embryo: it contains the
DNA necessary to replicate
the parent.

THE BIRTH OF GENETICS

What all these gardeners, from Father Cupani to Silas Cole, had done
reach the scented heights with their favorite blooms was dabble in t
little-known science of genetics, selecting and breeding from their plant
(Curiously, the one color that eluded them then and ever since was a pu
yellow flower.) The science of selection relied on the most detailed stu
of plants and animals, as amateur naturalists like the Reverend Gilbe
White was well aware. But writing to his friend Thomas Pennant
August 1771, White was concerned over who was, or was not, compete
to carry out the duties of what he called the Faunists.

"Faunists, as you observe, are too apt to acquiesce in bare descri
tionism and a few synonyms," he wrote to his friend. The reason wa
obvious: "The investigation of the life and conversation of animals, is
concern of much more trouble and difficulty, and is not to be attaine
but by the active and inquisitive, and by those that reside much in t
country. "Foreign systematics," he concluded, were particularly dubiou
and "much too vague in their specific differences."

Gilbert White's assertion that "foreigners" were not up to the task
properly studying plants ignored the contribution of Andrea Cesalpin
Born in 1519, Cesalpino, who studied botany at Pisa University, publishe
in 1583 *De Plantis Libri XVI*, which included his treatise on studyin
plants and classifying them according to their reproductive organ
White was proved wrong twice over by a chaste and celibate Moravia
monk named Johann (later Gregor) Mendel. Mendel exchanged his Chri
tian names when, in 1843, he joined St. Thomas' monastery on the ban
of the river Svratka in Brünn, the provincial capital of Moravi
now Brno in the Czech Republic. At St. Thomas', which wa
more a university than a monastery in some respects, t
monks were encouraged to pursue their own academ
interests, to research and teach. Gregor Mend
did so assiduously. Coming from a farmin
background, he was naturally inte
ested in animal and plant selection—i

INHERITED TRAITS
Using a the edible pea
(*Pisum sativa*), Mendel
observed that pure-bred lines
of the plant produced
offspring with constant
traits, while the characteristics of hybrids varied.

how, for example, a generation of chickens change, adapt, and hopefully produce some progeny that lay eggs better than others, and yet remain essentially hens.

Mendel started working with mice, but when a visiting bishop banned the unsavory smell of rodents emanating from Mendel's quarters, the monk turned, not to the sweet pea, but its close cousin, *Pisum sativum*, the pea. *Pisum* and *Lathyrus* are genera within the same family Leguminosae, differing from each other only in their stiles and stamens. *Pisum sativum* could be bred for consistency, green peas producing new green peas, yellow peas producing yellow. Gradually Mendel realized that traits are inherited independently of one another, in pairs, from each parent. He presented his findings in a scientific paper six years after the British naturalist, Charles Darwin, published *The Origin of Species* in 1859. Darwin had set out to show that plants and animals change over time, and that natural selection aided the survival of the fittest. His book caused a furor because of its implication that humans, too, were part of evolution, and not the natural masters of the universe, created by a benevolent God. While Darwin's findings caused howls of derision, and more importantly, deep debate, Mendel's work was ignored. The eminent Swiss botanist Carl von Nägeli wrongly persuaded Mendel that his work was incomplete and that he needed to do more research.

Mendel went to his grave, humbly accepting that his lifetime research amounted to nothing—many of his papers were destroyed—and that the national recognition he would have appreciated had eluded him. In the end it was a student of Nägeli, the German botanist and geneticist Carl Correns, and two other scientists (see box) who rediscovered Mendel's work after his death. It was left to them to show the world the true significance of the Bavarian monk's work on *Pisum sativa*.

MENDEL'S HERO

✦

Three botanists rediscovered Gregor Mendel's work at around the same time: the German Carl Correns, Austria's Erich Tschermak von Seysenegg, and the Dutch botanist Hugo Marie de Vries. De Vries had been working on his own theory of heredity without realizing that Gregor Mendel had already done the work on his peas. The word "genetics" was coined by the British academic William Bateson after he had read Mendel's papers. He became a champion of the Austrian's work.

Lavender

Lavandula spp.

Native range: The Mediterranean, India, Canary Isles, North Africa, and the Middle East

Type: Shrubby evergreen perennial plant

Height: Up to 6.5 feet (2 m)

+ EDIBLE
+ *MEDICINAL*
+ *COMMERCIAL*
+ *PRACTICAL*

A truly Mediterranean plant that roots itself in the wild even among the hot rock and thin soils of the Provençal maquis, lavender went on to become a cottage garden classic. But the plant, which was named by the Romans after the Latin *lavare* (to bathe or wash), proved to be a startling asset for the perfume trade.

FIRE PLANT

Cutting the flower stems immediately before flowering and then drying them under a Mediterranean sun locked in the plant's natural aroma. The name seems to have arisen from the Roman practice of steeping scented bundles of lavender in the villa bathing water.

Despite its languid, heavy-scented associations, this is a fire plant. Certain Mediterranean species are so packed with volatile oils that—like the Australian eucalyptus—they will spontaneously combust in the summer heat, setting fire to neighboring plants and triggering a heath fire. Only after such a fire will the seeds of these species germinate, which is why commercial growers have developed a "smoke water" to persuade them to germinate in the nursery.

Aside from the roots, lavender oil is present in all parts of the silver-leaved and white- to blue-flowered plants, which belong to the mint family (Lamiaceae). The long, thin leaves and the natural oils provide the plant with its natural protection in the wild, enabling it to survive midsummer droughts, rendering the plant unappetizing to most grazing animals, and yet, with its heady fragrance attracting potential pollinating insects. (Bees that have browsed on lavender produce an especially rich, intensely flavored honey.)

Lavender's reputation as a culinary and medicinal herb has been recorded for as long as herbals have been written. Lavender was used by every civilization from the Egyptians, Greeks, and Romans to the Arabs, who led the way in medicine (as in most other arts) in the Mediterranean region from the seventh century. Traditionally grown close to the laundry

> Of lavender hedges there are several of varying ages in different parts of the garden. Lavender for cutting should be from plants not more than four or five years old, but for pictorial effect the bushes must be much older.
>
> *Gertrude Jekyll*, Colour Schemes for the Flower Garden, *1914*

d used as a strewing plant to freshen
,ors, lavender also had a reputation as
 insecticide. In the twelfth century,
e German Abbess Hildegard of Bingen
ted its effectiveness against fleas and
ad lice, while in 77 CE, Dioscorides,
thor of the *De Materia Medica*, noted
 healing qualities, especially for burns
d wounds. From Roman times to the
oody campaigns of World War I,
vender was put to good use.

   Culpeper, however, warned in his *Complete Herbal*: "the chemical oil
awn from lavender, usually called oil of spike [it was known in India as
pikenard"], is of so fierce and piercing a quality, that it is cautiously to
 used." He went on to acknowledge lavender's healing qualities in rela-
on to "falling sickness, the dropsy, or sluggish malady, cramps, convul-
ons, palsies, and often faintings" as well as a dozen further ills, including
ming to the aid of the patient who has lost his or her voice. But it was
 the world of perfumery that lavender played a particularly significant
le. In 1709, the Italian perfumier Giovanni Maria Farina included a
btle blend of lavender in the perfume he named after
s new hometown, Cologne. His Eau de Cologne was
unched some time after four grave robbers, arrested
r plundering corpses during an outbreak of plague in
arseille, claimed to have included lavender in their
ague protection potion. The preparation, which also
cluded rosemary, cloves, and distilled vinegar, was
bbed "The Vinegar of the Four Thieves." Farina's
mily continued to sell their much-copied Eau de
ologne from the German city into the twenty-first
ntury (using the shop's street number, 4711, for their
mous brand), but serious perfume production was
ready switching to that part of Europe best known
r its iconic blue rows of lavender: Provence.

   Perfumes burned in Grecian and Roman times to
ent the air—hence the Latin *perfumare*, to smoke
rough/thoroughly—were beginning to give way to
nthetic perfumes by the mid-nineteenth century. But
ey could never match the qualities of that essential
l, lavender.

SCENT OF SUCCESS

✦

Each of the 28 or so species of
lavender produces different
quantities, and qualities, of oil.
The craft of the commercial
producers lies in producing the
perfect blend. *Lavandula angusti-*
folia, the true or English lavender,
produces the best quality when
grown at between 2,600 and 4,300
feet (800 and 1,300 m), while
L. latifolia, grown at lower levels,
yields around three times the
quantity, although the oil is of lower
quality. The hybrid produced by
L. angustifolia and
L. latifolia, *Lavandula* x *inter-*
media produces more low-quality
oil and grows at lower altitudes.

Crab Apple
Malus pumila

Native range: Central Asia: the Caucasus, Himalayan India, Pakistan, and western China

Type: Tree

Height: Up to 25 feet (7.5 m)

✦ **EDIBLE**

✦ MEDICINAL

✦ **COMMERCIAL**

✦ PRACTICAL

You would not want to eat *Malus pumila*, the bitter fruit of the wild crab-apple tree, but you might award it a place in any horticultural history of the world. Having parented the edible apple tree, it helped with the formulation of the theory of gravity by Sir Isaac Newton. Why the fruit is the subject of so many myths and legends is a mystery in itself, but the economic impact of this compact little lunchbox is beyond doubt.

STRANGE FRUIT

When a country stallholder in the market village of Alma-Ata in Kazakhstan first added a sack of seedling trees to his wares 1,500 years ago, his neighbors looked askance at what he was selling. The conventional trade, both with the locals and the menacing-looking tribespeople who passed by on the Silk Road (see White Mulberry, p.130), consisted of sheep's heads and live hens, and baskets of wild apples, walnuts, and apricots lifted from the nearby forests. But the trial sales of the saplings, also taken from the surrounding forests, must have gone down well with

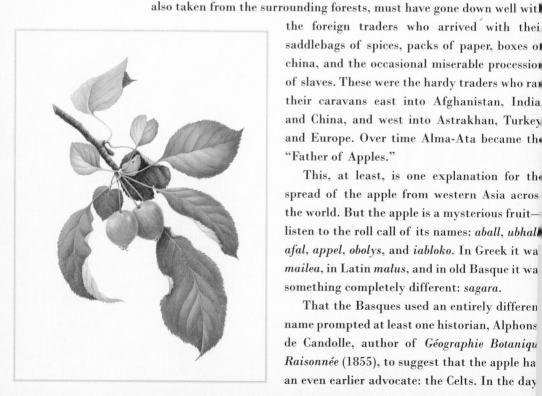

the foreign traders who arrived with their saddlebags of spices, packs of paper, boxes of china, and the occasional miserable procession of slaves. These were the hardy traders who ran their caravans east into Afghanistan, India, and China, and west into Astrakhan, Turkey, and Europe. Over time Alma-Ata became the "Father of Apples."

This, at least, is one explanation for the spread of the apple from western Asia across the world. But the apple is a mysterious fruit—listen to the roll call of its names: *aball, ubhall, afal, appel, obolys,* and *iabloko*. In Greek it was *mailea*, in Latin *malus*, and in old Basque it was something completely different: *sagara*.

That the Basques used an entirely different name prompted at least one historian, Alphonse de Candolle, author of *Géographie Botanique Raisonnée* (1855), to suggest that the apple had an even earlier advocate: the Celts. In the day

when Rome was in the process of becoming the superpower of western Europe, the Celts were drifting from their ancestral homelands in eastern Europe, also the home of the wild apple, into western and southern Europe. Although the Celtic people have tended to be romanticized, they were almost certainly as brutal as any self-sustaining tribe of the day. They recorded their history in poetry and ...ation, in storytelling and hand-me-down legends. A pertinent story, as ...gards the apple, is that of Merlin, Merddin, or Myrddin. Spell him how ...u will, tales of the wild wizard with his staff and brown gown circulate ... word of mouth in the old Celtic pastures of Wales, Brittany, Galicia, ...eland, and western Scotland to this day.

Here, in a sixth-century poem by "Merddin the Caledonian," are our ...cient apple trees:

. what was shown to Merddin before he became aged, namely seven score ...d seven, delicious apple-trees of equal age, length and size, which sprang ...m the bosom of mercy. They are guarded by one maid ...th crisped locks.

...nother Celtic tale suggesting the Celts as the early ...chardists was that of St. Brieuc, who began planting ...ple orchards in Brittany after he was expelled from ...estern England by warring Saxons. The Dwll Gwnedd, ... ancient Welsh code of laws, lays down a pricing ...ructure for apple trees: ". . . an increase of two pence ... added every season until [the tree] shall bear fruit ...d then it is three score pence in value, and so it grad- ...tes in value as a cow's calf."

The apple features prominently in Greek and ...oman legends too. Atalanta, the tomboy of Greek ...ythology, was the unloved child of Iasus of Arcadia, ...andoned on a mountainside and suckled by a bear. ...aised by hunters, she became a famed huntress ...rself, and a young woman who resisted the advances ...' potential suitors. Each who asked for her hand was ...tted against her in a running race. They ran naked, ...e in her diaphanous gown. Each time she won, the ...ouse-who-was-not-to-be was put to death. Then the ...ddess Aphrodite took pity on a new suitor, Melanion,

A-WASSAILING

✦

The business of corralling apple (and any other fruit) trees into one place, or orchard, is an ancient one and the customs surrounding its maintenance equally ancient. None is stranger than the practice of meeting in the cold, dark orchard on the Twelfth Night after Christmas and shooting the largest tree in the orchard. Wassailing, the fertility rites revived in the English counties of Herefordshire, Gloucestershire, and Somerset especially, involved hanging pieces of toast in the largest tree (to attract the good spirits of the robin), discharging weapons into the branches (to dispel the bad spirits), and carousing with song and cider for as long as possible.

and advised him to drop three golden apples on the track. As Aphrodite expected, the apples arrested Atalanta's attention long enough for Melanion to win the race and her hand. The apple features again in the eleventh labor of Hercules. In the garden of three nymphs, the Hesperides, stands a tree of golden fruit inhabited by a dragon whose job it is to protect the fruit. Hercules finds the garden with the aid of a helpful sea god, Nereus, and takes away the golden apples, but they start to decay the moment they leave the garden and must be returned so they can regain their former beauty.

Although the story of the "golden fruit" and Adam and Eve in the Garden of Eden could refer to the more common pomegranate, there is no mistaking the apple in that mysterious Celtic tale of the misty isle of Avalon. Avalon, or Annwn, was the island of apples and the earthly paradise in the western seas where the noble ruler of the Round Table, King Arthur, was taken on his death. Celtic mythology took the apple to its heart: Morgan le Fay, the Queen of Avalon, carries an apple bough as a symbol of peace and plenty. Sometimes portrayed as a scheming sorceress, she is also the winter goddess, the complementary of the lord of summer, Arthur. The dying Arthur was taken to Avalon (sometimes identified as Glastonbury in Somerset, England) in the hope that he would return to fight and defeat any future invaders of the realm. Yet, when the Normans beached their boats on the English shores in the invasion of 1066, they brought with them a new set of apple and orcharding techniques along with new ideas on *le cidre*. The Romans had already brought the arts of Pomona, the goddess of fruit trees, with them into France (then known as Gaul) and England together with their vines and vineyards. A cooling climate saw Bacchus, the god of grapes, give way to Pomona.

Cider was a taxable commodity and tax records show cider in production in most of southern England by the 1300s. For the next 600 years it became the staple agricultural drink in the cider-growing districts. Cider was not so much a byproduct of apple growing, but the sole purpose for planting and harvesting the cider apple. This account of Shropshire farmer Stan Morris, from Bucknell, was recorded in the 1980s.

Sum Venus, orta mari, toti gratißima cœlo,
Exhilarans homines, ætherosſsæ Deos.

MAGIC AND MYTH
The Greek goddess Venus, the Roman equivalent of Aphrodite, with her son Cupid and the golden apple, the "apple of discord," given to her by Paris. The apple is surrounded by myth and legend, particularly when it comes to Celtic tales and the story of King Arthur.

der making, that took the best part of a week.
etween October and Christmas was cider making time.
he horses were used to grind yer apples up, in a
rtable mill, set down by the river. The place down by
e river was special because you got your river water;
ere used to be ten or a dozen made their cider there
ery year.

orris described filling the barrels with the pressed
ple juice, a liquid with a reputation as a fierce laxa-
ve, and waiting for the natural yeasts to start to
rment the liquid.

u'd see how he was working like and topped him up
ith a drop of water . . . We used to buy our barrels off
firm that had rum and there'd be a certain amount of
e rum in there: well, that was left, obviously! In the
der house at home we'd have one or two, 120 gallons,
d about two hogsheads (that's a hundred gallons) and
en about two or three 50s or 60s put down."

he quantity of cider (up to 620 gallons [2,820 l] a
ar, or just over 100 pints [57 l] a week) for an average
usehold of six, plus half a dozen workers, highlights
e importance of farm cider.

HE BIG APPLE

y the middle of the eighteenth century, the apple
ee—and cider—had been taken around the world.
ne grower, Thomas Smith, a farm laborer who had
migrated from England with his wife, Maria, and their
ve surviving children, settled in New South Wales,
ustralia. At Ryde they grew oranges, peaches,
ectarines, and some of the estimated 1,000
ifferent apple varieties. After Maria's death
1870, one particular strain that
ney had developed was exhibited
t the Castle Hill Agricultural
how as "Smith's seedlings"; it
ent on to become the famous
ranny Smith.

APPLE HEADS

✦

Not all tales involving apples are
true. The story of the Swiss hero
William Tell defying reason to split
an apple, placed on his son's head,
with a bow from his arrow, is
untrue. There is also the anecdotal
tale of the mathematician Sir Isaac
Newton (1642–1727) contemplating
his theory surrounding the laws of
gravity. He was sitting in his garden
at Woolsthorpe Manor in Lincoln-
shire pondering these radical
notions when a ripe apple broke
from its bough and, borne down by
gravity, fell to earth. The variety was
said to be Flower of Kent.
Despite circumstantial evidence,
there is no actual proof that the
event took place.

SUCCESS STORY
The Granny Smith, first
grown by the Smith
family of New South
Wales, became one of
the big apples of the
twentieth century.

APPLE JOHNNY
Nurseryman and conservationist Johnny Appleseed introduced his apple seedlings to the American states of Indiana, Illinois, and Ohio.

In America, too, new varieties developed. Since apple seeds rather than apple trees were initially shipped to America, the North American varieties developed a wider genetic stock. One Captain Simpson was said to have planted the seed of an apple he had eaten at his farewell dinner party in England, which, in 1824, became one of the first cultivated apple trees in Washington State. Henderson Luelling, meanwhile, had set off west from Iowa with a wagonload of apple trees. The weight of the wagon so slowed his progress he ended up stopping in Washington State where, with another Iowa man, William Meek, he began planting the great orchards that made Washington State the largest apple-producing region in the States. The arrival of the railroad came just in time and enabled the apple crop to be shipped right across the continent.

Luelling and Meek were helped in their efforts by the strange figure of John Chapman, a nineteenth-century itinerant apple-tree grower (he acquired his seeds free from cider mills) and preacher. Chapman, who established apple nurseries all around Ohio, Indiana, and Illinois, was later known as the folk hero Johnny Appleseed.

RICH PICKINGS
A garden apple tree can produce around 30 apples a year, while a commercial variety yields upward of 300 fruits.

In the mid-1800s, Jesse Hart, a Quaker farmer, produced from the rootstock of an otherwise dead tree a productive, bright red apple, which he named the Hawkeye. Three years after Granny Smith came to market in Australia, Hawkeye was judged "delicious" by an apple judge and marketed two years later under its new name. Delicious was to become the world's most widely grown apple.

What wondrous life is this I lead!
Ripe apples drop about my head;
The luscious clusters of the vine
Upon my mouth do crush their wine.

Andrew Marvell, "The Garden," 1681

A GLOBAL MARKET

America's apple growers received a boost at the end of World War II. Europe's apple orchards had fared badly in the war and the U.S. stepped in, shipping the small fruit, which the American consumer tended to reject, to Europe. However, by the 1990s, China's orchard-planting program was bearing fruit. Initially, China had broken into the fruit juice market, but by the turn of the century, had become the world's top apple exporter too, overtaking Europe, India, and America. Outside China, producers complained that the cheap Chinese labor undercut their home markets, but found themselves bringing in migrant labor (from eastern Europe in France and the UK, and from Latin America in the U.S.) for their own apple harvest. Some environmentalists argued that, in a well-managed market, farmers would source their labor locally, paying local rates and passing the costs on to the buyers. But the fruit farmers knew only too well that their big buyers, the supermarkets, would simply take their business elsewhere.

In a footnote to the Big Apple story, the Global Trees Campaign, working to save the world's most threatened tree species, published a list of trees under threat in Central Asia in 2008. It listed 44 original wild trees in the ancient forests of Kazakhstan, Kyrgyzstan, Uzbekistan, Turkmenistan, and Tajikistan, where an estimated 90% of the old forests had been destroyed in 50 years. As a consequence of the breakup of the former Soviet Union, excessive grazing, harvesting, and timber extraction was threatening trees considered to be among the progeny of the first fruits and nuts. They included the wild apricot (*Armeniaca vulgaris*), the wild walnut (*Juglans regia*), the world's most threatened apple species, *M. niedzwetzkyana*, and *M. sieversii*, which is thought to have provided the genetic roots for all modern domestic apples.

PAUL GAUGUIN
The apple, the most widely planted fruit in the world's temperate regions, also had the power to inspire painters such as Paul Gauguin.

White Mulberry
Morus alba

Native range: China and Japan

Type: Deciduous shrub or tree

Height: Up to 49 feet (15 m)

✦ EDIBLE

✦ MEDICINAL

✦ **COMMERCIAL**

✦ PRACTICAL

The Silk Road was the world's first superhighway, a 5,000-mile (8,000-km) overland trail imbued with all the mystery and romance of long journeys to exotic places. The first trade route to link East with West, the Silk Road not only carried news of the latest religion to hit the East, Tibetan Buddhism, it also carried that curious "fruit" of the mulberry tree: silk.

SILKEN GIFTS

The Silk Road was not a road as such, only a spidery collection of tracks and trails that, for a thousand years or more, arose one by one and wound their way between China and Europe. The name "Silk Road" took hold after a German geographer, Ferdinand von Richthofen, coined the term *seidenstraße* in the late 1800s. The most easterly part of the trail started up in Xi'an (Siam, now Thailand) and skirted the Gobi desert before passing through Turkistan. A later southern trail began in Calcutta and rose up alongside the Ganges before crossing to the south of the Himalayas and into the wild hills of Pakistan and Afghanistan. While the northerly routes ran on through Kazakhstan and Armenia, these southerly tracks passed through Iran, Iraq, and Syria before reaching the relative safety of cities such as Alexandria, Constantinople, Athens, Genoa, and Venice.

The silk roads were all about safety. Some of the earliest routes were established during China's Han Empire (206 BCE–220 CE), whose farmers and merchants were plagued by the raiding Xiongnu. The ancestors of the Hun tribes, the wild horsemen of the Xiongnu so harried the Chinese that delegations were dispatched to their neighbors to form alliances against the Xiongnu. Sometimes the strategy worked, and sometimes it failed. On his first mission among them, the patient Chinese

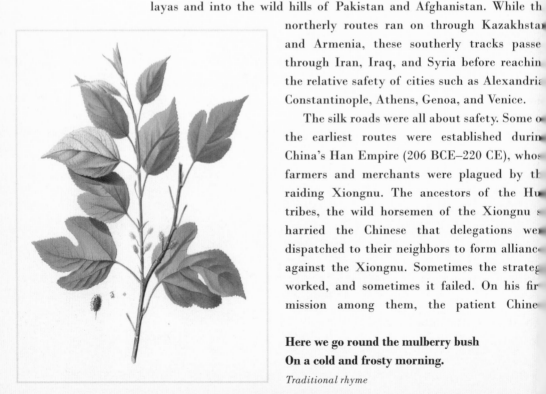

Here we go round the mulberry bush
On a cold and frosty morning.

Traditional rhyme

diplomat Zhang Qian was captured by the Xiongnu. He spent 11 years as their prisoner, even settling down among them with a new wife and children. Whenever envoys like Zhang Qian were sent out, they took offerings to soften up their neighbors, presenting gifts of princesses, gold, and silk. By the first century CE, the imperial economy was sending out almost a third of its revenue. The economy would have been hemorrhaging had not the gifting of silk matured into the silk trade.

The Chinese had mastered the art of silk-making many years earlier: remnants of silk have been found that could be well over 4,000 years old. Silk was dependent on the native Chinese white mulberry, a tree valued by cabinet and musical instrument makers for its hardwood. The mulberry's thick broad leaves, however, were manna to the silkworm (*Bombyx mori*). In China it was common practice to plant the sturdy wild mulberry first and, once it was established, graft a cultivated stock onto the old rootstock. Once the tree had reached five years of age the leaves could be gathered, finely cut, and fed to the silkworm.

To begin with, the eggs of *B. mori* were stored and carefully nurtured so that they could be hatched in simultaneous batches. The hatched caterpillars were then laid on beds of chopped straw, spread out on screens, and for the next 35 days allowed to gorge on the mulberry leaves. By the end of this time the silkworms had spun the cocoons that would provide the silk. The cocoons were removed, some for breeding stock and the others to meet their maker, destroyed in a Turkish bath of hot steam or plunged into a pool of scalding water. The empty cocoons could now be gently unraveled to yield a thread of natural silk up to 5,000 feet (1,500 m) long. The silk thread could be dyed, decorated, and woven into a fabric. The white mulberry remained key to the whole process: a single silk blouse, for example, required no less than 8,800 pounds (4,000 kg) of leaves.

Chinese silk (but not the know-how needed to make it) fed the trade routes of the silk roads. The merchants who plied the tracks with their packhorses, dromedaries, and even elephants, added tea, paper, spices, and ceramics to the payloads traveling west. The "new" faith, Tibetan Buddhism, found its way out along the Silk Roads while the traders carried grapes, glass, incense, and lucerne, used as cattle fodder, back to the east. Silk remained the most valuable commodity, often

HARD BARGAIN
Traders haggle over the price of silkworm cocoons at a market in Antioch around 1895. The now deserted sea port, near Antakya in Turkey, was close to the silk routes out of China.

STOLEN SEEDS
✦

Alternative stories of how silk-making found its way out of China rest on various legends. One of the most popular tells of the King of Khotan, an ancient Buddhist kingdom on one branch of the Silk Road (now in China), who respectfully asked for a bride from the East. He sent word to warn her that his kingdom had neither the silk nor the mulberry tree. The royal bride disobeyed the rule forbidding anyone to remove silkworms or mulberry seeds and hid both in her headdress as she crossed the border.

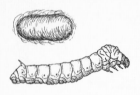

being employed as a currency in itself. At one point, a skein of silk and a horse was valued at five slaves (although records failed to show whether the animal had to be a high-born Arab stallion or a nag that was ready for the knacker's yard). In the first century BCE, silks reached the heart of the Roman Empire, where the Romans treated it like jewelry. Small items of *sericum* (silk) were stitched onto cushions or pinned onto fashionable items of clothing.

TENDER CARE
Women minister to the needs
of a carpet of silkworms
with a shower of mulberry
leaves in this print by
Utamaro Kitagawa, dated
around 1800.

The Roman author Pliny the Elder endeavored to describe the harvesting of the legendary tree in his *Natural History* (77 CE): "The first men who were involved in it were the Seres, famous for the wool of their forests," he explained. "They detach the white down from the leaves by sprinkling it with water, and so their women perform the double task of separating the strands and reweaving them." Because the Chinese so successfully kept the secret of silk-making from the West, there were constant rumors as to how it was made. Silk was said to have been spun from fine soil, from the petals of a rare desert flower, even from an insect that ate and ate until it burst, revealing a body full of silk. The tall tale that silk came from the white down found on certain trees was closest to the truth, referring as it did to the wild silk moths. By now, sufficient silk was reaching Rome for its wealthier citizens to wear whole dresses made from the material; certain senators took to wearing silk themselves. A succession of moralists including Seneca, Solinus, and the Emperor Tiberius condemned these effete and "disgraceful" practices, which, according to Tiberius, "confuse the men with women."

Gradually the methods of making silk, and intelligence on the vital role played by *Morus alba*, were carried out along the silk roads. Seeds and saplings of the white mulberry were taken into Persia and Greece and the island of Sicily became a focus for silk-making. By the late 1400s, as the sea trade overtook the old silk roads, the French started their own silk industry, planting thousands of mulberries in the south. The English King James I tried to follow suit, but while the mulberry tree thrived, silk-making did not. Finally, during its colonial period, the United States introduced the tree and its trade. The silken mulberry had crossed the world.

FUSSY SILKWORMS

✦

The legendary farmer-emperor, Shennong, is said to have taught the Chinese people how to grow the mulberry tree for the silkworm. In the 1300s Wang Zhen, in his *Shonshi Tongku*, offered useful advice on caring for the silkworms as they ate their mulberry leaves. The caterpillar, he wrote, must be protected not only from the smells of fried fish or meat, but also from any woman who had recently given birth or any man who was "carrying" wine. Furthermore, the worms would not tolerate dirty people, the sound of rice being pounded, nor wet or hot mulberry leaves.

Nutmeg
Myristica fragrans

Native range: Tropical islands of southeast Asia

Type: Seed of evergreen tree

Size: Up to one inch (2.5 cm)

+ *EDIBLE*
+ *MEDICINAL*
+ *COMMERCIAL*
+ PRACTICAL

From coriander, crocus, and cardamom to pepper, chocolate, vanilla, and ginger, herbs and spices are an intrinsic part of human history. Their sources have been subject to secrecy, protectionism, restrictions, and thefts. The battle for control of the little nutmeg, however, was more bitter than most.

THE NUTMEG TRIP

Although herbs and spices like mace and nutmeg have for a long time been employed to flavor food and drink, the idea that they were employed to mask the smell of none-too-fresh food is a fiction. Undoubtedly they used to be more important than they are currently, given that today almost every neighborhood shopkeeper in the West stocks fresh-frozen fish, meat, or fowl along with crates of fruit, herbs, and flowers that were ripening under an equatorial sun only days earlier. Some, such as lavender and the South American lemon verbena (*Aloysia citriodora*) served to override the everyday stink of the street; some, like cloves (*Eugenia aromatica*), sweetened the breath. But the real secret of their success, as John Gerard noted, was as "meates to maintain life, and for medicine." They kept people in good health.

There is no doubting the efficacy of nutmeg. *Myristica fragrans* produces fist-sized, apricot-like fruits from its pale yellow fragrant flowers. The fruits split to reveal the nutmeg encased in a skein, which is then dried and ground into the spice mace. The nutmegs are also dried and sold whole or as a finely ground powder, and the spice was adopted by physicians in ancient China to stimulate appetite and boost digestion. It was also known to ease insomnia, diarrhea, and stomach upsets while its beneficial oil lessened rheumatic pain. Nutmeg also contains the toxic alkaloid myristicin, and taking large quantities can induce disturbing, hallucinogenic side effects.

In the first ages of the world [plants] were the ordinary meate of men, and have continued ever since of necessary use both for meates to maintain life, and for medicine to recover health.

John Gerard, Herbal, *1597*

erhaps not surprisingly, all this served to add to the
nse of mystery surrounding the spice.

The more difficult it was to source a particular
ant, the wilder the tales of its origins. As with silk
ee White Mulberry, p.130), nutmeg was rumored to
me from some strange places. The secrecy
rrounding its origins was propagated by the Arabs
d Indians who sold it. Nutmeg was described as one
those silent trade items, left on some empty, exotic
ore in exchange for tradable items like metals and
irrors. It was unknown to the Greeks and barely known in Rome, but it
ached Europe one day in the 500s in a consignment of spices delivered
om Constantinople. For the next seven to eight centuries, as the Arabs
rried it in overland, the Venetians profited by it, as they had with
pper. Europe broke into the maritime trade of the Indian Ocean when
asco da Gama sailed around the Cape of Good Hope in 1497. The source
nutmeg was revealed in the acres of nutmeg trees spread across the
opical Moluccan Islands.

The nutmeg trade, however, was not to be controlled by the Portu-
ese, but by the world's first multinational, the Dutch East India
mpany. In the 1600s, the Company elbowed out the opposition,
otecting its new commercial interests by razing to the
ound nutmeg trees growing on neighboring islands.
eral fruit pigeons continually frustrated their efforts
y spreading the seed.) Employing mercenaries,
eheading rivals, and shipping in slave labor, the
mpany ran its business affairs like most colonial
wers of the time, to the inevitable detriment of the
digenous population. Its monopoly held fast for two
d a half centuries, but was dented in 1776 by Pierre
oivre, the French botanist, who managed to smuggle
fficient seed out of the Moluccas to start a plantation
Mauritius. Just over a decade later, the British began
ipping seedlings to Penang, Calcutta, Kandy in Ceylon,
d Kew Gardens (see box).

The nutmeg monopoly, enjoyed first by the Moluccan
landers and then by the Portuguese, Dutch, and
rabs, was finally broken. Nutmeg could now be added
other crossover plants (sugar and ginger being among
e earliest) that were taken from their native soil and
t down to flourish and turn a profit elsewhere.

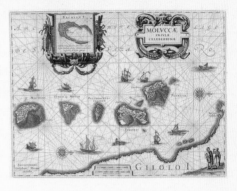

SPICE VICTORS
Willem Blaeu depicted a sea
battle between Dutch and
Portuguese sailors on his
1630 map. The first known
map of the Moluccan
Islands, Blaeu shows the
islands in the hands of the
eventual winners: the Dutch.

NUTMEG AWAY

✦

"List of nutmeg plants collected at
the Banda Islands, December
1796," ran the delivery note written
by Christopher Smith of the East
India Company to Sir Joseph Banks
at Kew Gardens, near London. He
elaborated: "I remained at these
islands for upwards of 18 months
during which time I have collected
64,052 cloves, nutmeg and other
valuable plants. I fear much that
the miscarriage must have been
great in consequence of a long
voyage . . . and no person of
practical knowledge on board (ship)
to take care of them." Smith's fears
were unfounded.

Tobacco

Nicotiana tabacum

Native range: Possibly Bolivia and northwest Argentina

Type: Annual

Height: Up to 8 feet (2.4 m)

+ EDIBLE
+ MEDICINAL
+ **COMMERCIAL**
+ PRACTICAL

It rivals cotton as the world's most important non-food crop, but *Nicotiana tabacu* has no other competitor when it comes to courting controversy. It took cigare' manufacturers a while to concede that this processed plant kills, yet it remains a leg and a popular poison and was once even heralded as a miracle cure.

CURE OF THE CENTURY

Portugal was just beginning to organize the early transatlantic ship ment of black slaves and had set up an embassy in the African tradin center of Timbuktu when France appointed a new ambassador, Jea Nicot. While he attended the Portuguese court from 1559 to 1561, b familiarized himself with some of the strange plants returning on th empty slave ships from the Americas. One, the henbane of Peru, esp cially interested him, and he successfully used it as a poultice to trea ulcers. He also dispatched seeds to Catherine de' Medici, the Quee Mother, in Paris. It not only proved a useful addition to the apothecary medicine box, but also started a fashion for sneezing. The "Nicotia habit" involved inhaling a pinch of ground tobacco leaf, and in arist cratic French circles it became all the rage. The fashion was helped alon

nicely in 1571, when Nicolas Monardes unveiled a new cu for up to 20 common, and often fatal, ailments, includin migraines, gout, toothache, dropsy (edema), and the ag (fever). Monardes was a Spanish physician who lived i Seville, one of the busiest ports of entry for plants fro the Americas, and he wrote up his findings in the som what optimistically titled *Joyful Newes Out of the Ne Founde World* (1577).

As happened with so many of the "new" America plants, there was serious confusion over names, wit numerous possibilities put forward. Two decades later, th physician John Gerard ventured an explanation of "Tabac or Henbane of Peru. Nicolaus Monardus names it Tabacum, although, he added, "the people of America call it Petun. Latin names included *Sacra herba*, *Sancta herba*, and *Sanc sancta indorum*. But he said: "Of some it is called Nic tiana." The French ambassador was becoming more closel associated with *tabaco*.

erard recorded his thoughts in his 1597 *Herbal*, where he also detailed, to astonished readers, the method of taking the tabaco: "The dry leaves are used to be taken in a pipe set on fire and suckt into the stomacke, and thrust forth againe at the nosthrils."

As regards setting out all the medicinal benefits of tabaco, admitted Gerard, it would require a whole volume. Nicholas Culpeper, writing in his *Complete Herbal* in 1653, was equally enthusiastic: "It is a

A BIG MISTAKE?
Jean Nicot presents his tobacco plants to Queen Catherine around 1868. Tobacco promised to be a great healing plant.

native of the West Indies, but we raise it in our gardens," he explained, before launching into a list of remedies. Made into an ointment with hog's lard, it got to the bottom of "painful and inflamed" piles. It banished toothache, killed lice, countered corpulence, and, as a distilled oil, "will destroy a cat." The diarist Samuel Pepys could testify to its efficiency as he recorded in his Diary of May 3, 1665: "Saw a cat killed with the Duke of Florence's poison, and saw . . . that the oyle of tobacco . . do the same effect." Reports that no London tobacconist suffered ill effects of the plague prompted at least one boys' school, Eton, to compel their charges to smoke the weed, with a threat of a thrashing for any who demurred. Culpeper, however, was not convinced that tobacco acted as "a preservative from the plague": "Rivinus says, that in the plague of Leipsic [Leipzig] several died who were great smokers of tobacco." But the great physician did produce one further claim for this extraordinary medicine: blowing tobacco smoke, by means of bellows, into the bowels "in the manner of a clyster" (an enema) was not only an excellent treatment for loosening the bowel and ridding the body of "small worms," but also for reviving persons who had "apparently drowned."

Where, then, did this fine and wholesome plant come from? And what was it like? Gerard ably described the plant with its stalks the size of a child's arm, growing 7 to 8 feet high (up to 2.4 m) with long, broad, smooth leaves. The plant, he noted, perishes at the first approach of winter. Another Englishman, John Rolfe, had planted the first cultivated crop of tobacco in Virginia county in 1612. Within seven years, tobacco was that county's biggest export, grown by slaves and sold at auctions held from August to the late fall as the buyers followed the harvest from the southern Geor-

ALKALOIDS

✦

Many plants contain natural chemical compounds called alkaloids, which have a pH value higher than 7. Some have a medicinal effect on our bodies, while others are poisonous. Many can be processed and extracted in a purified form for medicinal or recreational purposes. Included among these are cocaine, caffeine, morphine, quinine, and nicotine.

gian tobacco belts to the "old Belts" of Virginia in the north. Consume took their medicine in different ways, including French snuff, America chew, the Spanish cigar, and the British pipe. But a growing fashion fo the little cigar (which would become known as the "cigarette") ha manufacturers vying with one another for that distinctive blend o different tobaccos, from the dark-leaved "burley" to th Virginia "bright," which would corner the market.

When it came to rolling and packing the cigarette there was only so much a pair of nimble hands could d The nineteenth century was a period of industrial innova tion, and James Bonsack from Roanoke, Virginia, playe his part. In 1880, he patented a cigarette-rolling machin that could turn out 12,000 an hour. Within ten years, such machines we rolling in the dollars for men like James Buchanan Duke—"Buck" to h friends, and "Mr. Cigarettes" to the American market. By 1890, Bu controlled 40% of the market in America.

THE NIGHT RIDERS

He was not universally popular, especially in the earl 1900s, when he was accused of using strong-arm tactics to take control of the smaller tobacco growe of Kentucky and Tennessee. The Night Riders, a vigi lante group, led by the elusive Dr. David Amoss, wa formed to force reluctant tobacco growers into joinin an association opposed to Buchanan's tactics. Burnin and dynamiting tobacco warehouses at night, th Riders played a successful cat-and-mouse game wit the authorities (although after a raid on Hopkinsvil in December 1907, a posse led by local militia leade James Birch Bassett pursued and killed one of th riders). By now the cigarette was a universal panacea thanks to another of tobacco's properties: its capacit to calm people down. Stressed-out soldiers had smoke during the Thirty Years' War (1618–1648) and th Peninsular War (1807–1814); the Crimean (1853–1856 and the American Civil War (1861–1865); the two Boer Wars (1880–188 and 1899–1902)—when British soldiers learned not to stretch on match to ignite three cigarettes (this was the time it took for the night time Boer snipers to pick off another victim), and World War I. Whe Buck Buchanan died in 1925, his daughter Doris became the riches girl in the world. She was just 12 years old.

COMMON CONCERNS

✦

What did Siegfried Sassoon, Greta Garbo, Che Guevara, Winston Churchill, and Sir Walter Raleigh have in common? Yes, they all smoked. In 2002, the World Health Organization (WHO) estimated that a third of all men, globally, smoked. They also reckoned that ten million cigarettes were sold every minute and that tobacco was killing one in every ten people. By 2030, it is projected to cause the deaths of one in every six people. According to WHO, every eight seconds someone somewhere dies because of smoking-related disease.

bacco was the cash crop with no limits. Yet even as rly as the seventeenth century it had its detractors. t seems to me that here we have a bad and pernicious habit," speculated Gonzalo Oviedo while nceding that it did appear reasonably successful in eating syphilis. In 1606, the Scottish physician Dr. leazar Duncan suggested it be renamed "Youth's ane" since it was "so hurtful and dangerous to uth." In 1622, a Dutchman, Johann Neander, clared its "excesses ruined both mind and body." he most outright condemnation came in a 1604 amphlet, *A Counterblaste to Tobacco*, claiming that noking was "a custom loathsome to the eye, hateful the nose, harmful to the brain, dangerous to the ngs." Eyebrows were raised when the anonymous thor was revealed to be King James I, especially as introduced the first tobacco tax. In one sense, the yal critic was only anticipating the activities of the thorities 400 years later after tobacco was revealed, the *Reader's Digest* declared on its front cover in 1952, as "Cancer by e Carton." By 2008, countries from Bhutan to Cuba had introduced noking restrictions for health reasons (see box).

CIGARETTE BREAK
A cigarette advertisement from 1899. Who could have predicted that a century later tobacco would be the cause of death for one in every ten people across the globe?

Olive

Olea europaea

Native range: The Mediterranean

Type: Evergreen tree

Height: Up to 66 feet (20 m)

+ *EDIBLE*

+ MEDICINAL

+ *COMMERCIAL*

+ PRACTICAL

It's hard to imagine the Mediterranean without its figs, vines, citrus fruit, or olive The last came late to the region, presumably cultivated from fruit in the wild mo than 5,000 years ago. Once it arrived, olive oil powered up the city state Athens, which went on to give us democracy, the Olympic Games, the Partheno and a taste for the arts that lasts to this day.

OLIVE IDOLS

In 1907, the Impressionist painter Pierre-Auguste Renoir purchased h home, Les Collettes, in the town of Cagnes-sur-Mer in southeast Franc because he wanted to save its grove of ancient olive trees. He had bee looking at property on the French Riviera when he heard of Les Collette a smallholding whose ancient olive grove was to be felled to make way f a market garden. In the early 1900s, there was better money in roses tha olives. Renoir bought the house and rescued the olive grove. He then sper the last 11 years of a restless life at Les Collettes struggling to capture th essence of this Mediterranean tree, which, as he wrote in a letter to friend, was "full of colors. A gust of wind, and the tonality of my tree changes. The color is not on the leaves, but in the spaces between them.

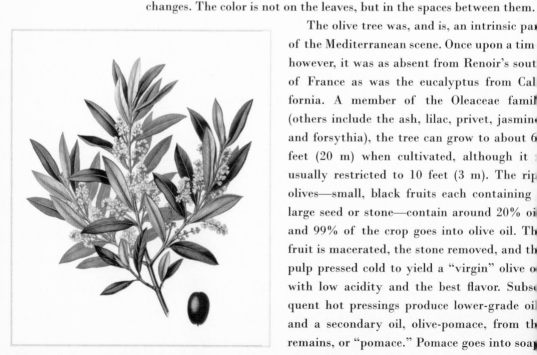

The olive tree was, and is, an intrinsic pa of the Mediterranean scene. Once upon a tim however, it was as absent from Renoir's sout of France as was the eucalyptus from Cal fornia. A member of the Oleaceae famil (others include the ash, lilac, privet, jasmin and forsythia), the tree can grow to about 6 feet (20 m) when cultivated, although it usually restricted to 10 feet (3 m). The rip olives—small, black fruits each containing large seed or stone—contain around 20% oi and 99% of the crop goes into olive oil. Th fruit is macerated, the stone removed, and th pulp pressed cold to yield a "virgin" olive o with low acidity and the best flavor. Subse quent hot pressings produce lower-grade oil and a secondary oil, olive-pomace, from th remains, or "pomace." Pomace goes into soa

while the olive oil industry sometimes burn the stones, or pits, to provide heat for processing. Although the olive has fired the Mediterranean economy for 5,000 years, Herodotus, writing in the fifth century BCE, claimed there was not an olive tree anywhere in the world except Athens. The rarity of the olive prompted him to advise one settlement, which had suffered a crop failure, to build their idols from olive wood rather than stone in future.

Legend would have it that the goddess Athena, daughter of Zeus, gave the olive to the Athenians. It is said she caused an olive tree to spring up in the Acropolis, which became the parent tree of many others. This gift reputedly left Athenians forever in her debt.

Athens was the cultural and commercial center of a loose federation of Greek "city-states" that came gradually to power in the wake of the fall of the Mycenaean civilization around 1120 BCE. While the states, including warring Sparta, frequently did battle among themselves, they were nevertheless able to unite against outside threats, such as in the late 500s BCE when Persia threatened their ascendency.

Athens itself was governed by wealthy landowning "tyrants" (rulers who had absolute and unrestricted power). In the 540s BCE, one of these, Pisistratus, brought political stability long enough for the olive groves—which took a decade to settle in—to become

VENERABLE ANCIENTS
Olives growing on a ridge at the Mount of Olives, the main burial ground in Jerusalem. Given the trees' lack of age rings, it is difficult to determine their true age.

PEACEABLE OLIVES

✦

From biblical stories (when, in the great flood, Noah sent his second dove from the Ark, it returned with an olive branch) to the American Revolution, the olive branch was seen as the symbol of peace. (The Continental Congress signed the Olive Branch Petition in 1775 in a bid to prevent all-out war with Britain.) The flag of the United Nations ("its main purpose, peace and security") depicts the world as seen from the North Pole symbolically surrounded by olive branches.

established. (These same trees were eventually turned into battering rams and siege ladders and used by the Roman general Lucius Sulla to lay siege to Athens.) In time, the tyrants gave way to a more collective form of governance in the shape of an assembly of representatives voted into power. The arrival of liberalizing democrats (from *demos*, meaning "the people," and *kratos*, meaning "power") was in part a response to the Athenians' growing affluence (it is possible to trace a similar process in America in the nineteenth century).

Just as the Ancient Greeks paved the way for the world's first democracy, they also established what would become the world's first international sporting event. The Olympic Games, held every four years in honor of Athena's father, Zeus, saw athletes converge on Athens to compete in now-familiar events such as javelin, discus, and running. It wasn't just in the sporting arena that the Athenians excelled; three centuries later they set a benchmark in architecture with the building of the Parthenon, which was regarded as presenting the "correct" proportions for architecture in Georgian Britain more than 2,000 years later. In the same way that a fossil-based oil would transform the Arab states into the world's wealthiest powers in the twentieth century, Greece developed into an artistic, sporting, and democratic superstate thanks, partly, to its olive oil.

ELUSIVE SUBJECTS
While Renoir struggled to capture its likeness, the olive tree was second nature to Vincent van Gogh, as seen in his painting *The Olive Trees* (1889).

Moving so much oil around demanded new crafts and technologies: a currency in which to trade it, ships to carry it, naval vessels to protect the merchant ships from piracy (Athens possessed a formidable navy), and potters to make jars such as the amphora to carry the stuff. As well as producing utilitarian objects, the potters also created a unique and beautiful ceramic art with plates, bowls, vases, and cups decorated with scenes of domestic life as well as those from myth and legend.

GRECIAN GOLD
Olives contain around 20% oil and the first press, a cold press, yields the top-quality "virgin" oil. Subsequent pressings produce lower-grade oils.

Greek soil was too thin and too stony to grow cereals, but revenues [fr]om the production of olive oil helped fund the cultivation of wheat in [oth]er colonies. From the eighth century BCE onward, the Greeks had [ex]tended their sphere of influence into Spain, southern France, southern [It]aly, North Africa and the Nile Delta, the Black Sea, and the Aegean [Se]a. Each had its key port: Byzantium (Istanbul), Gados (Cadiz), [Sa]guntum (in Valencia), and Croton (in Calabria), as well as Crete and [C]yprus. From the local governance down to the layout of these new city [st]reets, each colony was a clone of the mother ship, Athens.

Edward Hyams, in his book *Plants in the Service of [M]an* (1971), concluded that, the legend of Athena and [he]r gift aside, the olive tree did not reach Greece until [c. th]e 700 BCE. Once it had taken root and fueled the Greek [ec]onomy, it was shipped around the Mediterranean. The [p]arent trees of Renoir's Provençal olive grove first [ar]rived on board a Greek ship docking at the port of [M]assilia, now Marseilles. Italy was devoid of olive trees [un]til around 370 BCE: thanks to the gift of the Greeks, [th]at country became the world's leading olive oil producer [w]ithin two and a half centuries.

When the canvas sails were unfurled on ships in the [fif]teenth century—the ships that heralded the great age [of] European seafaring—olive seedlings were transported [ac]ross the globe. And yet today, when olives are grown in [S]pain, Italy, Turkey, Greece, Tunisia, Morocco, Japan, [So]uth Africa, India, China, New Zealand, and California, [it] is still the Mediterranean countries that consume the [li]on's share—80%—of the global olive crop.

OIL SEED RAPE

✦

Rapeseed was already growing in the Netherlands by the mid-fourteenth century, and it was Dutch farmers who showed their French, German, and English counterparts how best to harvest the crop. For centuries, poorer households relied on either olive or rapeseed oil ("stinking tallow") to fuel their lamps. These vegetable oils were gradually replaced by cleaner-burning oils, including coconut fat and palm oil, before the discovery in 1854 that petroleum oil could be distilled and used to make high-quality paraffin wax.

Rice

Oryza sativa

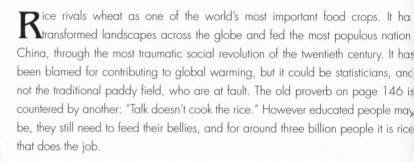

Native range: Asia

Type: Grain-bearing grass

Height: 2 to 5 feet
(0.6 to 1.5 m)

- **✦ EDIBLE**
- ✦ MEDICINAL
- **✦ COMMERCIAL**
- ✦ PRACTICAL

Rice rivals wheat as one of the world's most important food crops. It has transformed landscapes across the globe and fed the most populous nation, China, through the most traumatic social revolution of the twentieth century. It has been blamed for contributing to global warming, but it could be statisticians, and not the traditional paddy field, who are at fault. The old proverb on page 146 is countered by another: "Talk doesn't cook the rice." However educated people may be, they still need to feed their bellies, and for around three billion people it is rice that does the job.

THE GLOBAL CROP

Rice falls into four main categories: upland rice grown on hillsides; rain-fed rice raised in shallow water; irrigated rice plugged into the paddy field; and deep-water rice planted in estuaries and places that flood naturally. It is the oldest continuously grown cereal in the world, and it is raised in more than 100 countries. To grow one of the most important crops in the world, 4.6 million square miles (12 million sq km) of land in southeast Asia, America, Africa, Australasia, and southern Europe (Italy especially) are devoted to rice fields. It is not enough. Rice makes up 30% of world cereal production and, thanks to new varieties, yields have doubled in the last 30 years; but in less than 30 years, by around 2025, an extra 1.5 billion people will come to depend on rice.

In the dry, it grows just like wheat or barley. In the wet (and this applies to more than 90% of global rice production), it grows in the paddy field. Around half of the world's rice is harvested by hand and eaten on the farm where it was grown—it is a backbreaking, labor-intensive business. In the paddy (*padi* in Malay means "rice"), rice is started from seed in nurseries and planted out after four weeks, where it is grown on in the warming paddy field. It takes between 90 and 260 days to grow and seeds about 30 days after flowering, with the grains forming on numerous florets clustered together at the head of the stalk. Traditionally, women planted and weeded the crop while men irrigated and plowed the fields. The ideal draft animal in the paddy field was, and still is, the water buffalo—a lumbering beast that can simultaneously draw the plow and manure the crop.

the same way that wheat
ansformed the landscape of
e West, the little grains of
sativa have dictated the lie
the land in much of Asia,
pecially in the paddy field.
e paddy probably originated
China, although those in
uth Korea are among the
rld's oldest. The rice is
opped in September and dried
the sun before being taken to
arket. In places such as the
and of Java, the paddy fields
e stepped into the hillside in
series of tumbling terraces,
tted with temples dedicated

the rice deities. Surrounded by bunds, or low walls of mud, they are
d with irrigation water. Every spring, the banks are repaired before the
e is transplanted into the freshly flooded field in May.

It was not just in the Far East that the crop changed the land. "During
e summer months, rice crops waved over fields of thousands of acres in
tent"—this observation, made in the 1830s, concerned the lower
etches of a series of South Carolina rivers between
pe Fear in the north and St Johns in north Florida.
he view of the rice fields," added the correspondent
. S. S." in the *American Monthly Magazine*,
Sketches of the Santee River," October 1836), looked
t on "a surface so level and unbroken, that in casting
e's eye up and down the river, there was not for miles
intervening object to obstruct the sight." Until the
vil War and the loss of the slave trade, rice was big
siness on the former tidal swamps of South Carolina.
troduced from Madagascar (one Henry H. Wood-
rd planted seed given to him by a Madagascan ship's
ptain in the 1680s), rice was planted in estuarine
ddy fields, wrested out of the wilderness by black
ves. Shipped in from West Africa and the West
dies, they faced the backbreaking labor of clearing
e native vegetation, digging drainage ditches, and
ilding levees to create miles of flooding fields that

COLOR COORDINATION
✦
Little else except rice can be grown
in a paddy field. This "monocrop-
ping" leads to a buildup of diseases
like blast, yellow dwarf, grassy
stunt, foot rot, and stem rot, and
pests such as locusts, rats, crabs,
and rice weevil. Traditional
protective measures include a host
of rituals such as placing a special
flower over the first seed of the
season to wearing the most
auspicious colored clothes (as
instructed by the village astrologer)
when planting up the paddy field.

filled and emptied with the rise and fall of the tide. These hydrau[l]
paddies were productive: Charleston was selling over 20 million poun[ds]
(9,072 tonnes) of rice by the 1730s. This transformation of the Sou[th]
Carolina landscape continued until, after the Civil War, no one could [be]
compelled any longer to carry out the grueling work of maintaining t[he]
paddies. Finally, in the 1890s, a series of hurricanes obliterated the Sou[th]
Carolina rice fields.

Nowhere has rice so marked the landscape as in China. Althou[gh]
Latin America, for example, grows around 75% of the upland rice (trac[ts]
of rainforest have been cleared to make way f[or]
the crop), Asian farmers grow about 90% of t[he]
world's rice and the paddy fields of India a[nd]
China grow more than half the global total [of]
around 710 million tons (645 million tonnes). [At]
the turn of the 1900s, China was struggling [to]
emerge from the devastation of the opium trade (see Opium Popp[y,]
p.148). This paved the way for the most radical social change of t[he]
twentieth century, in a revolution that would be driven, not only by ri[ce]
but also by the "Great Teacher, Great Leader, and Great Suprem[e]
Commander," Mao Zedong.

In 1931, Mao, the son of a Hunan peasant, was leading a precario[us]
Communist republic with Zhu De in Jiangxi Province in opposition [to]
the ruling Nationalist Party, the Kuomintang. When the Nationali[st]
Chiang Kai-shek attacked Jiangxi, the Communists performed a[n]
unthinkable act: they took their rice and weapons and set off on a 6,00[0-]
mile (9,700-km) journey west to seek sanctuary. The 100,000-stro[ng]

> **If you are planning for a year, sow rice; if you are planning for a decade, plant trees; if you are planning for a lifetime, educate people.**
>
> *Ancient Chinese proverb*

POLISHING RICE
This woodblock is from a sequence called *36 Views of Mount Fuji*, by the Japanese artist Katsushika Hokusai (1760–1849). Produced between 1826 and 1833, this scene shows the traditional Japanese way of rice polishing.

dre was confronted by 18 mountain ranges and
nstant harrying from the Kuomintang. Despite the
dversity, 20,000 survived what became known as The
ong March, reaching Shaanxi Province in 1935. In
uly 1937, both sides were compelled to join forces in
der to counter an invasion from another rice-
ependent nation: Japan. On August 6, 1945, America
ropped the first atomic bomb on Hiroshima, killing
me 150,000 people and helping to bring about the
d of World War II. In the aftermath, the battle
tween the Nationalist Party and Mao's communist
rigades resumed in earnest. With the declaration of
e People's Republic of China on October 1, 1949,
hina turned into the world's largest communist state
d in 1958 Mao launched the First Five-Year Plan—a
ntral part of the wider economic and social plan
own as the "Great Leap Forward." It was designed
 take the small farming collectives and merge them
to larger "people's communes" in order to increase
od production. Farm animals and implements were

ought under collective ownership and the private growing or raising of
od was forbidden. In 1966, Mao launched the Cultural Revolution,
hich saw his zealous young supporters, the Red Guard, herding intel-
ctuals out of town for a bitter taste of peasants' life. What happened
uring the turmoil of plan and counterplan under Mao's rule as the Great
elmsman remains a source of controversy and dispute. Claims that this
as a peasant revolution led by a benign dictator are met with counter-
aims that an estimated 30 million people died from overwork and star-
tion. Mao's measures may yet prove to have caused the largest famine
 human history. It was the first time since 2800 BCE that the golden
ain had failed its farmers.

 Controversy of a different kind surrounded the paddy fields in the
te twentieth century, when climate change scientists identified methane
 one of the major contributors to the greenhouse effect. Western scien-
sts blamed 18% of greenhouse gas emissions on livestock and suggested
at the traditional paddy field, with its combination of decomposing
ffalo manure, rice stalks, and roots, released over 37.8 million metric
ns of methane into the atmosphere. But studies by Indian scientists
ggested that the figure could be at least ten times lower. The blame,
ey said, was not the rice paddy field, but statistical extrapolation based
 relatively tiny surveys.

Opium Poppy
Papaver somniferum

Native range: From Turkey across the East, especially Afghanistan, India, Myanmar, and Thailand

Type: Fast-growing, upright annual

Size: 3 feet (1 m)

+ EDIBLE
+ **MEDICINAL**
+ **COMMERCIAL**
+ PRACTICAL

The opium poppy has proved to be both a blessing and a curse on history. Its healing balm, morphine, has been recognized for its used in easing extreme pain since Neolithic times, while its derivative, heroin, has had nightmare consequences in the West. Arguably, it was opium, once administered to nursing mothers and babies alike, that changed the course of history for the world's most populous nation, China.

DECEPTIVE BEAUTY

The opium poppy is disarmingly pretty. A member of the same family as the field, scarlet, or corn poppy (*Papaver rhoeas*), the blowsy white, pink, red, or purple blooms of the opium poppy have decorated genteel garden borders, and the dried stems featured in flower arrangements in well mannered drawing rooms for centuries. When the flower head dies back it reveals a swollen seed head resembling an upturned pepperpot with a fringe on the top. This dispenses the mass of minute black seeds inside like salt from a cellar. During the final ripening stages, however, the seed head produces a milky-white narcotic sap, the source of opium, morphine, and heroin.

Opium is harvested by scoring the surface of the ripening poppy head in the evening and, in the morning, collecting the sap that has oozed from the scars overnight: raw opium. The sap is scraped from the plant, rolled into pellets, and dried in the sun. Raw opium contains morphine, from which heroin is made, together with codeine and thebaine—both are alkaloids that relieve pain and induce deep drowsiness. It has been exploited for at least 6,000 years, primarily by Neolithic tribes who ranged across eastern and southern Europe. The Greeks celebrated it for its calming, medicinal qualities, and the Romans were as familiar with it (Homer mentions it in the *Odyssey*) as were the terary lights of the nineteenth-century: Wilkie Collins, Samuel Taylor Coleridge, Charles Dickens, Percy Bysshe Shelley, and Thomas De Quincey. But it was Arab merchants who first introduced opium to China in the East, and Europe in the West as they worked their land trade routes.

Heroin was first isolated in 1874 in Germany. During the early trials, some of those who tried it said it made them feel *roisch* (heroic). Heroin was soon being marketed as a non-addictive substitute for morphine. When Americans, trying to clear a troublesome cough in the early 1900s, found their cough remedies curiously addictive, it was because heroin was an active ingredient in them. Some 50 years later, the number of troops addicted to both heroin and morphine was alarming U.S. authorities. A report to Congress in 1971 suggested that 15% of American servicemen involved in the Vietnam war had become heroin addicts. More recently, Russia became the largest per capita user of heroin after the return of heroin-addicted Soviet soldiers from their war in Afghanistan. By the end of the last century, an estimated eight million young people in the West suffered from heroin addiction.

This was nothing compared to the number of Chinese people who had fallen under the somnolent spell of the source of opiates such as heroin; in the early part of the twentieth century, over a quarter of all grown men in China were using narcotics derived from the opium poppy. The world has not seen such levels of mass addiction before or since, nor has a narcotic caused such damage as it did to China. As the effects of opium seeped into every level of Chinese society, the nation was left weakened and vulnerable to attack by aggressors such as the Japanese.

The source of China's addiction lay not in its own native fields, but in India. The cartels that controlled the opiate supplies, and that spread misery among both the Indian growers and the Chinese consumers, were the clandestine representatives of Western nations including Britain, France, and America. A dogged historian could trace the problem back to the 1490s, when the Portuguese navigator Vasco da Gama sailed

PEOPLE'S OPIATE
Pure opium dribbles from an incision in the head of a poppy. The source of both heroin and morphine, raw opium is scraped from the flower head before being dried in the sun.

CURE AND KILL
✦

Opium has always been used medicinally, and the opium poppy is the source of around 25 different alkaloids. They include papaverine (used to treat intestinal problems), verapamil (used to treat heart-related problems), codeine (a painkiller and cough and cold cure), and morphine (used for pain relief). Unlike many other natural drugs, morphine cannot be chemically synthesized and must be extracted from poppy itself. Heroin too started out as a legal medicine—it is made from morphine—but is now banned in most countries around the world.

his ship around the Cape of Good Hope and into the rich mercantile sou
that was the Indian Ocean. Da Gama had pioneered the new sea rout
between East and West at a time when Europeans entertained som
strangely unimaginative ideas about the people in this part of the glob
The Eurocentric view (which did not change greatly over the course o
the next 400 years) was that Africa, India, and the East were populate
by foolish, uncivilized natives who could be persuaded to part with the
valuable spices and precious metals in return for cheap jewelry an
worthless knick-knacks. Europeans also assumed that "The East" woul
welcome cutting-edge Western technologies.

Da Gama sailed in on a productive trade betwee
Africa, India, and China of salt, gold, ivory, ebon
slaves, ceramics, cowrie shells, beads, and silks. Portuga
and its Iberian sister Spain were quick to monopoliz
the sea trade in these commodities between East an
West. Eventually and inevitably, Dutch, French, an
British traders began to muscle in on the action.

While African countries and India were willing t
do business, China was proving to be a coy tradin
partner. The self-contained Chinese enjoyed their ow
silks, porcelains, and tea, and while they welcome
some solid silver bullion in exchange, they wante
virtually nothing else from the West. In 1793, th
British ambassador, Lord Macartney, visited China i
the hope of establishing some trading concession
Macartney was an old-school European who perceive
his negotiators as inscrutable, feudal Orientals. H
convinced himself that they needed only a glimpse o
what the West had to offer in order to be persuaded t
throw open their doors to trade with the West.

China's Manchu leaders were not so easily seduce
While they were amused by the mechanical clocks tha
Macartney presented to them, they still saw his lord
ship as little more than a provincial leader with a pett
petition. They certainly did not see themselves as eith
Eastern or Orientals. Their dynasty was positioned a
the center of the world, stable, safe, and self-sufficien
One Chinese delegate told Macartney with som
sympathy that he was mindful of "the lonely remot
ness of your island, cut off from the world by inte
vening wastes of sea."

MORPHINE

✦

Morphine was isolated by Friedrich
Wilhelm Sertürner from opium in
the early 1800s. He named his
discovery after Morpheus, the
Greek god of dreams. The field
trade in legal opium, used for
medical purposes, is centered on
India, although other producers
include France and Turkey. The
prime source of heroin has, since
2000, been Afghanistan. Other
producers include Burma, Thailand,
Vietnam, Laos, Pakistan, Mexico,
and Colombia and the drug is
blamed for a whole range of
problems in the West. Opium is still
seen as an acceptable recreational
drug in some remote, rural areas,
particularly in Afghanistan.

It was all the more remarkable, then, that within 50 years the social system that governed China, and had done so for more than a thousand years, was about to be brought to its metaphorical knees by a foreign field of poppies.

POISONING PEOPLE

Frustrated by China's resistance to the profitable possibilities of trade, the Western nations cynically created their own trade routes. They introduced tobacco from Portugal's Brazilian fields and Indian opium from British-owned Bengal. It was a powerful combination. Britain had taken control of Bengal's opium fields after Robert Clive defeated the Indian Mogul armies at Plassey in 1757. Clive would later become an opium addict himself. Meanwhile the British East India Company, under the protection of the British government, organized the business of buying and processing the drug in India, enslaving the opium growers to the Company. Taking care not to carry the opium themselves, they ran opium into China through the sea ports, using freelance agents equipped with fast boats. The Company was as guilty of drug trafficking as any cartel boss, but the setup allowed them to refute any accusation of drug smuggling. As the ships slipped in and out of the Chinese ports, and as more and more Chinese officials had to be bribed into denying the opium trade to their seniors, the East India Company controlled the supply of opium, and, more importantly, the price.

The opium of the eighteenth century was as lucrative as the crack cocaine (see Coca, p.70) of the twenty-first century, and its glutinous profits soon attracted dealers from other parts of the world. Rival supplies of Malwa opium began seeping in from western India, while Turkish opium started arriving on board the ships of American profiteers. As more of the yellow stuff flooded in, the price fell and the addiction rate rose.

The China authorities resisted. Imperial orders banning opium smoking had been issued as far back as 1729, but the people's exposure to opium was

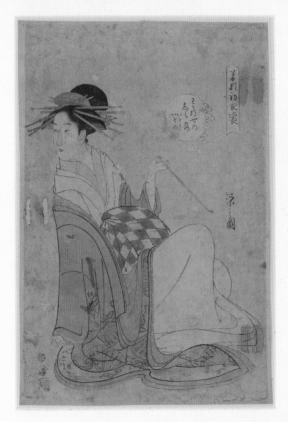

RECREATIONAL DRUG
Many colonials fell for the seductive attractions of a pipe of opium, especially when prepared by a pretty young woman. Robert Clive, "Clive of India," was not immune to opium's narcotic appeal.

MESSAGE IN A BOTTLE
Before they withdrew it from sale, the German pharmaceutical company Bayer marketed heroin as, among other things, a non-addictive cough remedy. Morphine was isolated from opium by Friedrich Wilhelm Sertürner.

beginning to penetrate, and destabilize, every aspect of life in China. Eventually efforts to resist the drug runners were met with gunboat diplomacy: in the early 1840s and 1856, the British, with much "gung-ho" support from back home, sent war ships in to assert the "right to trade." The Chinese were ill equipped and no match for the British soldiers. They lost both of the Opium Wars and, in the aftermath of each defeat, the amount of opium flowing into China promptly increased.

Thou has the keys of Paradise, oh just, subtle, and mighty opium!

Thomas De Quincey, Confessions of an English Opium Eater, *1821*

By now, China's population had risen to 430 million. The hitherto stable rule of the Qing Dynasty (1644–1912) and their Manchurian leaders had helped the nation to prosper, and the country experienced a sharp increase in population. The peasant farmers, however, were struggling to feed so many people in a country that was increasingly debilitated by the effects of opium addiction. It was no surprise when, between 1850 and 1864, insurrectionists started a revolt, known as the Taiping Revolution. They seized land, expelled private landowners, graded the fields according to soil quality and potential yields, and handed over management of the land to the community.

BAD DREAMS
An opium smoker photographed in 1870. The spread of opium so devastated the Chinese economy that it paved the way for the peasant movements and eventually the rise of communism.

FOREIGN POWER

The weakened Manchu government was compelled to turn to the foreign powers they had so despised for help in defeating the revolutionaries. They enlisted the assistance of France, the United Sates, and Britain to provide logistical and technological aid. Their new allies were more than happy to cooperate, but at a price. They insisted that China introduce a crippling concession: the legalization of opium. Reluctantly, China agreed.

Opium addiction eventually permeated every level of Chinese society and cost the country its sovereignty. By the end of the nineteenth century, China was a nation in decline. The last emperor, the child Puyi, abdicated in 1912. He would die in 1967 working as a humble archivist during yet another peasant move ment, the Cultural Revolu

tion, which hauled this nation into the twenty-first century. Not until World War II would opium addiction in China finally be brought under control (see Rice, p.144).

Now it was the Western world's turn to deal with the drug that was potentially even more destructive than opium: heroin. Heroin was becoming an increasingly popular recreational drug in America and Western Europe by the early 1900s. Initially, the trade came directly from the country that had been duped into opium addiction: China. While heroin laboratories were set up to process the drug, organized crime, in this case, triad gangs, stepped in to shift the drug and launder the profits. The outbreak of World War II saw these heroin supplies cut, both because of the battle lines drawn up between Japan and America, and because China's communists were assiduously clearing out the heroin racket.

After World War II, the heroin trade was controlled by the Mafia in Italy and by drug cartels in Latin America, the Far East, and, by the end of the twentieth century, Afghanistan.

THE FLOWER OF REMEMBRANCE

There is a postscript to the story of the poppy, however, involving the species known as the corn poppy (*Papaver roeas*). In 1920, it was adopted as the symbol of remembrance after an American teacher, Moina Belle Michael, sold silk poppies to friends to raise money for injured servicemen. She had been inspired by a poem by John McCrae, a doctor with the Canadian Forces during World War I, in which he writes, "If ye break faith with us who die, We shall not sleep, though poppies grow, In Flanders Fields."

PEDESTRIAN CURE

✦

Opium and its derivative laudanum were popular recreational drugs for many nineteenth-century literary figures, including the author Thomas De Quincey. He became a household name in 1821 after the publication of his *Confessions of an English Opium Eater*. He had started taking the drug as a student at Oxford and now, while he continued taking it, offset its lethargic effects by walking. "(I) am never thoroughly in health unless when having pedestrian exercise to the extent of fifteen miles at the most, eight to ten miles at the least." He walked off the opiates with the faith of the neurotic, hatless and in all weathers.

PERNICIOUS PLANT
Raw opium made ready for being processed into heroin. Man has managed to turn the innocent and elegant opium flower into one of the world's most addictive drugs.

Black Pepper
Piper nigrum

Native range: India

Type: Tropical evergreen vine

Size: Up to 23 feet (7 m)

+ *EDIBLE*
+ *MEDICINAL*
+ *COMMERCIAL*
+ PRACTICAL

The black peppercorn was once the most valuable spice in the kitchen, and was partly thanks to the lucrative pepper trade that the world of banking foun its feet in Venice.

PEPPERCORN RENTS

The nations and islands of the Mediterranean are rich in ancient arch tecture, the visible remains of the superpowers that dominated Europ for centuries. In the Middle Ages, their mariners set sail in flotillas o leaky little ships to explore the Atlantic Ocean. They were driven t search for a particular plant, the source of the peppercorn. Instead the found America.

When Geoffrey Chaucer's characters set off on their journey in h famous fourteenth-century story, *The Canterbury Tales*, the English po placed them in the rough side of London city, Pepper Alley in South wark. Pepper Alley, Pepper Gate, Rue d Poivre: almost every medieval European cit seems to have named at least one distri after the common or garden spice. Why Because, along with its brothels, bear-baitin squares, and public baths, every town had it spice street, an alleyway where the spic traders gathered to sell their wares. An King of the Spices in the market, the mos expensive commodity there, was pepper.

Of all the spices on sale, pungent peppe was probably the only product whose arom could be detected above the everyday stin of the medieval street. Yet when the popula poet and hymn-writer William Cowper wrot in *Table Talk*, in 1782 ". . . the courtl laureate pays/His quit-rent ode, his peppe corn of praise," the peppercorn had come t symbolize a mere trifle. The King of Spic had so fallen in value that it symbolized nominal sum, a token paid for the rent of place. (The word also slipped into militar arlance with lead pieces shot from cannon being used to "pepper" the enemy. And while Swedish people were inclined to dismiss someone with the words *dra åt skogen dit pepparn växer*—get off to the forest where the pepper grows—Welsh people might describe a voluble neighbor as *siarad fel melin bupur* or talking non-stop, like a pepper mill.)

Scratching away with his pen, Cowper was writing not long after an historic event in the East: the British, under Robert Clive (Clive of India), had recently routed the Bengal Mogul leader, Nawab Sirajuddaula, and begun collecting *diwani*, the rich revenues from its new territories. Now that the Europeans had finally gained a sound trading position in India, pepper was far easier to come by than it had been.

SAILORS' PEPPER

An unassuming wrinkled little grain, the black peppercorn is the fruit of the climbing vine, *Piper nigrum*, which still grows wild in parts of India. The vine, supported on stakes or trellises, produces long ribbons of small fruits in the third year, continuing to do so for another 15 years or so. The fruits, or peppercorns, turn red as they ripen on the vine. Picked and left to soak, the outer covering or pericarp of the corn can be rubbed away to reveal the white peppercorns inside. Black peppers, on the other hand, are harvested by picking the fruit unripe, still encased in the pericarp, and leaving them to wrinkle and dry in the sun.

To the native Indians, the pepper vine was but one of many spices available to flavor their food, but to Europeans in the Middle Ages the peppercorn was already an essential culinary ingredient. It was as vital to the cook in her kitchen as the salt she used to preserve her meat and vegetables. Every farmhouse had its salting bench—the stone slab where sides of meat were salted down before being hung from hooks on the kitchen ceiling. Every cottager had his salt safe, set in the wall by the hearth to keep the salt dry. And every kitchen had its pepperpot, sometimes full, often empty. So important was it to medieval cuisine that pepper commanded a price ten times higher than that of any other spice.

HOT DEALS
Theodor de Bry's engraving
shows Chinese pepper
merchants in Java weighing
out and selling their peppers
in the 1550s, evidence
that the Chinese were
marketing pepper before
the Europeans arrived.

It is said that no self-respecting seventeenth-century sailor ever set sa
without a gold earring, a token that could be traded by his shipmates t
provide the means for a proper burial if, as so often happened, it wa
needed. But maritime archaeologists have discovered that he and hi
fellow sailors were far more likely to be carrying a leather pouch of th
most precious stuff: black pepper.

MERCHANTS OF VENICE

The overland trade that brought the pepper from source to pepperpo
had been long and arduous. Pepper was originally traded in the bazaar
of India, loaded on to mules or packhorses and carried up into the foot
hills of Pakistan, into Afghanistan, through Iran, Iraq, and Syria. Fror
there it was transported through Turkey or overland through the Balka
States, to the hub of sixteenth-century trade: Venice.

The loyalty of the small north Italian tribe, the Veneti, to the Roma
Empire had been rewarded by the Roman rulers with the gift of th
marshy lands and island lagoons on the Adriatic coast of northeast Ital
Although susceptible to occasional invasions by Goths and Huns, th
people prospered from the region's key trading position, between th
spice-rich East and the spice-hungry West. By the 800s, the Veneti unde
their *doges*, or leaders, had established a capital, the Republic of St Mark
better known as Venice.

enice today is a small, elegant city looking out across
he sea that regularly invades its streets. By the early
500s, its boatmen operated, not fancy lacquered
ooden gondolas, but sturdy merchant ships, boats
at made Venice head of the strongest maritime
mpire since the rule of ancient Athens.

The Venetians governed the "Veneto," profitable
ties such as Bergamo, Brescia, Padua, Verona, and
icenza, and occupied swathes of the Dalmatian coast-
ne as well as the thriving trading isles of Crete and
yprus. By now the bronze horses, a symbol of the
ower of the Byzantine empire that once stood outside
he Hippodrome in Constantinople, had been removed
> St Mark's Square in Venice: the Venetians had prof-
ed from the sacking of Constantinople by the
rusaders. The bronzes are still there, a symbol of the
yzantines' defeat.

While the city's cash-rich merchants built sump-
uous palaces and raised fine churches in gratitude to
od for, among other commodities, the peppercorn,
he city's fathers worked on ways to cope with moving
heir prodigious wealth around. They developed the
ascent banking system. Italy's Vatican bankers, despite several edicts
gainst usury, were the medieval world's most successful, while the
lorentine Cosimo de Medici prudently managed the Medici Bank,
pening "branches" in Geneva, London, Rome, Milan, Pisa, and, natu-
ally, Venice.

The banks only began to run into trouble when the emerging Ottoman
mpire began to throttle the Venetian trade and the Spanish, Portu-
uese, Dutch, French, and English looked elsewhere for their expensive
pices. Portugal ventured across the Indian Ocean, sailing round the
ape of Good Hope to buy spices at source, while Spain headed for the
mericas. The price of pepper rose (it would at one time match
he price of gold) and, before Columbus had even set sail for
he Indies, the Venetian banks had crashed.

BLOODY SPICES

✦

Another famous spice, the clove
(*Syzygium aromaticum*), was
traded not from India, but the
fabled Spice Islands, the Moluccas,
a group of volcanic islands in
eastern Indonesia. They included
Tidore, Amboina (now Ambon), and
the Bandas Islands. This spice
trade, which included nutmeg and
mace, was zealously guarded by the
Dutch in the 1600s. Having wrested
the islands from the Portuguese,
they outlawed the export of the
plant and destroyed surplus trees to
maintain their monopoly. A British
attempt to set up a rival trading
station on Amboina in 1623 ended
with the "Amboina Massacre," the
trial and execution of the British.

BLACK PEPPER
The climbing vine *Piper
nigrum* produces a crop of
fruits, or peppercorns, which,
when picked unripe and
dried in the sun, wrinkle
up and turn black.

ariety's the very spice of life,
hat gives it all its flavour.

illiam Cowper, The Task, *1785*

English Oak

Quercus robur

Native range: Europe, Russia, southwest Asia, north Africa

Type: Deciduous tree

Height: 125 feet (40 m)

✦ EDIBLE

✦ MEDICINAL

✦ **COMMERCIAL**

✦ **PRACTICAL**

U sed to build castles, cathedrals, and battleships, that arboreal giant the Englis oak has largely survived man's depredations. Thanks to the wine industry, relative, the cork oak, has not been so lucky.

HEARTS OF OAK

In the nineteenth century, it was a finite resource that was being exploite for everything under the sun, from building, transportation, and heatin to dyeing, packaging, and porting millions of gallons of beer, wine, an spirits. Industry could not function without it and yet it was fast runnin out. This precious resource was the oak.

This king of the forest can live for more than a millennium, accordin to some sources, and grow up to 125 feet (40 m). Mature specimens ar usually home to many species of wildlife. It can take as long as 150 year before an oak is ready to be used for construc tion purposes, but it is well worth the wait. A estimated 5,000 mature oak trees were used i the construction of Admiral Nelson's flagshi HMS *Victory*, built between 1759 and 1765.

For such a huge and long-living tree, th oak is surprisingly bad at reproducing natu rally. First, it can take a full 50 years to produc its first crop of acorns, which contain the seeds Second, the overwhelming majority of the ten of thousands of acorns it drops are eaten b animals or simply rot. And so it is left t forgetful squirrels or jays to bury them fo future consumption for the lifecycle of thi giant of the countryside to continue.

The story of the English oak (*Quercus robur* is one of our earliest environmental succes stories. In the absence of man it thrived Burgeoning human populations put it unde increasing pressure. Along with the Nort American redwood and southern beech, oak appeared on Earth around 66 million years ag A million years ago, the tree carpeted the Euro

an landmass, although this receded
humans began felling them.

Oaks were shaped into Neolithic
onuments, or henges, 5,500 years
o and, 500 years later, into that
chnological breakthrough of the
ronze Age, the wheel. Oak tannins
ade animals skins wearable. Oak
as converted into charcoal, light,
rtable, and hot enough to smelt
ecious metals. When the Romans
me crashing through Europe to
under the natural resources of their
w territories, they turned the oak
to fortresses, ships' keels, and so
uch charcoal to extract lead, copper,
onze, iron, tin, gold, and silver that
e oaks of southern Britain almost disappeared.

The depopulation caused by the Black Death provided a brief
covery, but the old oak forests were decimated, leaving vestigial wood-
nds and venerable trees behind. Bede mentioned a meeting of bishops
d doctors at "St. Augustine's Oak" in 603 CE, while the Major Oak is
ckoned to have been growing in Sherwood Forest, England, for between
0 and 1,000 years.

The trees' demise prompted John Evelyn to write one of the first
nservation guides, *Sylva—A Discourse of Forest Trees*, in 1664: "Trees,"
e intoned, "come slowly on for our grandchildren's shade."

SHELTERING GLORY
The oak's distinctive,
rounded canopy makes
the tree instantly recognizable in the landscape. The
strength and durability
of the hardwood has helped
the tree secure its future.

OLE KING OF FORESTS

he oak is as iconic as the Californian redwood, as symbolic as the
otswana baobab, as sustainable as the Australian eucalypt (when
nfined to its indigenous territory), and as sturdy as, well, as an oak. An
ak-framed house is flexible enough to survive earthquakes and torna-
oes. The timber is as strong as steel and safer in a house fire: steel
uckles, oak simply smolders. Assets like these led to such epithets as
eart of oak, king of the forest, the monarch,
nd "the builder oake, sole king of forests all"
s the poet Edmund Spenser put it.

Hyperbole never changed the course of
istory, but the oak did. Tudor England was
uilt of oak; it drove the formative years of

Those grey, gnarled, low-browed,
knock-kneed, bowed, bent, huge, strange,
misshapen oak men that stand waiting and
watching century after century.
Francis Kilvert, Kilvert's Diary 1870–1879

MAJOR OAK,   AGE 1,500 YEARS, GIRTH 35 FEET, BASE 64 FEET.

SENIOR CITIZENS
The Major Oak, near the
village of Edwinstowe in
Nottingham Forest,
photographed in 1912.
With a 33-foot (10-m)
girth, the old oak was said to
have sheltered Robin Hood
within its woody folds.

the Industrial Revolution (contrary to popular opinion, the ironmaste[r]
did not decimate the oak lands to feed their industrial furnaces, b[ut]
instead husbanded the woodlands, managing them as a sustainab[le]
resource), and it equipped the British Navy with ships that turne[d]
Britain into a colonizer that, when Queen Victoria died in 1901, rule[d]
over one in every four people on the planet.

Within 50 years, England's oak woods were being dec[i-]
mated once again. The reason for this was the outbrea[k]
of the Great War. "The unprecedented war fellin[g]
swept away . . . much of the good oak," reported [a]
British forest survey in 1924. An old timber feller p[ut]
it more prosaically: "You don't get them kind o[f]
woods you used to get."

Yet by the end of the century the oak, a sustai[n-]
able timber source that was as kind to the clima[te]
as it was to the builder, was springing back. "Th[e]

FEATHERED FRIENDS
From little acorns great trees grow.
Acorns are a favorite food of jays,
which bury their hoard of acorns
in the forest floor.

ture of oak, both as a tree and a form of timber is
ight," concluded the authors of *Oak—A British
istory* in 2003.

For the cork oaks of southern Portugal, the situa-
on was the exact reverse. The oaks had been harvested
r their bark for three centuries. It was a French monk,
om Pérignon, who is sometimes credited with discov-
ing how to seal a bottle of wine with a cork stopper,
lowing wine to be stored for years and giving the wine
ade a huge economic boost. Sections of bark were
eled from the living tree, causing scarring, but no
rmanent damage. The thick, semicircular sheets were
tted and flattened before millions of bottle corks
re extracted from the sides of the sheet. Waste cork
s used for floor tiles, insulation, and the seals inside
tops of bottled beer.

"You could drive for miles through the south and
e nothing but cork oak at the end of World War II,"
called one worker. "But even then there were signs
at the cork boom was coming to an end as plastic
als, plastic 'corks,' and screw tops were being introduced." In 2000,
rtugal was still producing 40 million corks a day and, even though the
eat cork woods still cover large swathes of central and southern Europe,
ey are faced with an uncertain future.

ARISE AND PLANT

✦

The loss of Portugal's cork oak
woods, which soak up carbon
dioxide equivalent to 185,000 cars
a year, will exacerbate climate
change. Concerns over the
destruction of traditional woodlands
and the need for their sustainable
management were being aired back
in 1664 when English diarist John
Evelyn published *Sylva—A
Discourse of Forest Trees*. Evelyn
blamed a shortage of oaks on,
among other things, the "dispropor-
tionate spreading of tillage." The
book encouraged tree conservation
and gave rise to the idea of
nachhaltig, or sustainable yield.

BOTTLING OUT
The cork oaks of southern
Portugal have served as a
sustainable resource for three
centuries, thanks to the wine
trade. But now the
Mediterranean cork oak
woods face uncertain times.

English Oak **161**

Dog Rose
Rosa canina

Native range: Europe, North Africa, and western Asia

Type: Climbing prickly shrub

Height: Up to 10 feet (3 m)

✦ EDIBLE
✦ MEDICINAL
✦ **COMMERCIAL**
✦ PRACTICAL

The oldest ornamental plant in America, the rose became a favorite of th suburban gardener as it gave rise to the first specialist flower groups. It w central to the growing passion for gardening in the nineteenth century.

SCENT OF SUCCESS

The nomadic Sakai tribespeople of Malaysia might struggle to compr hend certain modern customs (life insurance, for example, or driving work in a steel box fitted with seats) but, like anyone else, they wou appreciate the significance of smell. From fresh river fish in Malaysia takeaway curries in Melbourne, goods across the world are marketed how they smell. The human olfactory sense lags behind that of dog cats, or the cecropia moth, which can smell a mate seven miles away, b the language of fragrance was always a common currency: the fema ancestor of the woman who dabs a finger of perfume on her inner wri before stepping out into the New York night was doing much the sam in ancient Persia 2,500 years ago.

It was in Persia, modern-day Iran, where the u of rose oil began. According to legend, a prince noticed that a pile of rose petals, lying in a po at her wedding feast, exuded aromatic oils und the hot sun. Persian (and more recently India Bulgarian, and Turkish) rose oil, mostly extract from the damask rose (*R. damascena*), became t perfumier's preferred blossom. It is still expe sive: 1 fluid ounce (25 ml) requires just und 10,000 blooms.

In his 1597 *Herbal*, John Gerard wrote th the dog rose, *R. canina*, was a gift to "cookes a gentlewomen (who) make Tarts, and such li dishes for pleasure." But for the yeoman's wi in the Middle Ages it was not simply the sce that persuaded her to nurture a rose or two amo her coleworts and peas, it was its medicinal pro erties. She would have known the Apothecary's ro (*R. gallica* var. *officinalis*), the one whose peta compressed into beads, formed the "rosary," and t

damask rose, brought back to England by returning Crusaders, and a first-aid flower used for coughs, colds, eye infections, and, according to John Gerard, to "staunch bleedings." Then there was the pale pink hedgerow rose (*R. canina*). Good for treating rabid dog bites, its leaves served as a laxative, its seeds as a diuretic, and its hips were such a rich source of vitamin C that during World War II British school children were sent out to hunt them out. (They returned with an annual harvest of 250 tons [226 tonnes].) The curative qualities of the rose have also featured in aromatherapy: its calming qualities were said to benefit both the griever and the melancholic.

PERFUMED PERFECTION
The source of scented rose oil, roses share a common ancestry: the wild roses of Europe, Asia, and North America.

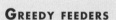

Today, new varieties (some with curious names such as South Africa's Lights of Broadway and Chasin' Rainbows) join the estimated 16,000 existing varieties. All stem from the wild roses of Europe, Asia, and North America. These sweet-scented naturals flower briefly and are gone. The flowering season for their cultivated offspring was still brief when in 1648 Robert Herrick, in his poem "To the Virgins, to Make Much of Time," advised:

Gather ye rosebuds while ye may
Old Time is still a-flying;
And this same flower that smiles today,
Tomorrow will be dying.

All was about to change with the arrival of the Chinese rose. In the late 1700s, making their way to the fabled Flowery Land, the Fa Tee nursery in Canton, traders discovered pot-grown specimens that were still blossoming in the fall. The Chinese hybrids were soon being shipped home for cross-breeding.

History is full of famous figures who, thanks to their prestige and bank balance, could indulge their roses and gardens. When the U.S.'s third president,

GREEDY FEEDERS

◆

Roses respond to heavy feeding. "Be avaricious for manure," advised the nineteenth-century gardener James Shirley Hibberd at a time when amateur rose growers relied still on the fertilizers that had been used by the Greeks: manure and vegetable waste. For 50 years, between 1840 and 1890, this was supplanted by mountains of sea bird dung. Guano was shipped from South America to Europe and America until the Englishman John Bennet Lawes, having converted his bedroom into a laboratory, discovered how to create a synthetic fertilizer based on phosphates.

Thomas Jefferson, remodeled the grounds at Monticello in the early 1800s, he made room for his favorite Gallica and sweetbriar roses along side some native varieties. In the early 1900s, France's Dr. Joachim Carvallo's makeover of Château Villandry (aided on the expenses side by his marriage to an American heiress) involved combining roses with 30,000 vegetables to create the world's most exotic potager. But as with the sweet pea (see Sweet Pea, p.118) the amateur gardener was making a significant contribution to the cultivation of the rose in backyards, *kleingärten* (allotments), and *les lopins de terre* (French urban garden squeezed between buildings).

RURAL BEAUTY

The work of painter Helen Allingham personified the charm of these cottage roses. A friend of John Ruskin, Alfred, Lord Tennyson, and Dante Gabriel Rossetti, Allingham (born Helen Paterson in 1848) studied at London's Female School of Art, supporting herself by illustrating magazines and books before marrying an Irish poet, William Allingham (he was 50, she 25). She devoted herself first to her family and then, after they had moved to Sandhills, Surrey, in 1881, to a series of cottage paintings that became the Allingham trademark. Here she portrayed a tranquil world where pretty working women gossiped in the sunset beside cottage porches wreathed in roses. (Romanticism aside, Allingham was distressed by the gentrification of Surrey's old cottages by insensitive home improvers and was trying to record the vernacular details before

HELEN ALLINGHAM
A Mother and Child Entering a Cottage.
Allingham (pictured above) saw Surrey's old, rose-covered cottages, not through rose-tinted spectacles, but with the eyes of a painter. She documented these prime examples of vernacular architecture before they were gentrified by commuters moving out of London.

they were lost.) Allingham's art captured a time when amateur gardeners, from Ghent to Gettysburg, bewitched by the guiles of the garden, devoted themselves to rose growing.

"He who would have beautiful roses in his garden must have beautiful roses in his heart," declared the man that Alfred, Lord Tennyson hailed as the father of the rose. This was the dashing Dean of Rochester and president of Britain's first rose society, Samuel Reynolds Hole. In the 1860s, he found himself dragged off to judge a rose show

n Nottingham. He anticipated a series
f florid, formal displays dutifully laid
ut by the head gardeners of the great
ountry estates. Instead he was met by
 group of Nottingham allotment
olders, some of whom had borrowed
he very blankets from their own beds
o keep the frost from their darling
pecimen roses. The event, at the
eneral Cathcart Hill Inn, was Brit-
in's first national rose show.

Shows like these continued to gain
opularity in Europe, America,
ustralia, and New Zealand (where
he Dean's sister lived) throughout the nineteenth century. In the 1840s,
he Reverend John Stevens Henslow, vicar of Hitcham, Suffolk, England,
hich had hit the headlines for its spiraling crime, advocated allotments
o reduce the crime wave. Local farmers, fearful that their workers would
ithhold their labor during the day only to expend it on the allotment of
n evening, threatened to blacklist anyone who dared
nt one. The wise Henslow invited landowner and
borer alike to participate in that great leveler, the
ower and vegetable show.

By now, nurseries were listing upward of 1,400
ifferent rose varieties. The rose was already North
merica's oldest ornamental plant. Philadelphia had
rganized the first public flower show in 1829, and in
844 Robert Buist rushed out his *Rose Manual* to meet
he demands of amateur rose growers.

All this failed to impress the gardener James Shirley
ibberd. "The question will occur where a rose garden
hould be formed, within view of the windows or far
way. We reply, 'far away'; for a rose garden should be
 its season a wonder to be sought, as, when its season
 past, it is a wilderness to be avoided."

ROSES ARE RED

✦

America's Valentine's Day is
estimated to produce more than
9,000 metric tonnes of carbon
dioxide as red roses, cut in Africa
or South America, are flown in. The
threat of climate change prompted
Colombian flower growers to
capitalize on their low-impact
technology and sustainable
horticultural practices (workers
walked or rode their bikes to work
in solar-heated greenhouses) and
set up a fairtrade-style, cut flower
group, Florverde. Standards
included social programs for the
workers, minimal water depreda-
tion, and reducing the use of
pesticides. Similar groups have
followed in their wake.

ar off, most secret, and inviolate Rose,
nfold me in my hour of hours.

 B. Yeats, "The Secret Rose," 1899

Sugarcane
Saccharum officinarum

Native range: New Guinea. Now grown in tropics and subtropics in the United States and as far as New South Wales in the southern hemisphere

Type: Tropical, tall-stemmed, reed-like plant

Height: 4–12 feet (1.2–3.6 m)

✦ **EDIBLE**
✦ MEDICINAL
✦ **COMMERCIAL**
✦ PRACTICAL

Heroin, cocaine, alcohol, tobacco, . . . and sugar. Refined sugar is a drug that has been causing serious harm to people's health for a long time. Given the havoc sugar has caused, no wonder then that people have dubbed it "white death."

WHITE DEATH

Civilizations managed well enough without sugar for thousands of years, but when it did arrive it enslaved millions of Africans and damaged the health of its consumers.

In the sugarcane plantations of the West Indies, African slaves made music as they worked. Like their fellow pickers in the cotton and tobacco fields, the slaves used songs to pace out the rhythm of their work. The music was the genesis of modern jazz and blues. Unlike that of the cotton or tobacco pickers, the tempo in the sugar plantations was fast, almost furious, and the life expectancy of the slave in the sugarcane fields was half that of those in the tobacco fields. As sugar was poisoning its consumers, it was killing its workers.

Sugar is an ancient food, but the way we process it is relatively recent. Originally a plant of New Guinea, sugarcane found its way across the Indian Ocean as canoe cargo and driftwood. The raw canes were, and still are, a delicacy, but around 2,500 years ago Indians at Bihar on the banks of the Ganges mastered the process of refining the local sugarcane into pure sugar. It would be a long, slow journey before sugar reached Europe and the West; it is said to have reached the Greek world shortly after the time of Alexander the Great.

When refined sugar did reach Europe (it was being traded in Scandinavia by the late 1390s), the Venetians took control of the trade, as they had the world's spice traffic (See Black Pepper, p.154). As was also the

If sack and sugar be at fault, God help the wicked.

William Shakespeare, Henry IV, Part 1, *1597*

ase with the spice trade, the Venetians eventually lost control and the ugar business moved north, away from the Mediterranean and into orthern Europe.

There was a defining moment in the history of sugar when the Iuslims, who had occupied Spain and brought with them their sophisicated horticultural methods, were being driven from the country by hristian forces during the Reconquista. In theory, Spain's rulers after he Reconquista could have adopted the farming methods of their onquered foes to grow and process the sugarcane. But with their ttention fixed on foreign conquests rather than on nurturing the omelands, the Spanish, instead of investing in their agriculture, vested in slavery.

But even as the Muslims were being expelled from Spain in the 1490s, olumbus was shipping cane sugar stem cuttings, or sets, to Haiti. Their eighboring colonialists in Portugal had begun to plant up their own tlantic holdings, Madeira especially; adding vines to their local sugar rop would eventually produce the sweet wines of Madeira. The Spanish, neanwhile, carried their sugar sets on to the Canaries and eventually the aribbean. They were soon introducing that other commodity that would e associated with the sugar trade for the next 300 years: African slaves. rom then until the 1850s, sugar and the slave trade would be inextriably bound together.

Slaves need never have been used: he approaching agricultural methods f seventeenth-century Europe, with s ox teams and deep-plowing techology, could have performed the job ıst as efficiently. But sugar, and eople's passion for it, had already kewed history to favor slavery.

Aside from its inherent barbarity, lavery proved to be a short-term conomic expedient and a long-term ocial disaster. Stealing people from ne part of the world and forcing hem to work to their deaths in nother creates deep hatreds that urvive for generations.

As with many of the plants featured ı this book, the trade in sugar had oth positive and negative conse-

quences. Particularly when sold into the right market, sugar was a
extremely lucrative commodity, and the more it was consumed, the mor
keenly it was desired.

Latin America was full of plunderable Inca and Aztec treasur
awaiting redistribution in Spain and Portugal, but the West Indies offere
precious little else to interest the conquistadors. While the sweet-toothe
Europeans provided the marketplace for refined sugar, the West Indie
including Barbados, Jamaica, Cuba, Haiti, and Grenada, became th
islands of choice for growing and processing it: by the mid-1660
Barbados was poised to become the world's number one sugar produce
By 1800, it was Jamaica's turn to be badged as the world's bigges
exporter. Cuba would follow in the sugar succession in the mid-twentiet
century (see box, p.171).

When the Scottish poet James Thomson penned his new play *Alfred
a Masque* in 1740, he added the rousing lines: "Rule, Britannia! rule th
waves: Britons never will be slaves." The lines were later turned into
patriotic chorus, as apt as it was ironic. After 1680 many Britis
merchants were able to buy for themselves the freedoms that came wit
wealth. These city freemen ran the great seaports, Bristol, Liverpoo
and London. They supported their banks with large loans and generou
deposits, using revenue from the sugar and slave trades. Money wa
loaned to the plantation owners for the purchase of African slaves; profi
were put back into the business from the domestic sales of refined suga

triangular shipping route developed in the Atlantic between the British seaports, the West African slave ports, and the West Indies' sugar harbors. This Trafalgar Triangle started in the 1600s and continued until slavery was outlawed in the mid-1800s. The trade involved buying guns, cloth, salt, and trinkets, made in the English industrial Midlands, and shipping them out to the native traders in West Africa. When the ships' holds were emptied of cloth, food, and other goods, they were refilled with people. The British goods were traded for black Africans, seized, kidnapped, and enslaved from the interior. They were routinely shackled together to prevent them from jumping overboard—suicide at sea was a preferable death to the nightmare of forced labor that lay ahead. The slaves who lived through their voyage of several months on this "Middle Passage" between Africa and the West Indies were extraordinary survivors: they were crammed below deck with no room to move, lying side by side in unimaginably terrible conditions.

On the third stage of the Triangle trade, the wretched survivors disembarked and were sold to plantation owners. The ships were reloaded for the last time, their holds filled with rum and sweet sugar, and sent home to England. Britain was the world's first nation to develop such a sweet tooth that, for example, drinking tea, coffee, or cocoa without sugar was

SWEET HONEYBEE
✦
Before the advent of refined sugar, honey was the natural sweetener, and for thousands of years the honeybee was accorded proper respect: for example, a hive of bees was always formally told of the death of its owner. But bees, which pollinate around 80% of the world's crops, are dying. In 2006, Colony Collapse Disorder (CCD) was reported in North America. Since then losses have spread through North America and Europe. Possible causes of CCD include habitat destruction, pesticides, GM crops, global warming, drought, changes in the bees' diets, and radiation from cellphone masts. Efforts to establish the cause have so far eluded scientists.

CANE CROPPERS
Cane workers in the sugar plantations near Guánica, Puerto Rico, in the 1940s. They were the inheritors of the social problems caused by the British monopoly of the slave trade.

unfashionable and unthinkable. It was also the first nation to embark o[n]
an industrial revolution: but for the profits of the Triangle Trade th[e]
revolution would have been severely delayed, perhaps even eclipsed b[y]
another European nation. Even before Richard Trevithick unveiled h[is]
fiery creation, the steam locomotive, sugar was England's single mos[t]
important and lucrative import.

SLAVE TO SUGAR

The dictionary definition of slavery ("the ownership of one person b[y]
another") does not hint at the humiliations that were inflicted by slav[e]
owners; encyclopedic explanations that "slaves are usually used for thei[r]
labor, but sexual rights over them may also be an important element" i[s]
a euphemism for rape. Such a miserable industry could not last foreve[r].
Denmark, in 1792, and France, in 1794, banned the Atlantic slave trade
In the same year, the U.S. legislated against American ships being use[d]
in the slave trade; Britain introduced a ban in 1807 and the British Wes[t]
Indies in 1834 before the final executive order abolishing slavery wa[s]
issued by President Lincoln in 1863. Although slaves were still bein[g]
traded out of Africa in the 1930s, the emancipation of the 1860s di[d]

CHILD'S PLAY
Long after the abolition of
slavery, children like these,
still working in sugar
plantations near Sterling,
Colorado, in 1915, spent
more time on the land than
in any school playground.

outlaw the slave trade. It did not bring it to an end in the sugar plantations: economics, however, did.

During the nineteenth century, horticulturalists had been experimenting on an unlovely-looking vegetable, *Beta vulgaris*. The root vegetable, beet, had long been grown to be fed to the hulking farm beasts of northern Europe to help them through the long winters. The root seems to have been domesticated first in Germany in the 1200s and when, 600 years later, the German scientist Franz Karl Achard succeeded in extracting around 6% of sugar from one strain of the root, nations like Germany and France seized upon its potential. Frustrated by Britain's virtual monopoly on West Indian cane sugar, they succeeded in hybridizing *Beta vulgaris* to the extent that the root became known as sugar beet and thousands of acres of European soil were devoted to its cultivation.

Emperor Napoleon, for one, saw the stolid sugar beet as a useful weapon in his war with England and ordered nearly 70,000 acres (28,000 ha) to be planted up. The root was a generous provider: cattle and sheep were fed on the pulp left behind after sugar had been extracted, while another by-product, beet molasses, could be usefully turned into alcohol. And it could be grown without slave labor. By 1845, sugar beet was seriously undercutting the West Indies trade; eventually it all but bankrupted the Caribbean trade. Although some of the sugar plantation owners were ruined, many of them, and the banks that loaned the capital for the slavers in the first place, stayed afloat with the compensation paid for their loss of "business." There was to be compensation paid to the freed slaves. If the slaves were poor and exhausted, so was the soil.

Sugarcane is a heavy feeder and a crop demanding plenty of fertilizer and water. In the year between the planting of sets and the harvesting of the cane, sugar

WAR WEAPON
When beet, grown as an animal feedstuff for centuries in northern Europe, proved to contain low but extractable levels of sugar, Emperor Napoleon planted thousands of acres during his war on the sugar-rich English.

CUBA

✦

The Spanish colony of Cuba became a major sugar producer after being overrun, briefly, by the British in 1762. Although Africans and Chinese "coolies" continued to be illegally enslaved after the emancipation of slaves in 1865, sugar production, especially in Cuba, was gradually mechanized. By the twentieth century, Cuba had become the world's biggest producer and America its biggest market. But with increased production at home, demand for Cuban sugar dropped away after World War II, and the country's economy slumped. It was against this backdrop that Fidel Castro, the son of a wealthy sugar landlord, seized power.

SUGAR PIRACY
The Dutch privateer Piet
Heyn seized more than 30
ships flying the Portuguese
flag, off the coast of Brazil
in 1627. The booty? Their
holds were filled with sugar.

rose like a field of giant grass. At harvest time, the leaves and tops, the bagasse, were sometimes set alight to burn them away, before the canes were cut and carried to the processing works where they were crushed and boiled. The process released high levels of sucrose and, like the refining of oil, involved initially extracting the heavy, crude, black sugars, before progressively extracting lighter, brown and yellow sugars, and finally the purest "plantation whites." When cane had been cut with the cane knife or harvested by machine, the old plant grew new stems, called ratoons, which could be cut for a further two or three seasons before the plantation was exhausted.

One potentially positive development, however, was to use the cane as a substitute for irreplaceable fossil fuels. In Brazil, fields of sugarcane have been grown to fuel a national program for substituting gasoline with cane alcohol, or "ethanol," but while the fuel causes less pollution than gasoline, like soy (see Soybean, p.84), this is another crop whose expansion threatens the shrinking Amazonian forest.

The social consequences of our desire for the white stuff continue to reverberate around the world. The working conditions of migrant Haitians who cross the border to work in the bateyes, or sugar towns of neighboring Dominican Republic, have come in for sustained criticism. The developed world, meanwhile, has been confronting another consequence of sugar: obesity.

For decades, the manufacturers of processed foods have reduced the fiber content and upped the sugar content in their foods. This has had disastrous consequences; the associated health risks of obesity include diabetes, cancer, and heart disease (see box). The World Health Organization estimates that, by 2015, obesity will affect 1.5 billion people. These problems, however, pale in comparison with the terrible suffering endured by the estimated 20 million African people who were enslaved as a result of the sugar trade.

NATURAL DISASTER

✦

All of the world's estimated 7,000 edible plants contain some sugars along with fats, starches, proteins, and fibers. Our digestive systems make enzymes that convert the natural sugars into energy and break down the fibers. But when pure, or refined, sugar hits the body, the digestive system has nothing to do. The body stops producing the enzymes and rejects the now indigestible high-fiber foods. This accelerates the body's chemical addiction to sugar, causing obesity and triggering other health problems such as alcoholism (alcohol hits the bloodstream even faster than sugar) and diabetes.

ONE LUMP OR TWO?
(Opposite) It had started out as a simple tea sweetener, but sugar from plantations such as this one in the West Indies eventually became an addictive additive used in a scores of foodstuffs.

White Willow
Salix alba

Native range: Europe, China, Japan, North America

Type: Fast-growing tree

Height: 80 feet (24 m)

+ EDIBLE
+ *MEDICINAL*
+ COMMERCIAL
+ *PRACTICAL*

I n the oil-rich days of the twentieth century, the craft of willow-working almost slipped into oblivion. And yet people with the potential to develop heart disease take their daily dose of willow . . . and no self-respecting cricketer would step onto the crease without a chunk of willow in his hands.

PAIN IN THE HEAD

In 1899, the pharmaceuticals giant Bayer released aspirin to an unsuspecting market. The arrival of the world's most frequently taken drug followed the work of nineteenth-century French and German chemists on a curious substance extracted from the bark of the white willow (*Salix alba*), which they called "salicin." This led to the discovery of salicylic acid in willow and meadowsweet—*Filipendula ulmaria* (see "Wayside aspirin" box).

The possibility that white willows had great curative powers had been known for centuries. Dioscorides describes it as a treatment for gout, and it was widely used for all manner of pains and ailments: rheumatic pains, childbirth, toothache, earache, and, naturally, for headaches.

John Gerard, the herbalist, had nothing to say for it in 1597, but Culpeper advocated it as a substitute for cinchona bark after experiments by "Mr. Stone," to whom, he thought, "the world will be much indebted." As Culpeper explained, cinchona prices were rising. "While the Peruvian bark remained at its usual moderate price, it was hardly worthwhile to seek for a substitute, but . . . [now] we must expect to find it dearer and very much adulterated every year."

In the 1890s, chemists who had been searching for a substitute for a treatment for rheumatic fever and arthritis came up with aspirin. The rest, as they say, was history—except for a terrible flu pandemic that broke out in 1918. One soldier returning from Italy to England recalled traveling in boxcars "with men dying like flies around me. We lost more men to flu than we had to war!" Estimated to have killed between 50 and 100 million people, Spanish flu, as it was known, is ranked as one of the worst natural disasters of all times. Sales of the new drug aspirin soared.

S. *alba* is one of many willows, all members of the Salicaceae family and including other water-lovers: the aspen, poplar, and cottonwood. It is fast-growing and, fed with spring water or river water, will live for around 120 years. The shorter pussy willow, *S. caprea*, lives half as long, and earned its name from the production of fluffy male and female flowers, or catkins, in early spring. They are a scented gift for pollinating bees and moths, and for schoolroom windows.

MIGRAINES, NÉVRALGIES
GRIPPES, RHUMATISMES

ASPIRINE
"USINES DU RHÔNE"

LE TUBE DE **20** COMPRIMÉS DE 50 cent. **2** FRANCS

DEMANDER DANS TOUTES LES PHARMACIES
LA MARQUE "USINES DU RHÔNE" CARTONNAGE VERT

Kashmir and English willows (*S. alba* "Caerulea," subspecies of the white willow) compete to provide the perfect material for the cricket bat. Willow is still regarded as the best material for hot-air balloon baskets (willow cases were used to air-drop ammunition in World War II because of their capacity to bend before they break), while the all-natural willow coffin has become something of a must-have for the ecologically minded recently deceased.

Yet the craft of weaving with willow, rooted in Celtic traditions, almost disappeared in the twentieth century. Beds of willow had been producing "osiers"—long, whippy willow wands used in basketmaking—since Neolithic times, but the craft of working the willow into anything from coracle river craft to eel and crab pots was almost killed off during the age of plastics.

As with so many plants that changed the course of history, the future for willow may be bright. Research has shown that routine use of aspirin can help prevent strokes and control angina. In Sweden, the use of willow has already overtaken oil for domestic and industrial heating, and research is being carried out into its further possible uses as a biofuel.

PAINKILLER
The willow tree had long been associated with pain relief. However, it became the source of the world's most widely used drug following the discovery of salicylic acid in the tree bark.

WAYSIDE ASPIRIN
✦
Meadowsweet (*Filipendula ulmaria*) is the quiet hero of the wayside. Now passed by almost unnoticed, in years gone by the presence of colonies of meadowsweet were well known and, if possible, carefully guarded. Together with plants such as bog myrtle (*Myrica gale*), it was used to flavor ale, and as a medicinal aid. Originally named by Carl Linnaeus as *Spiraea ulmaria*, the word "aspirin" has been said to have come from adding the "a" from "acetyl" to the first part of meadowsweet's old name.

"I'm very brave generally," he went on in a low voice: "only to-day I happen to have a headache."
Lewis Carroll, Through the Looking Glass, *1871*

Potato

Solanum tuberosum

Native range: Andes in South America

Type: Bushy perennial with edible tubers

Height: 3 feet (1 m)

+ **EDIBLE**
+ MEDICINAL
+ **COMMERCIAL**
+ PRACTICAL

The course of history was never altered by a single plant, only by the way which people use, abuse, or profit by plants. When it came to the potato, mo people were content to consume them, but the fate of one nation, Ireland, and th makeup of the population of another, the United States, was profoundly affected b the little tuber from South America.

HOT POTATO

In 1886, a photographer happened to be on hand with his glass-pla camera outside a charming old Irish cottage. His lens, however, reveale a stark scene. Three gaunt policemen stand guard as the landlord's agen evict a family, their few sticks of furniture piled up outside the tur roofed house. A grandfather, father, and two boys stand to one sid sullenly looking on. In a second photograph, an elaborate battering ra has been erected outside what was the cottage door. The ram has punche a hole in the turf wall and branches of furze have been crammed into th opening and through the two broken windows.

If the photographer stayed for the final scene, the image does not survive. Instead we must imagine the furze being lit and the turf roof catching fire as the former tenants hoist their few posses- sions on their backs and make their bitter way down the track. Some died. Some survived and were forced to live a life of poverty in the city slums of Dublin, Cork, or Belfast. Some made it onto the ships leaving for a new life in America, Australia, Canada, and New Zealand. All remained bitter to the end. The failure of the Irish potato

No one . . . will regard a potato as a mere vegetable, but rather as an instrument of destiny.

E. A. Bunyard, The Gardener's Companion, *1936*

rop in the 1840s was a national catastrophe with international implications. The subsequent famines and typhus outbreak killed a million and drove another two and a half million onto the emigration ships. Cobh near Cork may have been the

ort where the potato first landed in Ireland. For many Irish people, Cobh as their final glimpse of the Emerald Isle before the "coffin ships"—so amed after the conditions on board—bore them off on a 12-week oyage across the Atlantic.

"When famine and disaster came upon that unhappy country [Ireland] its citizens took shelter under the Stars and Stripes. There they nned the dying embers of hatred against the old country [Great Britain] ith a result that is with us today," wrote E. A. Bunyard in 1936.

In the 1960s, internecine warfare between Catholics and Protestants Ireland broke out. By then almost 34.5 million Americans could claim Irish ancestry. Many made it their duty to send money nd munitions to one side or the other. Thousands ould die during what became known as "the Troubles." one of the worst incidents, in 1987, a car bomb xploded among families at a Remembrance Day arade in the town of Enniskillen, killing 11 people. The rish republic's fraught modern history has its roots in e upheaval caused by the potato famine.

OISONOUS POTATO

eruvian people have been eating potatoes for thou-nds of years. 4,000-year-old shards of pottery from e region suggest they worshiped, or at least vener-ed, the crop as well. For the Inca, the vegetable served a useful companion to maize or corn, and when this vilization was destroyed by the Spanish conquista-ors the potato was among the booty brought home Europe.

The vegetable can be grown almost anywhere in the orld except in low-lying, tropical regions, and its arch content gives it a higher food value per acre than y cereal crop. The conquistadors' potatoes proved to

LAZY BEDS

♦

The Irish "lazy bed" was neither idle nor Irish. Lazy beds were laid down in many of the more remote parts of the British Isles, and made use of marginal, often peaty land. Provided the crop was disease-free, the lazy bed produced a harvest of spuds with very little effort. The beds were made by heaping a manure such as seaweed onto a rectangle of bare ground, and then digging a drainage trench around the patch. The average width of the raised beds was 3 feet (1 m), wide enough for three potato plants. Seed potatoes were cut in half and plunged down into the ground during the spring.

be worth more than all the Inca gold and silver.

Though all green parts of the potato are poisonous (including green tubers that have been exposed to light), the tubers themselves contain 18% carbohydrate, 2% protein, a little potassium, and around 78% water. They can be baked, fried, roasted, turned into soup or stew, processed into flour or crisps, or fermented into high-octane schnapps.

SIR FRANCIS DRAKE

Families can live, and have lived, on a diet of nothing but potatoes. S a versatile food might have expected a wide welcome when it arrive Europe. It was not to be.

According to the *New Illustrated Gardening Encyclopaedia* (19 "The importation of the plant is usually accredited to Sir Walter Ral who is supposed to have brought it from America, but later author claim that a Mr. Herriot was responsible for its introc tion." One version goes that Sir Francis Drake, return from Virginia in 1586 after collecting some home settlers, also picked up some "Virginia potatoes." T were delivered to Raleigh's agent, who planted then Raleigh's estate in Youghal, southern Ireland. When crop flowered, he cooked the poisonous green fruit served them to his master, who fell ill as a result. tale is as improbable as the story that Drake insiste finishing a game of bowls before going into ba against the Spanish Armada in 1588, or the tale placed the first potatoes on the west coast of Irel washed ashore from Armada ships wrecked in a sto A more likely explanation is that the potato, hav been successfully introduced to Spain, gradually sp north and east into Europe.

Europe in the sixteenth and seventeenth centu was a place of religious tension and superstition. T was conflict between Catholic and Protestant, e cially after the St. Bartholomew's Day Massacre of 1 when Protestant blood ran through the streets of P and after the unmasking of the Catholic gunpov plotters, hanged, drawn, and quartered after their fa

ttempt to blow up the English parliament in 1605. The British authorities
ere still hanging women for witchcraft in 1686 when poor Alice Molland
as sent to the gallows in the West Country for "conniving with the devil."
he work of Beelzebub was evident everywhere, and the suspicious
urned their gaze on the naked little potato with its voluptuous curves
nd suggestive shapes—not to mention its disturbing habit of swelling
nd multiplying even when buried, like a corpse, in the cold ground. And,
s the righteous, God-fearing Protestants pointed out: the Bible made no
ention of the potato.

An additional concern came from the fact that those who inadver-
ently ate raw potato suffered from eczema, which was then considered
o be a form of leprosy. "Though the potato is an excellent root, deserving
o be brought into general use, yet it seems not likely that the use of it
hould ever be normal in the country," concluded one David Davies in
795. The English writer and gardener John Evelyn (1620–1706), whose
iaries are largely contemporaneous with those of Samuel Pepys, advo-
ated eating the poisonous fruit pickled as a salad.

However, the Reverend Gilbert White—one of England's early potato
rowers and a well-known diarist—recorded a turning point for the

SLOW START
The herbalist John Gerard
was pictured holding a potato
flower in his *Herbal* (1597).
Most Europeans, however,
did not know how to prepare
the potato and were
superstitious about
its provenance.

At the outset, north
Europeans preferred their
parsnips to the upstart
potato. However, the
potato's higher yields and
a longer growing season
persuaded them to switch
their allegiance.

vegetable. He noted in March 28, 1758: "Planted 59 potatoes; not ver
large roots." By 1768 he observed: "Potatoes have prevailed in this littl
district, by means of premiums, within these twenty years; and are muc
esteemed here now by the poor, who would scarce have ventured to tast
them in the last reign." By 1838, William Cobbett was noting in *Th*
English Gardener that the potato "does very well to qualify the effects o
fat meat or to assist in the swallowing of quantities of butter. Ther
appears to be nothing unwholesome about it, and when the sort is good
it is preferred by many people to some other vegetables of the coarse
kind." By now Welsh laborers were accustomed to paying their *dyle*
tatw, a debt of labor to the landowner who allowed him to grow his *tatw*
on the land.

Germany, after a reluctant start, was persuaded to side with th
potato following a famine in Prussia. Frederick the Great (King o
Prussia between 1740 and 1786) sent in free potatoes and armed soldier
to persuade the peasantry to accept them. The citizens of Offenburg i
Germany took the unusual step of erecting a statue to Sir Francis Drak
in the town square, although it took to its plinth by default. The sculpto
Andreas Friedrich, had tried to sell his work to the city of Salzburg; whe

he good burgers failed to find enough money,
'riedrich donated his Drake to Offenburg on the
ondition that it was sited with its back to Salz-
urg. The statue was removed by the Nazis
during World War II.

French opposition to the potato was more
oncerted, despite the peasantry suffering
everal famines that left them starving on a diet
f grass roots and ferns. Pharmacist Antoine-
Augustin Parmentier had a better idea: *Qu'ils mangent
es pommes de terre* ("Let them eat the earth apple").
'armentier had survived on a diet of "earth apples" or
otatoes during the Prussian famine (he had been a pris-
ner of war). Determined to introduce the potato to France,
e persuaded Louis XVI to wear one of the delicate white
otato flowers at court. Louis' courtiers fawned in admiration.
he court gourmets were further intrigued when Parmentier arranged a
dinner where every course included *pomme de terre*.

In 1770, he dealt Gallic prejudice the *coup de grâce* when Louis allowed
im to use a field in the grounds of the Palace of Versailles to plant a
op-secret crop of potatoes. Guards were posted ostentatiously around
he field to protect the crop. The security arrangements doubled people's
uriosity and, under cover of darkness, the field was raided again and
gain. Citizens passed the illicit potato from hand to hand. The potato
ad arrived at last. In 1793, after French Republicans had executed King
ouis XVI, the monarch's fine gardens were dug up and planted with the
ractical potato. Parmentier, however, kept his head and is
evered still in French dishes such as *hachis parmentier*, a
neal of minced beef covered with mashed potatoes, and
randade de morue parmentier*, a dish that combines salt
od with potatoes and is typically served during the
vinter months.

OTATO BLIGHT

By the late 1700s, the potato was Ireland's key crop. The
ountry had struggled to survive as a British colony, not
east since its rout by the English general Oliver Cromwell,
vho had defeated the Royalists during England's Civil War.
romwell's repression in Ireland, and the massacres that
ollowed the sieges of the Drogheda and Wexford garrisons,
rove the peasantry to the brink of extermination. Most had

PARMENTIER'S POTATO
Antoine-Augustin Parmen-
tier used all his wiles to win
over the French and defeat
the Gallic prejudice to the
potato. It took a cunning
deceit to persuade the
housewife to adopt the
pomme de terre.

POTATO BLIGHT
In warm and humid
weather, the fungal infection
Phytophthora infestans can
devastate the potato crop,
causing the foliage to die
and the tubers to rot in
the ground.

subsisted on a largely cashless
economy, the main token of
exchange being the cow. John
Worlidge, writing his *Systema Agri-
culturae* in 1669, thought the
potato was useful enough as "food
for swine or other cattle." And, he
noted: "They are much used in
Ireland and America as bread and
may be propagated with advantage
to poor people."

Most of Ireland offered poor returns for the wheat farmer, and the
potato, ceremoniously planted at the spring religious festival, Good
Friday, and liberally sprinkled with holy water to keep the devil at bay,
served the population well enough. Despite their adversities (most Irish
tenants were paying import duties to the British government on everyday
items like tea and sugar and being bled dry by high rents, paid to absentee
landlords), the Irish population grew. By 1800 it approached 4.5 million—
thanks to the potato.

Families grew to depend on the vegetable, sharing their meals from
the *skib*, the shallow wickerwork bowl also known as a scuttle, *ciseóg*, or

sally saucer. The potato became a "spud" after the
broad-pronged fork or "spud" used to raise the crop.
It was planted with a dibber and it was the job of the
woman of the house to go "guggering," making holes
for the spuds. Every summer, the crop was sprayed
against blight with a mixture of bluestone (copper
sulfate) and washing soda. But in 1845 no amount of
spraying could save the crop.

The crop failed again in 1846. Thousands starved in
the 1840s despite a good corn harvest in 1847, because
the corn was exported to England.

**That one million people should have died in what was
then part of the richest and most powerful nation in the
world is something that still causes pain as we reflect on
today. Those who governed in London at the time failed
their people through standing by while a crop failure
turned into a massive human tragedy.**

Tony Blair, British Prime Minister, 1997

The potato famine destroyed the heart of a nation and it went on to transform the countryside. Ireland's regime of inflated rents, unmanageable mortgages, and systematic evictions was unsustainable and, eventually, land reform saw almost three-quarters of the land redistributed among former tenants. While bankrupted landowners abandoned their manor houses and walled kitchen gardens, large farm holdings were reorganized so that the fields formed a convenient series of rectangles spreading out behind the farmhouse—the so-called "ladder farms" that are still seen in Ireland today.

STAPLE DIET
The potato was the staple diet of the poor, as seen in *The Potato Eaters* (April 1885) by Vincent van Gogh. However, the bitterness caused by the Irish potato famine would persist for generations to come.

Cacao
Theobroma cacao

Native range: South American rainforests

Type: Tree

Height: 45 feet (15 m)

+ *EDIBLE*
+ *MEDICINAL*
+ *COMMERCIAL*
+ *PRACTICAL*

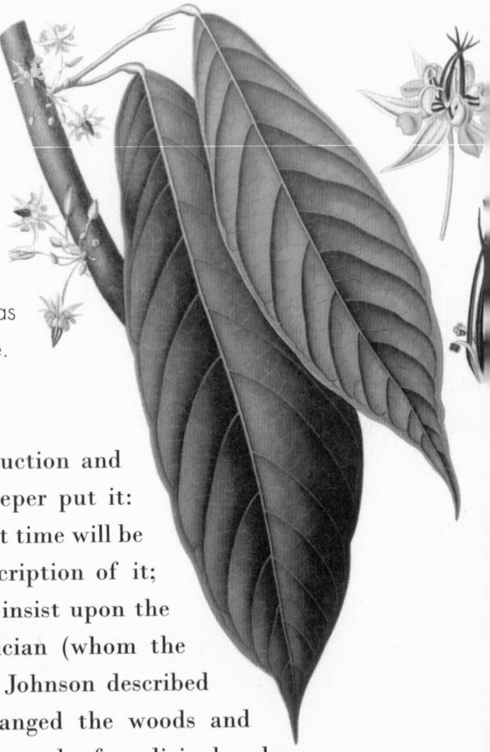

The cacao bean was a favorite fare of Quaker industrialists when it was seized on by a new breed of late nineteenth-century white-collar worker: advertisers. Thanks to them, the food of the gods was set to become a guilty pleasure.

FOOD OF THE GODS

Chocolate needs no introduction and little description. As Culpeper put it: "This is so well known, that time will be misspent in writing a description of it; and therefore I shall only insist upon the virtues of it." The physician (whom the famous lexicographer Dr. Johnson described as "the man that first ranged the woods and climbed the mountains in search of medicinal and salutary herbs") was referring to the ash tree, but could have said th same about chocolate, the prime product of the cacao bean.

The cacao bean is a native of the American tropics, a small tre dependent on a rich soil and plenty of rain. The tree crops at around fou years (it can live for 80 years or more bizarrely bearing pink, fuchsia-like flower and later the cacao pods, on the mai trunk. The mature yellow or red po contain a mass of cacao beans that mu be scooped out from their mucilagino surroundings, then fermented or sweat

You may go to Carlisle's, and to Almack's too . . .
For coffee, tea, chocolate, butter and toast:
How he welcomes at once all the world and his wife,
And how civil to folk he ne'er saw in his life.

Christopher Anstey, The New Bath Guide *(1766)*

beneath a pile of banana leaves before being dried in the sun. By now t bean, which contains caffeine and the related alkaloid theobromine, ready for processing.

Cacao is an exotic, a luxury, almost certainly, said some, a divi gift. Carl Linnaeus must have thought so, since he classed it, wittily, *Theobroma*, the "food of the gods." In pre-conquest Latin Americ where sugar was unknown, crushed cocoa provided a thick, viscous liquid. Stirring in the products of other native plants—peppers and vanilla, for example—created a rich, syrupy sauce, ideal for serving up at a celebratory feast.

In Aztec times, the cocoa bean was more likely to be roasted, ground, and added to a stew-like vegetable dish with corn and peppers, or served up as a bitter festival drink with which to toast Quetzalcoatl, the feathered serpent god. They may no longer be toasting Quetzalcoatl, but many Spanish people still like to start the day with their *chocolate con churros*, just as French people enjoy a bowl of chocolate and a *pain au chocolat*. These are the "new" chocolate consumers; four centuries ago, there was no other choice than bread and watered-down wine. When the Spanish conquistadors arrived in Latin America, however, they discovered not only gold and silver, but beans, potatoes, and the cacao bean. At first no one quite knew how to prepare this fat-rich but bitter dish, until someone thought to try it with West Indies sugar. Countering the cacao's bitterness proved a wonderful surprise: by the end of the 1500s, the taste of this sugar-sweetened chocolate drink was on the tongue of anyone who could afford it.

Initially, the dish traveled to the Spanish court. Like many royal societies, the court seethed with sycophancy and faddy fashions. When, in 1660, Maria Theresa wedded the French king, Louis XIV, she brought with her the gift of chocolate from her native Spain. It was a gift she had occasion to turn to herself, a consolation for the King's indulging his penchant for sharing the royal bed with anyone but her. But, though the fashion for curious hairstyles and bannier dresses, which left women occupying three times their natural space, were destined to go the same way as the twentieth-century bouffant and the mini skirt (which did just the opposite), the royal taste for chocolate endured.

The early European chocolate houses were no more than fashionable drinking dens, and chocolate continued to be drunk as a thick,

LOVE BEAN
The European lust for chocolate turned a cottage craft into an international industry, and saw an army of pickers descend into the Ecuadorian forests to collect the precious cacao bean for shipping abroad.

hot, sweet beverage until a Dutchman, Casparus van Houten, foun[d a]
new method of processing it at his chocolate factory in Amsterda[m.]
Cacao beans could be ground down, as they had been in America [for]
centuries, and made into a drink mixed with milk. Van Houten disc[ov]-
ered a method of reducing the fat to produce a cake of cocoa that co[uld]
then be pulverized into a powder. When the Van Houten patent expir[ed]
in 1838, the British chocolatier and Quaker Joseph Fry stepped in.

The Quakers were a band of religious observers who believed th[at]
there was a little of God in everyone, but that the pomp and ceremony [of]
most established religions fell far short of the ideal. The relationsh[ip]
between them and chocolate-making in nineteenth-century-England w[as]
extraordinarily strong. They included Henry Joseph Rowntree, who r[an]
a chocolate factory in York; Joseph Fry, who was based in Bristol; an[d]
Mr. Cadbury, of whom more shortly, in Birmingham.

As Van Houten's son, Coenraad, refin[ed]
the process of producing chocolate ba[r by]
"Dutching" it to produce a dark, m[ild]
confection, Rodolphe Lindt in Switzerla[nd]
was developing a process known [as]
"conching," which turned out a smooth[er]
chocolate. Meanwhile, on the night tr[ain]
from London Victoria, heading for t[he]
channel ferry, was John Cadbury. It w[as]
1866 and Mr. Cadbury was about to bu[y a]
Van Houten chocolate press direct fr[om]
the factory.

The Cadbury family came fr[om]
England's West Country. In 1831, Jo[hn]
Cadbury was in Birmingham, one of t[he]
new beating city hearts of the new ind[us]-
trial age, where he planned to open a coc[oa]
and chocolate factory. Chocolate then w[as]
still the bitter-rich concoction favored [by]
women for its medicinal and therapeu[tic]
properties. In 1875, Cadbury's Van Hout[en]
press was put to work.

When John's sons, George and Richa[rd,]
took over the business from their fath[er]
they proved to be not only astute bu[si]-
nessmen, but exemplary employers to[o.]
They gave staff half-day holidays a[nd]

improving cycling lessons. Free cotton was handed out to the women so they could stitch their own uniforms instead of having to buy them. When Cadbury's morning Bible readings from the factory floor were suspended, the workers petitioned successfully for their reintroduction.

Across the Atlantic in Derry Church, Pennsylvania, around this time (1894), Milton Snavely Hershey was recovering from his recent bankruptcy and establishing a new chocolate plant in town. The business did well. By 1905, it was rated as the biggest chocolate factory in the world. In 1907, when Hershey started to market little flat-bottomed teardrops of chocolate wrapped in foil, the iconic Hershey Kisses, it did even better. Derry Church was renamed Hershey. When, in the 1870s, the Cadburys moved to a green-field site by the Bourn brook near Birmingham, they named it, not Cadburys', but Bournville, and built a modern "garden city" for the workers.

At the time, most factory owners were content to let their workers live in terraces and tenements, homes that, as one perceptive commentator in 1850 noted, were "contrived to yield to their tenants the smallest possible quantity of comfort and convenience." George Cadbury wanted the best for his people and he specified even the smallest details of the Bournville homes, which he continued to build after his brother died in 1899. The density of houses was restricted to seven per acre (about three per hectare), each furnished with a garden three times its floor area, ready planted with six fruit trees and space for growing additional vegetable produce, reckoned by Mr. Cadbury to be worth half a crown (two shillings and sixpence) a week. Every house was to have three bedrooms, a sitting room, a kitchen, and a scullery with a bath that folded away into a cupboard. As Cadbury explained in an instructional booklet for his tenants: "Baths are provided in the back kitchens, so that it may be possible to have a warm bath at least once a week. And you have the advantage of drying by the fire."

Cadbury offered other words of wisdom: "Never allow water to stand on tea more than three minutes, or tannic acid is developed which is injurious"; and "Furnish your sleeping

CHOCOLATE FORTUNES Many nineteenth-century fortunes, including those of Milton Hershey, Henry Rowntree, Joseph Fry, and John Cadbury, were founded on the chocolate bean.

apartments with single beds; double beds are now little used in civilized countries except in the United Kingdom." If people followed these simple rules, he assured his readers, "they could expect to live at least ten years longer."

Aside from its paternalism, the Bournville experiment was not above taking risks with social housing. One was the construction of the Sunshine Houses, almost a century before the invention of photovoltaic cells. The Sunshine Houses (also dubbed the Ten Shilling Houses, this being the weekly rent) were built to make the most of their southerly aspect. Front rooms were placed on the south-facing side; kitchens, fitted with smaller windows, on the north. The effect of this passive solar power gave extra light and warmth and reduced coal bills.

Before his death, George Cadbury disinherited his children by turning Bournville into a trust so that "the speculator will not find a footing" and because "I have come to the conclusion that my children" (he had fathered eleven in two marriages) "will be all the better for being deprived of this money.

"Great wealth is not to be desired, and in my experience of life it is generally more a curse than a blessing." Cadbury continued to cycle the two miles (3.2 km) to work and to answer all his post by return long after he reached his 70s.

Yet when he and brother Richard had taken over the business in 1861, Cadbury's was actually on the verge of collapse. They put the chocolate empire into profit with a combination of new processes and advertising. In 1869, they launched the first decorated chocolate box, the progenitor of 150 years of kitsch art, with a picture of a girl with a kitten on her lap, painted by Richard Cadbury, a talented amateur artist.

In 1899, when the world of cinema was still in its infancy, Casparus van Houten ("Van Houten's Cocoa—Best and Goes Farthest") commissioned one of the earliest film commercials for their

> **[We are] securing to workers in factories some of the advantages of outdoor village life, with opportunities for the natural and healthful occupation of cultivating the soil.**
>
> *George Cadbury, opening the Bournville factory in 1879*

Dutch confection. It featured a tired office worker suddenly discovering new reserves of energy after eating a bar of Van Houten chocolate: the world of advertising burgeoning into life. Chocolate, as a breakfast drink, as a health food, even as an erotic experience (a reflection of some nineteenth-century claims for its aphrodisiac qualities), was a popular product with advertising copywriters (see box).

France's *La Presse* newspaper had started taking adverts in 1836, and 30 years later one William James Carlton hit on the idea of actually selling advertising space for his American company, J. Walter Thompson. Color printing transformed the appearance, if not the prose, of the chocolate advert in the second half of the nineteenth century.

Newspaper banner advertisements trumpeted strange claims: Baker's Chocolate and Cocoa was "an excellent diet for children and invalids," while an advert for Chocolate de Matias López depicted a couple before (weak and thin) and after (portly) indulging in a Lopez chocolate diet. Often advertisements were puffed up with testimonials that, like this 1879 one from a New South Wales gardener to a seed company, rang with insincerity. "I exhibited at the late Intercolonial Exhibition in Sydney, Bliss's American Wonder Pea, and they received a special diploma being highly esteemed on account of their quality and earliness, so that they have quite eclipsed the best English varieties tested against them."

Advertising men (and women: the industry was one of the first to value the opinion of women and, more importantly, to employ them on equal terms to their male colleagues) learned to be economical with the truth. Hershey's pure milk chocolate was dubbed "a nutritious confection"; Fry's cocoa powder provided "food that gives both staying power and nerve tone" to "men who have to control intricate and expensive machinery." Chocolate was even promoted as being good brain food: "Here's how I remember! Why don't you?" declared an advert featuring Bob Hope holding aloft a box of Whitman's chocolates.

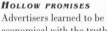

HOLLOW PROMISES
Advertisers learned to be economical with the truth when it came to packaging the products of *Theobroma cacao* and selling them to a gullible public.

STRANGE CLAIMS

✦

Early attempts to influence people with pictorial messages harked back to the religious paintings on church walls. Graphic depictions of the damned roasting in the fires of hell were designed to dissuade a largely illiterate population from a life of sin. Their effectiveness is impossible to quantify, but by the nineteenth century this billboard style was more popular than ever. *Il est vraiment bon* ("It is truly good"), insisted a poster for Chocolat Menier, picturing a charming truant graffitiing a wall with the instruction: "Drink Chocolat Menier."

Common Wheat
Triticum aestivum

Native range: Middle East and Asia Minor

Type: Upright-growing grass

Height: Up to 3 feet (1 m)

+ **EDIBLE**
+ MEDICINAL
+ **COMMERCIAL**
+ PRACTICAL

Without bread wheat, Europe might still be stranded in the Dark Ages. Civilizations are fueled by their foods, and in temperate climates the fuel of choice was wheat.

SEEDS OF REVOLUTION

Grains are the most important plants in the world. Every granule is a neatly packaged food store filled with energizing starches, proteins, minerals, and vitamins. Grains are not only edible; they are also portable, storable, and can be turned into bread—5,000-year-old loaves have been discovered in the tombs of ancient Egyptians. Wheat grains were almost certainly the first crops brought into cultivation by Stone Age people and they have fed much of the world and its farm animals ever since.

Qu'ils mangement de la brioche!—"Let them eat cake!"—suggested a bemused Marie Antoinette when told that her people, the French peasantry, had no bread and were being forced to eat grass in order to stay alive. The Austrian archduchess who had married the future king of France in 1770, and who often amused herself playing milkmaids at her mock farmhouse at Versailles, could not comprehend the plight of her people. Her husband was Louis XVI and under his dithering leadership the country's mounting debts and a succession of poor wheat harvests were turning the rumblings of discontent into revolution. Heads were about to roll. In 1793 after the Republicans had stormed Paris' Bastille prison, Louis XVI was put to death. Crowds watched with satisfaction as the head of the head of state fell from Dr. Guillotin's efficient execution machine set up in the Place de la Concorde. That October, Marie

Give us this day our daily bread
Matthew 6:11

Antoinette's own head rolled into the bloody laundry basket at the foot of the guillotine.

Marie Antoinette's callous (but possibly apocryphal) remark betrayed her naïvety over the profound importance of bread to the French *paysanne*. The baguette was as much a symbol of equality and freedom as the bare-breasted figure of Marianne who would later grace the French franc notes. Marie Antoinette would pay the ultimate price of her ignorance. All this for a loaf of bread.

Wheat is the primary milling cereal for making pastries, biscuits, cakes, and bread. It has been for perhaps 12,000 years. The early hunter-gathers who settled to farm in southwest Asia, Ethiopia, or the Mediterranean harvested wild wheat and stored it along with their other wild foods when the fall nights drew in. The merits of this wonder crop would have been debated around the evening fire: about how, when dried and ground in the stone quern or mill, the floury powder could be mixed with water and baked into sustaining breads and biscuits with a commendable shelf life. Or how, when sprouted and left to ferment, it turned water into ale. Or of how the dried seed, stored in rat-proof earthenware, could be persuaded to spring back to life when sown in the ground the following spring.

Farmers isolated better strains of the plant as the centuries passed. One of the difficulties lay in discovering a strain that did not shed its seed the moment it ripened, leaving the harvester scrabbling in the dirt to retrieve the crop. The basic varieties, einkorn (*T. monococcum*) and emmer (*T. turgidum* var. *dicoccum*), were programmed to regenerate the plant in even the most hostile soils: as soon as the wheat ripened, the grain, enclosed in a protective husk, burst forth from the parent plant. Under the right conditions, a warm fall night for example, the husks split open and drive the seed down into the earth, and fine hairs on the pod lock the seed into the ground.

Gradually (isolating a particular strain could take up to 1,000 years), varieties were selected that were easier to harvest and the grain economy grew—and grew.

MARIE ANTOINETTE
Give them brioche. An uncharitable Marie Antoinette failed to appreciate the importance of bread in the peasant's household. She and her husband, Louis XVI, would pay the ultimate price for their regal ignorance.

When a traveler from France arrived in Britain in 330 BCE, he noted that wheat fields were already growing in the southeast of England. A century later, when Rome sent its invasion forces out to conquer new territories in Sicily, Sardinia, North Africa, Egypt, and Spain, it was specifically to provide the empire with fresh wheat. When Vespasian became emperor after Nero's death in 69 CE, Egypt alone was supplying an estimated 20 million bushels of wheat a year. Wheat was power.

The collapse of the Roman Empire was accompanied by the loss of the wheat fields. They were not absent for long. In Europe, farming with slaves was giving way to farming through feudalism. In return for their lordship's protection, the serfs labored his land and the cash crop, once again, was wheat: what these Europeans called *hwaete* (Anglo-Saxon), *weit* (Dutch), *weizen* (German), or *hveiti* (Icelandic). The word (meaning "white," to distinguish it from the darker grains like barley and rye) came to symbolize prosperity.

Wheat even came to the assistance of the Iberian mariners as they explored the seemingly vast and endless Atlantic Ocean in the hope of reaching the rumored riches of the West. They traveled with the wind in

THE GLEANERS
Every grain counted for the field gleaners. But critics were shocked by Jean-François' Millet's portrait of the peasantry and his portrayal of workers in the field less than 75 years after the French Revolution.

heir sails and bags of grain in their
ips' holds. Landing on stepping stone
lands such as the Canaries, they would
ow and harvest a crop of wheat to
rovision themselves for the next leg of
e journey.

YMBOL OF CERES

he symbol of the sheaf of wheat stood
r farming and fertility, for harvest and
anksgiving, for the death of winter
nd the rebirth of spring. The harvesting
nd sowing of bread wheat involved an

CHANGE OF SCENE
As wheat fields advanced
through Europe, they
transformed the look
of the landscape and
changed forever the layout
of the countryside.

xtravagant amount of ritual, for this was the one crop that, if it failed,
reatened famine. If the hop, grape, or barley harvest died in the field it
as a setback. If wheat failed it spelled disaster.

Like her Roman counterpart, Ceres, Demeter was the Greek goddess
ost closely associated with corn. She even had her own cult following at
leusis, south of Athens, where a relief from the time shows Demeter
d her daughter, Persephone, handing Triptolemus the seed corn with
hich he will teach the Greeks to grow. From here on, the wheat fields
ere surrounded by ritual and superstitions: giving
ms or gifts of wheat to the poor was believed to help
e crop along. Little "harvest luck" wheat sheaves,
resented to the landlord by his most experienced
aper, were fixed above the hearth over winter to guar-
tee a safe sowing in the spring. In modern wheat
lds, wild flowers are a nuisance, but in medieval
mes, if a stranger happened to pass by the field during
e harvest, protocol demanded that he be brought
to the field and presented with a nosegay or a bunch
wild flowers. While today's arable farmers would be
rd pressed to find a posy of wild flowers to decorate
e tractor's dashboard, field flowers were still, in the
50s, being used to decorate the final wagon that
ought home the last sheaves of wheat.

In the northern hemisphere, as the big, red harvest
oon, the one closest to the fall equinox, rose in the
ening sky, the first loaf was ceremonially baked.
fts of sheaves were bestowed on the village, and
heat auctioned to raise funds for parish improve-

WHEAT ARCHITECTURE

✦

No other plant has so transformed
the rural skyline as wheat. Aside
from the mills, barns, granaries,
and grain silos used to process and
store grain, there were the great
cathedral-like "English" or aisled
barns. Built as big as a village
church, they contained storage bays
for the wheat sheaves and a central
threshing bay, set between two
great doors opposite one another.
During threshing or winnowing—the
two processes used to separate the
grains from the chaff—the huge
doors would be opened to create a
cross-breeze to blow away the chaff.

HORSE POWER
Farmers, with their horse-drawn corn planters and reaping machines, powered across the Western prairies in the 1800s. They converted all but a fraction of the Great Plains into croplands.

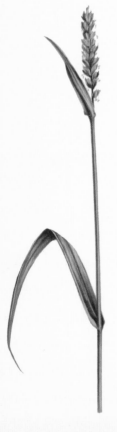

ments, or put to pay for the harvest thanksgiving. Once bucolic, pagan affairs, the harvest suppers (with strange local names like Mell Supper or Horkey) were turned into less boisterous events by the Church. Nevertheless, some distinctly pagan wheat rituals continued to lurk beneath the surface with celebrations like the crowning of the corn bride, the *Marie au Blé*, in France, and other brides being carried over the potentially fertile threshing place, the threshold.

Wheat yields, thanks to better husbandry rather than mystic rites, were already increasing by 1750, when they were two and a half times that of the Middle Ages. Across Europe, meanwhile, the medieval institution of feudalism was being dismantled. If the 1600s had been characterized by the rise of the first truly international economy, and the 1700 by battles for colonies and commerce, the 1800s seemed to be marked by social upheaval: France was settling down after its revolution, America was about to be embroiled in civil war, and Russia was gearing up for a revolution of its own. Much of England's common land had been hedged in for private profit and higher wheat yields under the Enclosure Acts and the English peasant usually judged it better to become a poorly paid laborer than stay a serf. Over the course of the centuries, those with wheat fields tended to triumph over those without.

By the beginning of the nineteenth century, the cultivation of wheat had spread across the temperate world, and the Industrial Revolution was signaling the start of a food revolution that would ultimately elevate America and many countries in Europe to being among the world's wealthiest nations.

THE BREAD BASKET

Bread, according to one seventeenth-century proverb, is the staff of life. "Taking the bread out of someone's mouth" deprived them of their most basic livelihood. Bread and butter, or more usually bread and cheese, represented life's bare necessities, at least in the world's wheat-growing regions where the colloquial "bread basket" referred both to the farmer's belly and to the open fields where he grew his wheat. In France it was the northern Beauce region that was dubbed Paris' bread basket.

In 1857, the French artist Jean-François Millet painted a portrait of the corn harvest. In *The Gleaners*, three women in headscarves stoop and, with nimble fingers, nip up the golden grains that fell as the reapers cut the corn. The picture shocked art critics over its intimate portrayal of the working peasants who had, in a kind of class action, topped Marie Antoinette less than 75 years earlier. But *The Gleaners* also revealed the world of farming at the dawn of a new era. In the background of the picture stands the revolutionary new horse-drawn reaper and binder. Nearby, laborers load sheaves of wheat onto wagons. Cut to the same scene 150 years later and the horses, wagons, and most of the men and women would be gone, replaced by monstrous machines sweeping through the plain in close formation. This

WHITE BREAD

✦

White bread is made from wheat flour that has had most of its fiber removed and has then been bleached. Other ingredients are added in an effort to make the flour more "nutritious." White bread has been fashionable since Periclean Athens, but was especially popular in England from the end of the eighteenth century. This, it seems, was the result of sugar addiction (see Sugarcane, p.166). People who were already beginning to consume a lot of refined sugar found wholemeal bread indigestible because their digestive systems could no longer cope with fibrous foods. They turned to white bread.

BREAD OF HEAVEN
From baps, bricks, and batons to Belgian rolls and bloomers, bread was known as the staff of life. "Bread of heaven," sang the Welsh miners to John Hughes' hymn of praise, "Cwm Rhondda."

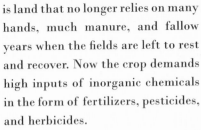

The hand-to-mouth business of sowing, reaping, winnowing, and storing wheat gradually gave way to mechanization in the twentieth century. When the horses had gone, field life was never the same again.

is land that no longer relies on many hands, much manure, and fallow years when the fields are left to rest and recover. Now the crop demands high inputs of inorganic chemicals in the form of fertilizers, pesticides, and herbicides.

During the intervening period between then and now, the technical advances of the Industrial Age initially provided farmers with steam-powered metal muscles to tame the huge resources of the new land coming on stream: the American plains, the South American pampas, the temperate regions of Australasia, and eastern Europe and Russia all fell before the plow. From the 1850s, the English yeoman farmer, his country at peace, enjoyed high wheat prices, an army of farm hands, and the profits to invest in new agricultural machinery, saw the wheat fields advance. Later, as petrochemicals and the oil industry came on stream to replace steam, the wheat revolution turned small farmers and artisans into clerks and machine minders.

GROUND DOWN

The miller and his flour mill, like this one in Sweden, was central to the wheat economy. The early entrepreneurs who survived the mill race went on to found fortunes.

THE HONEST MILLER

As so often happens, it was not the producer who profited so much as the middleman, in this case the miller. The engineers who created the water-

or wind-powered mills that could grind corn had mastered one of the earliest industrial processes. In non-mechanized communities, the hand-powered stone quern served local families. In northern Europe, the early mills were water-powered. They were built on the upper reaches of rivers, where the water ran swiftest, or on the lower levels, where large areas of water could be harnessed to provide free energy. The mill wheel was either fixed below the mill (known as a "click mill") or to one side.

In the Middle East and Mediterranean, millers made use of the winds, and this technology spread gradually—aided by Christian Crusaders—into northern Europe. Gradually, the watermill gave way to the more efficient windmill. On the typical nineteenth-century smock windmill (named after the land worker's traditional one-piece overgarment), four canvas-covered sails revolved in the breeze like a giant fan. The sails drove a geared shaft that turned the millstones, grooved to grind the grain and channel the flour into the miller's sacks below. A now-forgotten industry with its own skills and technical terms evolved to dress and service the millstones. Whether the stones were drawn from the famous French quarries in the Marne, where they were built up in sections of quartz bound with a ring of iron, or cut from the millstone-grit quarries of Derbyshire, England, the stone dressers would be called in to redress the stones to the miller's cry of "Show us your metal": a busy (and by implication more skilled) stone dresser's hands would be embedded with metal splinters from his mill bill. But the traditional millers went to the wind themselves when factory forges started turning out the oil-powered engines and spinning steel rollers that made the old mill redundant. Generations down the line, it was the millers who founded some of the wealthiest industrial dynasties of modern times and eventually the multinational corporations of the twentieth century such as Associated British Foods, Cargill, and Unilever.

STONE-BAKED BREAD

A 3,000-year-old etching on the tomb of Usimare Ramesses III, who ruled Egypt for just over 30 years from 1186 BCE, portrays the royal bakers at work with wheat. After threshing the grains to remove the chaff, wheat is shown ground into flour before being turned into dough and baked in a brick and clay oven that would not look out of place in a contemporary Italian pizza parlor. Unfortunately, the method of grinding the flour on a stone quern led to pieces of broken stone finding their way into the loaves. As well as discovering ancient loaves, placed in the tomb to assist the deceased on his journey to the life hereafter, archaeologists also found evidence of dental damage caused by too many gritty loaves.

PROTEIN PACKED
Filled with vitamins, minerals, starches, and proteins, and as portable as it was storable, wheat grain packed the power to feed the world. It has been doing so since the Stone Age.

Tulip
Tulipa spp.

Dutch tulips from their beds
Flaunted their stately heads.

James Montgomery, "The Adventure
of a Star," 1825

Native range: Mountainous parts of southern Europe, north Africa, and Asia

Type: Ornamental flowering bulb

Height: Up to 3 feet (1 m)

✦ EDIBLE

✦ MEDICINAL

✦ ***COMMERCIAL***

✦ PRACTICAL

It was the world's first "florists' flower" and the subject of a bout of "tulipmania" in seventeenth-century Holland when absurd sums of money were exchanged for a single bulb. An inspiration to Netherlandish painters, the tulip is still the focus of flower festivals worldwide.

GOING DUTCH

The Flemish master Peter Paul Rubens had an intriguing new subject of conversation for his young bride, Hélène Fourment, in 1629: the astronomic price of tulip bulbs. Rubens was 53; Hélène, whom he had married three weeks before Christmas, was 16, the same age as Rubens' oldest son, Albert. Despite the disparity of their ages it was a good match. In what proved to be the final decade of his life, Rubens' second wife made him a happy man and bore him five children. By now, the artist was a pillar of society and looking to improve the garden at his home, the Rubenshuis in the center of Antwerp.

Winds of change were whistling across the Flemish flatlands and through the ordered Dutch gardens. No longer was the home focused on a practical kitchen and herb garden. Following the Italian fashion, the Netherlanders were creating formal gardens decorated with geometric shapes, arbors, loggias, and trickling fountains—anything to provide a backdrop for the new plants that were finding their way into the country. Foremost among them was the tulip.

Today, people gather every spring to witness the flowering of the Dutch tulip fields. Covering more than 25,000 acres (10,000 ha), they represent a trade that exports 60% of the world's cut flowers and some 10 billion bulbs.

In the early seventeenth century, even before tulips were fashionable, gardens were changing. Flowers, previously the province of the physician and the cook, were being "botanized" and revered for their decorative qualities. And Holland was about to become the bulb's spiritual home. The tulip, found most abundantly in the Tien-Shan and Pamir-Alai Mountain Ranges in central Asia, had spread to China and Mongolia before it reached Europe. Turkish gardeners were renowned for bringing the tulips that now decorate the Netherlands to bloom a thousand years ago. (Although it became the signature flower of the Netherlands, the tulip was also the national flower of Hungary, Turkey, and the "Tulip state" of Kyrgyzstan.

It was Charles de L'Écluse, who, when he took up the post of botanical professor at Leiden University in 1593, introduced the tulip. It first flowered in the Netherlands in 1594. (Or did it? L'Écluse reported the case of a foolish Antwerp merchant who, some years earlier, had received a consignment of cloth from the east that contained some tulip bulbs. The merchant chewed on a few and threw the rest into his garden in disgust.)

L'Écluse had procured his bulbs through a friend, Ogier Ghiselin de Busbecq, who was stationed in Istanbul as the Flemish ambassador. A popular story of the time suggested that Busbecq or a colleague was traveling in Turkey when he came across tulips growing wild. Pointing at the plant, he asked a turbaned farmer for its name. Thinking the visitor was admiring his headgear, the farmer replied "tulipand"—turban. The diplomat recorded the name, only to discover later that its true name was *laâle*. (The heyday of the Ottoman Empire was described as the *Lale Devri*—the tulip era.)

At Leiden, L'Écluse continued to propagate his flowers. Generously, he dispensed bulbs to fellow enthusiasts and artists such as Jacques de Gheyn II and Rubens (whose work he admired) in the interests of botanical science. But he refused to sell his bulbs to money-grabbing bulb dealers. The business of bulb dealing was spiraling out of control: one bulb sold in 1637 for 6,700 guilders, equivalent to a house and garden on a smart Amsterdam canal, and 50 times the average annual income. Frustrated buyers found a way round L'Écluse's principled stand: they stole the collection, a theft that would form the basis for the flower industry of Holland's future.

Back in 1630, Rubens had begun his final body of work, drawing heavily on his own domestic circumstances: his house, his wife, his garden, and his new flowers. Among the most affectionate portraits was one of his family strolling through the garden toward the Rubenshuis' Baroque portico. As if predicting the approaching mania, Rubens added a stand of tulips.

TULIP MANIA
Flora's Wagon of Fools by Hendrik Pot (c. 1637) is an allegory of the tulip mania in which Flora, goddess of flowers, and her followers are being blown toward destruction in the sea.

GIFT OF GRATITUDE

✦

The Dutch royal family fled to Canada when Germany invaded Holland in 1940. (Their daughter, Princess Margriet, was born at Ottawa's Civic Hospital.) After Germany's defeat in 1945, the royal family returned and presented the Canadian government with 100,000 tulip bulbs as a token of their appreciation. (Every year they send another 20,000 bulbs.) This led to Ottawa's annual tulip show, an event replicated worldwide with tulip shows in Spalding, England, the Skagit Valley Tulip Festival, Washington State, and Australia's Royal Botanical Gardens at Bowral in New South Wales.

Vanilla

Vanilla planifolia

Native range: Coastal rainforest of Mexico and Central America

Type: Tropical climbing orchid

Height: Can grow as tall as 100 feet (30 m)

+ *EDIBLE*
+ *MEDICINAL*
+ *COMMERCIAL*
+ *PRACTICAL*

Gifted to the Spanish in the 1500s by the last of the Aztec leaders, Montezuma, and carried across the world onto the Indian Ocean islands, the dried beans of *Vanilla planifolia* have become a lucrative commodity. Widely used in foods such as ice cream, vanilla extract is an essential flavoring in the modern kitchen.

LONG HARVEST

Tourists wander through the market square or mount the steps leading up to the city gardens at Antananarivo, the Madagascan capital. Wherever they go, they are pursued relentlessly by women and children, proffering plastic bags containing a few withered-looking twigs. The price, even for the tourists, is unusually high. It is because these are vanilla pods—one of the most expensive spices in the world and, due to a quirk of fate, one that requires a great deal of time to prepare.

When news of the arrival of a group of armed men reached Montezuma in 1519, the mighty Aztec leader and his advisers took it as a signal that their creator had returned. From his capital city, Tenochtitlán (the city was five times the size of London), Montezuma had ruled his empire for 17 years, scrupulously careful to keep the serpent god Quetzalcoatl pacified with regular human sacrifices at the Great Temple.

Montezuma ordered up some of the city's most precious gifts for these pale-skinned gods and, shortly before he was murdered by his guests (no one knows how), presented the leader, Hernando Cortés, with his nation's most delicious drink, *chocolatl*. Although it was mostly made of ground cacao (or chocolate), Cortés's drink contained mysterious flavors drawn from exotic plants no European had ever tasted before. They included annatto seeds, chili pepper, and, rarest of all, vanilla.

It takes a huge, historic leap to leave the ill-fated Montezuma and arrive at some quayside in Florida, U.S.A., Sydney, Australia, or Wellington, New Zealand, where—in that order—people eat the most ice cream. The flavor of choice is vanilla (although a Kiwi preference for hokey pokey—a combination of vanilla and toffee—comes a close second). While people find it difficult to distinguish between real and artificial vanilla in some foods, test taste scores with ice cream flavored with real vanilla remain high.

Vanilla contains more than 250 active ingredients including vanillin, the substance responsible for creating that irresistible flavor. The cost of vanilla prompts its users to be temperate, but its taste is so distinctive that vanilla still finds its way into foods such as chocolate and custard, and into perfumes and toothpastes. It has been used in aromatherapy, and experiments with vanilla-scented patches suggest that the chemical can even reduce a person's desire for chocolate.

Why is vanilla so expensive? The answer lies in its cultivation. In South America, the vanilla pod (or bean) forms after the flowers of the orchid *Vanilla planifolia* have been pollinated by bees and humming-birds. Following Montezuma's untimely death, the Spanish kept as tight a control as they could on vanilla production, running it in tandem with their chocolate manufacturing works, and providing the accompaniment to the traditional *churros*—strips of deep-fried batter that are often dipped into a thick hot chocolate.

By the early 1800s, the plant had been taken to Mauritius and from there to Indonesia, the Bourbon Islands, Tahiti, and Madagascar. But the growers ran into a problem: the pale green orchid flowers lacked any natural pollina-tors in their new surroundings. Instead, every plant had to be hand-pollinated with a small, pointed stick inserted into each flower. The seed pods were then allowed to mature on the vine for six to nine months, before being harvested, laid out to dry in the sun, and subsequently wrapped in special woolen blankets to prompt fermentation. For the next few months, the pods were cured, or sweated, in airtight metal boxes.

The price and the effort required to harvest vanilla resulted in intensive research to find a suitable substi-tute. It proved difficult to meet the world demand for the estimated 5.5 million tonnes of vanilla consumed every year. Nevertheless, experiments to create vanilla from other sources—including from clove oil, lignin (a compound found in wood), and a soil bacterium thought capable of transforming a common chemical found in fruit and beet into vanillin—suggest that the street sellers of Madagascar face an uncertain future.

DECEPTIVE DELIGHTS
Vanilla planifolia is the only orchid cultivated for the practical purpose of flavoring food. The unattractive appearance of the dried and fermented vanilla pod belies the sweetness within.

Sweet, sweet is this human life
William Johnson Cory,
"Mimnermus in Church," 1858

CHILLED VANILLA
✦

Ice cream was enjoyed in the royal courts of England in the 1600s and was being flavored with vanilla by the time Thomas Jefferson collected his own recipe for it in the 1780s. Nancy Johnson invented a hand-powered ice-cream maker in the 1840s, and, by the late eighteenth century, a large market for ice cream had emerged.

Wine Grape
Vitis vinifera

Native range: Western Asia

Type: Climbing vine

Height: Up to 50 feet (15 m) depending on cultivation

+ **EDIBLE**
+ MEDICINAL
+ **COMMERCIAL**
+ PRACTICAL

Country people have been laying down their fall wines for 5,000 years at least. It was only when the Romans took to exploiting the wine vine, however, that the business began to go global.

BIG BUSINESS

Grapes can be turned into raisins, vinegar, and, above all, wine. The Egyptians claimed wine as the tears of the god Horus. Around 3,000 years later, at the turn of the twenty-first century, vintners were making 30 billion bottles a year and the market, worth around over $100 billion, was still growing. The fruits of the grape were big business.

By 2000, it would have been difficult to find even an island where a glass of wine, however challenging to the palate, was unavailable. Wine was not only being consumed in almost every non-Islamic country in the atlas, it was also being made in most of them. The vineyards of western Europe, California, Australia, New Zealand, and South Africa, along

with those of the Balkans and South America, amount to an impressive 20 million acres (8 million ha). Under a gracious sun, these vineyards typically yield between 60 and 70 million tons of grapes a year, which is potentially a lot of wine.

Within the *Vitis vinifera* species are a large number of varieties, including the spicy Germany Gewürztraminer or a subtle-scented Spanish Rioja; a piquant New Zealand Sauvignon or an Italian Chardonnay aged in an oak barrel. Down the centuries, wine merchants have worked to stabilize and standardize their product to maximize profits and minimize costs. The industry is achieving its goal: the average supermarket wine shelf may be weighed down with numerous different wines, but almost all are mass-produced, shipped in bulk around the globe, and trucked to the final retail outlet with a low price that seems at odds with how far the wine has traveled from the vine.

In 2004, the World Health Organization (WHO) estimated that excessive alcohol consumption was killing just over 3% of the world's population and harming another 4%. According to their figures, alcohol causes between 20% and 30% of all cases of cirrhosis of the liver, epilepsy, and esophageal and liver cancer. Along with whiskey (see Barley, p.104) and beer (see Hop, p.110), wine has undoubtedly played a part in this.

MASS MARKET

The vine berry is a little fruiting miracle that started life in the guise of *V. sezannesis* around 60 million years ago. Its wild descendent, *V. vinifera* subsp. *silvestris* (sometimes referred to as *V. sylvestris*) took root in eastern Europe, but proved a capricious grape when it came to wine-making: being dioecious—that is, carrying both male and female flowers on the plant—it had to be pollinated before it gave up the gift of the grape. The domesticated *V. vinifera*, a hermaphrodite, was more generous when it came to providing the wine-makers with their fruits.

When and where those wine-makers started out is debatable. Wine may have been made first in Iran 5,500 years ago. It may have started in what is now Turkey or Georgia 2,000 years earlier. Paintings and sculptures from both China and Egypt illustrate wine being made and consumed before the Greeks turned viticulture into a commercially lucrative enterprise.

The first wines were almost certainly a happy accident. As grapes, like many other fruits, contain juice and sugars, they have an inherent tendency to ferment. The crushed fruit needs only to encounter a wild yeast (and there are plenty around, including those that live on the grape skin itself) to start fermenting. The knack of managing wine is to stabilize the drink as the fermentation finishes and to preserve it in a bottle or cask. Herein lies the difference between a good and poor-quality wine. Whatever the origins of wine, it was destined to become the universal

CHUBBY CHERUB
Crowned with a coronet of *Vitis vinifera*, Guido Reni's Bacchus celebrated the serious business of drinking wine in 1623. Italy was, by that time, at the forefront of the Mediterranean wine industry.

drink of southern Europe before the advent of tea, coffee, and chocolate Outside the Islamic world—where Muslims abstain from alcohol—wine making was a classic cottage industry; as rustic as beer brewing and a rough and ready as cider-making. On market day, flagons of the stuff rattled their way into town on the farm cart or were delivered by *burro* t the village cave or *bodega*. Children were weaned on the same watered down wine that their grandparents drank—it was a safer drink tha water—and guests were greeted with a glass or horn cup of the stuff.

Outside the cider regions of Normandy and Brittany, in France, an Galicia and the Asturias, in Spain, the vineyard was one of the centra village enterprises. The lawyer, the doctor, and the mayor might each pa a little more for his wine, but everyone, from the *vigneron* to the woodman was a connoisseur when it came to judging the annual *vin du pays*—th local country wine.

The craft of wine-making had been perfected by the big wine dealer of the medieval age: the monasteries. In the Eucharist ritual, brea and wine respectively represented the body and blood of Christ. Sinc they required wine for this service of communion, the great monasti settlements devoted themselves both to God and the grape. The Cister cians of Burgundy, for example, established themselves on some of th

best grape-growing land in France. Here the monks took great care cultivating the grape, creating walled vineyards or *clos* to shelter their vines.

They learned to use the geography of the surrounding land to their advantage—in northern Europe, vines were planted in lines running down south-facing slopes to maximize their exposure to sunshine. They were planted close together to help them retain heat at night and, on seriously cold nights, small fires and torches were lit to keep frost at bay. In the hotter climes further south, the vines were positioned so as to provide shade to one another and were cultivated to fruit higher up the stem, thereby allowing cooling breezes to pass through their lower reaches.

The Church, major landowners, and centers of science played a central role in the development of the wine industry. Centuries of cultivation saw the vine produce more than 5,000 different varieties, around 30 of which would become the grapes most commonly used to produce wine. Among these are Cabernet Sauvignon, Pinot Noir, Syrah, Merlot, Chardonnay, Riesling, Muscat, Chenin Blanc, Sauvignon Blanc, and Sémillon.

When the monasteries went into decline, the old vineyards continued to sustain the land. In the 1400s, the Burgundian wine dukes were so powerful that they threatened the very stability of France. It was only the loss of their leader, Charles le Téméraire (Charles the Rash), during the siege of Nancy in 1477, that transformed the province into a profitable jewel in the French crown. Despite the uncharitable claim that Burgundian vines were only popular because foreigners could pronounce names like Chablis, Chambertin, Pommard, and Mâcon, Burgundy today boasts more *appellations d'origine contrôlées* than any other region in France.

WINE WORSHIPERS

✦

According to legend, it was the twice-born son of Zeus, the Greek god Dionysus, who brought the vine to Greece from Asia Minor (Turkey). Reputed by his female followers, or maenads, to hide in the guise of a bull, Dionysus was represented as the youthful and beautiful god of wine. In Roman mythology he was Bacchus. In earlier times, it was Egypt's Osiris who was celebrated as the wine god, and in even earlier days the Sumerians paid tribute to Gestin, the "mother vine-stock."

WORLDWIDE WINES

The rise of fine wines was helped along by the advent of the cork and bottle (see English Oak, p.156). The invention of a bottle that would lie on its side and keep the cork damp marked a significant stage in the development of wine.

From the 1700s to the 1800s, sales and exports of bottled wine steamed ahead. By this time, eight out of ten Italians worked in wine, while on big estates such as Latour, Lafite, and Margaux in Bordeaux, France, had followed the example set by Arnaud III de Pontac. In the 1600s, as the owner of the Château Haut-Brion, Pontac had pioneered the business of producing fine wines, rigorously selecting vines and carefully controlling cellar practice. Despite the long-standing enmity between France and England, the English could not resist French wines and the best of Bordeaux commanded prices three times that of other wines.

Vitis vinifera was also making its mark in other parts of the world. While the Spanish had brought the vine to their conquered territories in Latin America, particularly Chile, Australia started out with cuttings taken there by Captain Arthur Phillip in 1788. In the 1850s, what would become New Zealand's oldest vineyard had been planted by the Catholic Church at Hawke's Bay.

But the introduction of the vine to America—which marked the start of an industry that would make the U.S. the fourth biggest wine producer after France, Italy, and Spain—had an unforeseen problem: phylloxera.

FUNNY BUSINESS
"The phylloxera, a true gourmet, finds out the best vineyards and attaches itself to the best vines," ran this caption from *Punch* magazine in 1890.

LAYING DOWN
Mastering the simple technology of corking a bottle of wine heralded the advent of fine wines. However, the phylloxera outbreak caused a serious setback to European wine-makers.

Phylloxera is an insect no larger than a pinhead, but it has a serious appetite, not for the American *V. riparia* but for the European *V. vinifera*. The problem would have been confined to America were it not for the inventions of the steam ship.

In 1837, the British engineer Isambard Kingdom Brunel saw his purpose-built steamship, the SS *Great Western*, launch from its dock in Bristol, England. A year later, the *Great Western* made a record-breaking dash across the Atlantic to New York. Before the journey, Brunel fell and injured himself, prompting all but seven passengers to cancel their tickets. Despite this inauspicious start, steam travel significantly reduced journey times between Europe and America, so much so that the deadly phylloxera, which would have succumbed during a longer, wind-powered crossing, survived. In the 1860s, phylloxera struck. Aided by outbreaks of mildew, it devastated the European vineyards. The eventual solution, to graft *V. vinifera* onto the phylloxera-resistant American rootstock, came too late to save most of Europe's vineyards and it took almost a century for the industry to recover. Aided by technological and scientific advances, vineyards in America, Australia, South Africa, and New Zealand rose to fill the gap. Although nothing would be quite the same again in the European vineyards, by the end of the twentieth century the big four—France, Italy, Germany, and Spain—were still producing and consuming more wine than anyone else.

Why was wine such a big deal in Europe but not in India or China, for example? The sophisticated Mayan

Who planteth a vineyard, and eateth not of the fruit thereof?

1 Corinthians 9:7

SMASHING CHAMPAGNE

✦

In 1910 and 1911, Champagne workers broke into their own wine factories, smashed bottles and barrels, and threw cartloads of grapes into the river. The rioters were venting their frustration at the decision to truck grapes in from outside the region, to make up for the loss of local fruit to phylloxera and several poor harvests. It prompted the French government to send in the troops, and later to apply the *Appellation d'origine contrôlée*, to Champagne. In effect this prevented any sparkling wine made outside the region being called "Champagne."

and Inca civilizations had wild vines available, but made no wine. India had grown grapevines and made wine 2,000 years ago, but established no great wine industry. China's wine-makers had an even longer vintage, yet wine was never as much a part of the culture as it was in Europe.

The reason behind the success of European wines lay with the civilization that not only created underfloor heating, hot tubs, reinforced concrete, sensible street plans, and well-built roads, but also killed the first Christian: the Romans.

Before his assassination in 44 BCE, one of the great men of the ancient world, Julius Caesar, masterminded an eight-year campaign to turn Gaul, or France, into an Italian province. His great-nephew (and adopted son), Augustus, continued Caesar's work, and during the Pax Romana, the Roman peace that existed between his death in 14 CE and the death of Marcus Aurelius in 180, this progressive civilization planted vineyards. Although they patriotically regarded their native vineyards—such as Falernum, south of Rome—as superior to all others, they planted the vine right across their territories: Spain, Greece, Gaul, Germany, and southern Britain. When their empire collapsed, the Romans' *vinum* could have gone the way of the hypocaust and the hot tub, forgotten for a millennium or two, only to reemerge as something of an afterthought, but for the expansion of Christianity. It was tied, inexorably, to the Roman Empire.

In crucifying Jesus, the Romans unwittingly guaranteed the future of the vine. At his last supper, Jesus bade his followers share food and drink with him. He might have chosen fish and spring water, or cake and ale; instead he chose bread and wine. The Romans, who became Christian converts, turned the religion, and its celebratory drink, into a major element of Western culture. While Christianity promoted the idea of universal benevolence, a glass of good wine inspired much the same sentiment.

LATIN INFLUENCE
As the Roman conquest spread across Europe, vineyards were planted in Spain, Portugal, France, and Algeria.

VINEYARD CHURCH

◆

The association of the vine and Christianity was repeated in the 1970s with the founding of Vineyard Churches. The movement arose out of Bible study groups meeting in the houses of Californian musicians and briefly attracted the attention of one of America's most famous singer-songwriters, Bob Dylan. Among its founding fathers, the "hippy" priest Lonnie Frisbee was forced out of the Church because of his homosexuality.

MIRACULOUS DRINK
According to the Gospel of John (John 2 1–11), Jesus's first miracle was to turn water into wine at a wedding feast at Cana in Galilee.

Corn

Zea mays

Native range: The Americas

Type: Annual cereal

Height: 5–6 feet (1.5–1.8 m)

+ **EDIBLE**
+ MEDICINAL
+ **COMMERCIAL**
+ **PRACTICAL**

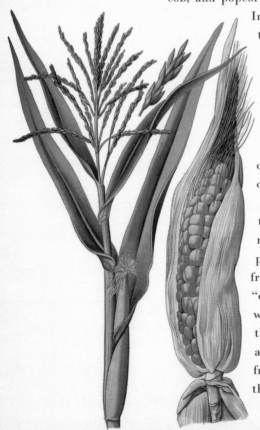

A t day break a young laborer, bare to the waist, strides down the road, heading for the fields. A picture of health and vigor, he is testament to the protein-rich crop he is about to pick, corn, or, as they say in Europe, maize.

MYSTERIOUS ORIGINS

After rice and wheat, corn is the third most important cereal on the planet. It gave rise to two of the greatest civilizations ever seen in South America, before being shipped to the Old World. Within the space of two centuries, the golden grain had become an industrial commodity as versatile as petrochemical plastics, as renewable as an apple. As supplies of fossil fuels dwindle, will *Zeta mays* become the fuel of the future?

Variously known as corn, sweetcorn, Indian corn, mealies, corn on the cob, and popcorn, corn was originally cultivated by Native American Indians. It not only sustained the great civilizations of the Toltecs, Aztecs, Mayas, and Incas, but also the "new" American civilization. As William Cobbett had pointed out in his *Cottage Economy* of 1821, "the finest hogs in the world" were "fatted upon this corn." It did a good job of feeding the people too: in 1810, the American population was around seven million. Largely fed on corn, it rose to 92 million within a century. After it was imported to Spain in the 1700s, corn helped feed a rapidly growing population.

Planted every year from seed, corn takes between three and five months to flower. First to emerge are the male tassels at the top of the stalk. Anemophily (wind) pollination allows the female flowers to be fertilized in a frond of delicate, silky styles borne on the tips of the "ears" lower down the stem. The ears, husks, or cobs, wrapped in leaves, produce a sleeve of fat, yellow grains— the corn on the cob. Each plant carries up to two ears, and the hand-harvester walks the rows, breaking the ears free and stripping back the leaves of the husk to reveal the glistening rows of sweet, protein-packed grains. The sugar in the corn starts to convert to starch the moment

Although it has yet to be conclusively proven,
corn is thought to have first been cultivated in
southern Mexico from where it spread to North
and South America.

It is picked, which is why sweetcorn is
best eaten fresh from the kitchen
garden (eaten on "the principle of the
lathe," recommended the author E. A.
Bunyard in *The Gardener's Companion*
of 1936). Equally, the cobs can be
baked in their leaves; stripped and
steamed or boiled; shelled from the
husk and eaten raw, cooked, dried, or
crushed into breakfast cereal flakes; ground into flour
for tortillas; or put in a hot pan and turned into
popcorn. Corn is a seriously versatile vegetable.

Its physical makeup, however, sets it at a biological
disadvantage: it does not naturally reseed. To create
next year's corn, someone somewhere must pick a grain,
preserve it until planting time, and then physically
drop it in a hole in the soil. This interdependence
between man and plant was key to the history of corn
and how humans learned to make the most of this
miracle food.

The earliest cultivated corn may have been grown in
southwest Mexico near Oaxaca. The corn fields would
have spread to the Tehuacán valley, out along the Gulf
and Pacific coasts, north into southwest U.S.A. and
down into the highlands of South America. Every time
the farmer's fingers prized free the grain and selected
those to be sown the next year, he chose the best of the
crop. This process of selection saw corn evolve and
improve everywhere it was grown.

Rice can be traced back to its wild origins over 6,500
years ago in the Hupei Basin and Yangtze Delta of
China. Wheat has identifiable wild ancestors in emmer
and einhorn. Yet the genetic link between cultivated
corn and its wild cousins has yet to be conclusively
established. In the absence of a biological history, is
there any truth in its legendary origins?

MAIZE OR CORN?

✦

The Mexicans called it *cintli* in
deference to their god of corn,
Cinteotl; Cuban Indians dubbed
it *maisi*. Columbus wrote of the
crop that "the Indians call *maiz*
. . . the Spanish *panizo*." To the
Europeans it was, at first, just
another grain: *polenta* (from the
Latin for pearl barley), explained
the Italians; foreign feed, said the
English, dismissing it as Indian or
Turkey corn. But botanist Carl
Linnaeus had some inkling of its
potential; he renamed *Turcicum
frumentum*, its original classification in 1536, as *Zea* ("cause of
life") *mays* ("our mother").
Europeans adopted maiz, mays,
or maize. But to the Americans,
who were expanding their crops
west into the old buffalo plains,
it was pure corn. As one Chicago
slogan put it in 1893, it was
the "Agricultural Conqueror of
the World."

One myth tells of a North American Indian who, when the Indians were first made, grew tired of digging for roots and lay down dreaming in the prairie grass. His reveries were interrupted by a vision: a beautiful woman with long fair hair standing close by. "If you do my bidding," she told him, "I will be with you for always." Taking sticks, she showed him how to rub them together in a tinder of dry grass and make a fire that burned the ground. "When the sun sets," she said, "drag me by my hair over the hot embers." He did as he was bid and wherever he dragged her, a grass-like plant sprang up in her wake. This gift meant his people no longer had to rely on roots for food.

In another legend, the Indian brave Hiawatha is anxious about his people's predicament: food is scarce and they face starvation. He leaves his village and begins a fast. On the fourth day, the god Mondamin appears. He challenges Hiawatha to a wrestling bout, promising that, if Hiawatha can defeat him, his people will be saved. The match begins and for three successive evenings the two wrestle. Hiawatha is weak with hunger, but finally defeats his foe. Mondamin is killed and buried and, in due course, corn rises from his grave.

Corn was already mesmerizing the indigenous people of the Peruvian coast 4,500 years ago. It continued to grow and evolve until the wandering Aztecs arrived in the Valley of Mexico in the thirteenth century. By 1325, while Europe was struggling with the Black Death, the Aztecs were building Tenochtitlán, now Mexico City, settling on two marshy islands in the south of Lake Texcoco. Floating great baskets of earth into the lake and planting trees to consolidate the land, the farmers created "chinampas"—raised fertile fields for their corn. The Aztecs kept peace by forging political alliances with their neighbors while their farmers assiduously followed their detailed, 365-day plant and harvest guides. Dividing the year into 18 months of 20 days each left five days spare these were the equivalent to our "Friday the thirteenth" and were regarded with deep superstition as unlucky days. Another profound superstition was that, without the regular sacrifice of human hearts, the terrible sun god, Huitzilopochtli would desert them and their crops.

Meanwhile, a group of Native South American craft workers and farmers, the Incas, were settling the Cuzco Valley in the Peruvian mountains. The horticultural Inca

VERSATILE VEGETABLE
Along with wheat and rice, corn is one of the world's great grain crops. It can be baked into breads, eaten as it is, or brewed into the beer *chica*.

built terraces and aqueducts to feed their corn and its sister crop, the potato, which was grown on higher ground and cultivated as a storage crop to complement the corn. By the 1400s, under their King, Pachacuti, the Inca empire expanded into Bolivia and Chile to the south. They were soon spreading north into Ecuador too, creating an empire networked by 19,000 miles (30,000 km) of roads used by relays of couriers who could deliver administrative messages across the region at the astonishing rate of 150 miles (240 km) a day. This was at a time when, in Medieval Europe, the English were burning a farmer's daughter—Joan of Arc—at the stake for her supposed heresy.

In 1519, Aztec astrologers spied a comet over the capital, Tenochtitlán, and predicted an impending disaster. It came in the form of a Spanish soldier, Hernando Cortés, who, like his force of 500, wore metal helmets and breastplates, carried guns, and rode on horseback.

The Americas, populated by perhaps 25 million natives before the arrival of the Europeans, was the biggest and emptiest fertile landmass in the world. Cortés, with his small army in tow, reached Tenochtitlán and—once the ceremonial welcomes were over—slaughtered the Indian nobility. By 1520, the great Aztec leader, Montezuma was dead and Cortés had became governor of Mexico.

MEAL MAKERS
Women grind corn flour to make and bake their flat tortillas in a Mexican hut in the 1830s. The corn was soaked and cooked in lime water before being ground into flour.

In 1532, it was the turn of the Incas to suffer at the hands of the Spanish conquistadors. Francisco Pizarro slaughtered all the Inca leaders except the emperor, Atahualpa. His release was offered in return for a ransom of gold and silver bullion. Once it had been delivered, Atahualpa was strangled. Within 30 years, two great South American civilizations had been routed and replaced by Spanish colonial rule.

Native Americans were as respectful toward grain gods such as Mondamin as Roman farmers had been toward their grain goddess, Ceres. Traditional rituals were performed as the Indians buried a fish (it acted as a slow-release fertilizer), planted their corn and later the squash and lima beans that used the corn stems for support. When the first cobs were cut they were ceremonially baked in the embers of the fire for the Green Corn Festival.

THE MIGRATION OF CORN

It was Columbus who brought the plant to Europe from the New World, and within a century it had reached China. It was taken to Russia, where it was used for cornmeal, *mamaliga*, and to Ghana, where they supped on *sofki*. It returned to favor in America when the Jamestown colonists kept starvation at bay by resorting to the native corn that they had originally dismissed as "savage trash." John Gerard wrote in his 1597 *Herbal* that the "turkie corne" came "not (as some suppose) out of Asia minor, which is the Turks dominions; but out of America and the Islands adjoining. It is planted in the gardens of these Northern regions, where it commeth to ripenesse when the summer

HAND TO MOUTH
Corn kernels were planted by hand, seed by seed. Once the seed was sown, Florida Indians like these could look forward to the Green Corn Festival and the start of a new year.

> **I, last April, sent parcels of the seed into several countries, to be given away to working men. This corn is the very best for hog-fattening in the whole world.**
>
> *William Cobbett*, Cottage Economy, *1821*

falleth out to be faire and hot; as my selfe have seen by proof in myne owne garden."

It was still a relatively new plant when the agriculturalist William Cobbett wrote his book for English country laborers, *Cottage Economy*, n 1821: "The stalks or ears come out of the side of the plant, which has eaves like a flag and which grows to three foot high." He omitted to mention that when the Mexicans baked their corn tortillas they first soaked the kernels in lime water (they used lye in the north and lime in Mesoamerica and the southwest) before grinding them down to flour and making their flat "breads" (lacking gluten, cornbread did not benefit from yeast). This compensated for the absence in corn of the natural amino acid lysine. As Cobbett warned, people could poison themselves with too much corn, suffering "corn sickness or rough skin, what the Italians called *pellagra*." The cause was identified as a lack of niacin. Nevertheless, the golden grain was lucrative—the more you grew, the more you profited.

In America, the four elements that allowed the expansion of corn into the West were coming together (the plow, the "steam horse," the mill, and plant selection), while in the South corn became a slave crop and a useful companion to cotton. The two staple plants of the Deep South provided year-long work for the slave, who was estimated to be able to manage six acres (2.4 ha) of cotton and eight (3.2 ha) of corn each year.

Before corn crossed from the New World into the Old, plant and animal life was already developing along separate, evolutionary lines. Once Columbus had triggered the two-way exchange of plants, natural evolution was supplanted by human intervention. Corn reversed the balance of world economic power, moving it away from China and toward Western Europe. A consequence of this was the elevation of Christianity to a greater status as European missionaries took the teachings of the Bible to the New World. Corn, in the end, proved to be one of the great history-changers.

CORN ADVOCATE
The English farmer and agricultural reformer William Cobbett was a champion of what he called "Indian corn."

A QUESTION OF DEGREE

✦

Supporters of biotechnology claim that the use of genetically modified (GM) crops will result in an increase in food yields of up to 25%, which could feed an extra three billion people. Opponents say that farming monocultural crops like GM corn leads to a loss of biodiversity, unpredictable side effects such as superweeds, and an increasing reliance on herbicides and pesticides. A more balanced agriculture, they argue, could meet the demand for food without using biotechnology.

Ginger

Zingiber officinale

Native range: East Indies

Type: Bamboo-like plant with edible rhizomes

Height: 3 feet (1 m)

+ **EDIBLE**
+ **MEDICINAL**
+ COMMERCIAL
+ PRACTICAL

G inger, which shares the same family as turmeric and cardamom, was a popular plant in the Middle Ages, esteemed for its sweetness especially when preserved. But it was expensive. In the 1300s, a pound of ginger cost the same as an entire sheep.

RELIGIOUS REVIVAL

Ginger was a familiar spice in Greek and Roman times. Although the northern Indians named it *srngaveram*, the horned root, the Romans called it *zingiber* and traded it across southeastern Europe from its native origins in the East Indies. It was the plant's knotty rhizome that first endeared it to the Mediterraneans, who used it to flavor food after first washing, boiling, peeling, and grinding the root down to release its pungent and aromatic qualities. In those relatively sugar-free days, the young rhizomes preserved in a honey syrup were a particular luxury.

The fall of the Roman Empire left the knobbly roots languishing in the shallow Indian soils and the ginger farmers more impoverished than ever. That was until the birth of a new era and a new religion: Islam. Until the 600s, three religions dominated Asia and southern Europe: the world's oldest, Hinduism; Buddhism; and Christianity. Now, with the death of the Prophet of Islam, Mohammed, in 632, and the rise of his father-in-law, Abu Bakr, and Omar, the next caliph (meaning successor or ruler), the new religion of Islam began to bed itself in until, by the fourteenth century it had spread across the Middle East, Spain, the Balkans, central Asia, the Indian subcontinent, the East Indies, and into North Africa.

Rarely does the founding of a new empire represent good news for those countries that bear the yoke of occupation. However, there is usually one beneficial side effect: safer trade routes. With its capital in Damascus and later Baghdad, the Islamic empire oversaw the reopening of the traditional overland routes between East and West. If you took a pencil to any sixteenth-century map of Africa and shaded in the Islamic territories, most of the east coast, from modern-day Eritrea, down through Somalia, Kenya, Tanzania, and Malawi, would be covered. The coast included

Nose, nose, jolly red nose,
Who gave thee this jolly red nose?
Nutmegs and ginger, cinnamon and cloves.

Francis Beaumont, The Knight of the Burning Pestle, *1607*

the shipping ports of Gedi, Kilwa, and Sofala, where ivory, salt, and Zimbabwean copper and gold were traded with China and India in exchange for ceramics, beads, and cowrie shells. Almost a third of North Africa, from Morocco to Timbuktu, was also under Islamic rule and the markets of Jenne, Gao, and Timbuktu—then a center for Muslim scholars as well as a booming trading post—received the silks, ceramics, and spices that had been transported from India through Iran, Iraq, Jordan, and Egypt.

APHRODISIAC CHARMS

In time, the dromedary camels, which had proved a *force majeure* when the Arab armies fought for their new territories, were complaining as only camels can as they were loaded up with ginger and other precious cargoes, including kola nuts and ivory. Accompanied by that other "commodity," black African slaves, the caravans headed for the North African coast where they could be shipped to Europe. With each pair of hands that ginger passed through, its value increased. Despite this, it became once again an essential culinary and medicinal spice thanks to the Arab traders.

However, the promise of powers outside the kitchen no doubt helped to prop up prices in the West as the ginger traders relayed rumors from the East that the spice was a reliable aphrodisiac, suitable for both internal and external use. As late as the nineteenth century it was claimed that the seducer who rubbed his hands in soft, ground ginger was assured of success in the bed chamber. King Henry VI of England suggested a more prosaic use: he advised the Mayor of London to include it in any preparation used to counter the plague.

It was a later royal, "good Queen Bess" or Queen Elizabeth I, who was reported to have invented that favorite childhood confection, the gingerbread man—introduced to amuse her courtiers.

GINGERED UP
A warming herb with a pungent flower, ginger helped drive the spice trade. Ginger-based ale was a popular drink during the American Prohibition, when it acquired a racy image.

Further Reading

Beerling, David, *The Emerald Planet –
How plants change Earth's History*,
OUP, Oxford, 2007

Blackburne-Maze, Peter, *The
Apple Book*, Collingridge Books,
London, 1986

Campbell-Culver, Maggie, *The Origins of
Plants*, Headline, London, 2001

Cobbett, William, *Cottage Economy*,
Kanitz Publishing, Herefordshire, 2000

Cornell, Martyn, *Beer: The Story of
the Pint*, Headline, London, 2003

Crouch, David and Ward, Colin,
The Allotment, Faber and Faber,
London, 1988

Culpeper, Nicholas, *Complete Herbal and
English Physician*, 1826

Dalby, Andrew, *Dangerous Tastes:
the Story of Spices*, British Museum
Press, London, 2000

Dájun, Wang and Shao-Jin, Shen,
Bamboos of China, Christopher Helm,
London, 1987

Doughty, Robin W., *The Eucalyptus:
A Natural History of the Gum Tree*,
John Hopkins University Press,
Baltimore, 2000

Drège, Jean-Pierre and Bührer, Emil,
The Silk Road Saga, Facts on File,
New York, 1987

Eastwood, Antonia, Lazkov, George, and
Newton, Adrian, *The Red List of Trees
of Central Asia*, Fauna and Flora
International, Cambridge (UK), 2009

Farrelly, David, *The Book of Bamboo*,
Sierra Club Books, San Francisco,
1984

Fernández-Armesto, Felipe, *Pathfinders*,
OUP, Oxford, 2006

Frey, William H. with Muriel Langseth,
*Crying: The Mystery
of Tears*, Winston Press
Minneapolis, 1985

Frost, Louise and Griffiths, Alistair,
Plants of Eden, Alison Hodge,
Penzance, 2001

Girardet, Herbert, *Cities People Planet:
Urban Development and Climate
Change*, John Wiley & Sons, Oxford,
2008

Grigson, Geoffrey, *A Dictionary of
English Plant Names*, Allen Lane,
London, 1974

Hammond, Claudia, *Emotional Roller
Coaster*, Fourth Estate, London, 2000

Harris, Esmond, Harris, Jeanette and
James, N. D. G., *Oak: A British
History*, Windgather Press, Cheshire,
2003

Harrison, S. G., Masefield, G. B. and
Wallis, Michael, *The Illustrated Book
of Food Plants*, OUP, Oxford, 1969

Hibberd, Shirley, *Profitable Gardening*,
Groombridge & Son, London, 1863

Hobhouse, Henry, *Seeds of Change*,
Pan, London, 1985

Howe, William L., *"Global Trends in the
Condom Industry,"* 2005, Institute of
Historical Research, digital article

Hyams, Edward, *Plants in the service
of man*, J. M. Dent, London, 1971

Huxley, Anthony, *An Illustrated
History of Gardening*, Paddington
Press, New York, 1978

Irish, Mary and Gavin, *Agaves, Yuccas
and related plants*, Timber Press,
Oregon, 2000

Fukouka, Masanobu, *The one-straw
revolution*, Frances Lincoln,
London, 2009

Kilvert, Francis, *Kilvert's Diary 1870 –
1879*, Century, London, 1986.

Laws, Bill, Collins *Field Guide: Fields*,
HarperCollins, London, 2010

Laws, Bill, *Artists' Gardens*,
Ward Lock, London, 1999

Lewington, Anna, *Plants for people*,
Eden Project Books, London, 2003

Leathart, Scott, *Whence our trees*,
Foulsham, London, 1991

Lovelock, Yann, *The Vegetable Book*,
Allen & Unwin, London, 1972

Murphy, Bryan, *The World Book
of Whisky*, William Collins,
Glasgow, 1978

Musgrave, Toby and Musgrave, Will,
An Empire of Plants, Cassell,
London, 2000.

Nobel, Park S., *Remarkable agaves and
cacti*, OUP, Oxford, 1994

Pelling, Margaret, and White, Frances,
*Medical Conflicts in Early Modern
London: Patronage, Physicians, and
Irregular Practitioners 1550 – 1640*,
OUP, Oxford, 2004

Rackham, Oliver, *The History of the Countryside*, J. M. Dent, London, 1986

Rajakumar, Kumaravel, *Infantile Scurvy: A Historical Perspective*, Pediatrics Vol. 108 No. 4, October 2001, University of Pittsburgh School of Medicine, electronic article

Rackham, Arthur, *The History of the Countryside*, J. M. Dent, London, 1986.

Simons, A. J., *Vegetable Grower's Handbook*, Bakers Nurseries, Wolverhampton, 1941

Stocks, Christopher, *Forgotten Fruits*, Windmill Hill Books, London, 2008

Smith, A. W., *A Gardener's Handbook of Plant Names*, Harper and Row, New York, 1963

Thoreau, David, *Walden and Other Writings*, Bantam Books, New York, 1962

Tudge, Colin, *The Secret Life of Trees*, Allen Lane, London, 2005

Winch, Tony, *Growing Food: A guide to food production*, Springer, Dordrecht, 2006

White, Gilbert, *The Natural History of Selbourne*, Cassell and Company, London.

Woodward, Marcus, Editor, *Gerard's Herbal*, Studio Editions, London, 1990

Woodell, S. R. J., Editor, *The English Landscape, past, present and future*, Oxford University Press, Oxford, 1985.

USEFUL WEBSITES

American Botanical Council
www.herbalgram.org

American Museum of Natural History *www.amnh.org*

Australian Network for Plant Conservation *www.anbg.gov.au*

Botanic Gardens Conservation *www.bcgi.org*

Canadian Botanical Conservation Network *www.rbg.ca/cbcn/en*

Champion Trees *www.championtrees.org*

Claude Monet *www.giverny.org*

Conservation International *www.conservation.org* *www.biodiversityhotspots.org*

European Bamboo Society *www.bamboosociety.org*

Fairtrade *www.fairtrade.org.uk*

Global Partnership for Plant Conservation *www.plants2010.org*

GLOBIO *www.who.globio.info*

Helen Allingham Society *www.helenallingham.com*

National Audubon Society *www.audubon.org*

National History Museum *www.nhm.ac.uk*

National Maritime Museum *www.nmm.ac.uk*

National Society of Allotments and Leisure Gardens *www.nsalg.org.uk*

Royal Botanic Gardens *www.kew.org*

Royal Botanic Garden Edinburgh *www.rbge.org.uk*

Royal Horticultural Society *www.rhs.org.uk*

Royal Society for the Protection of Birds *www.rspb.org.uk*

UNESCO Programme on Man and the Biosphere *www.unesco.org/mab*

United Nations Environment Programme *www.unep.org*

World Health Organization *www.who.int*

World Wildlife Fund *www.wwf.org*

Index

IMAGE CREDITS

7 top	© Tomas Bercic | iStockphoto
16	© Getty Images
18	© Annsunnyday | Dreamstime.com
19	© Jonas Hamm | iStockphoto
21	© Adrian Beesley | iStockphoto
22	© Creative Commons | Sanja565658
27 top	© Jonphoto | Dreamstime.com
29	© Markus Unger | iStockphoto
32	© Creative Commons | Georges Jansoone
33	© The Stapleton Collection
35	© Jojojojo | Dreamstime.com
40	© Floortje | iStockphoto
41	© Michal Galazka | iStockphoto
43	© Tomasz Zachariasz | iStockphoto
46	© Libby Chapman | iStockphoto
50	© Creative Commons | John Wilbanks
53	© Chris Hepburn | iStockphoto
59 bottom	© Antimartina | iStockphoto
62 bottom	© Arkadiy Yarmolenko | iStockphoto
66	© Kit Sen Chin | iStockphoto
69 top	© Alina555 | iStockphoto
73	© Sayarikuna | iStockphoto
79	© Olaf Loose | iStockphoto
81	© dgmata | iStockphoto
84	© Lizzie Harper | Science Photo Library
89	© Juthathip Tybon | iStockphoto
94	© Nicolas Robert | Getty Images
95	© Takk | Creative Commons
96 bottom	© James McQuillan | iStockphoto
101 top	© Luis Fernández García | Creative Commons
109	© Vladimir Vladimirov | iStockphoto
110	© Sheila Terry | Science Photo Library
111	© Stephen Sparkes | iStockphoto
112 top	© Tamara Kulikova | iStockphoto
112 bottom	© Trevor Moore | iStockphoto
115 bottom	© Bjorn Heller | iStockphoto
117	© Science Photo Library
120	© Tamara Kulikova | iStockphoto
124	© Jeni Neale
128 bottom	© Jan Will | iStockphoto
142 top	© Susib | iStockphoto
144	© Ikopylov | Dreamstime.com
145	© The British Library Board. Add.Or.1740
147	© Angelogila | Dreamstime.com
156	© Getty Images
157	© Gabor Izso | iStockphoto
159	© Julien Grondin | Dreamstime.com
160	© Mary Evans Picture Library
161 bottom	© Lindsey Johns
163 right	© Gee807 | Dreamstime.com
167	© Phbcz | Dreamstime.com
173	© Mary Evans Picture Library
175	© Getty Images
187	© Floortje | iStockphoto
195	© Floortje | iStockphoto
197	© Tjanze | iStockphoto
201	© Brent Melton | iStockphoto
204	© Museo della Civilta Romana, Rome, Italy | The Bridgeman ArtLibrary
206 bottom	© Luoman | iStockphoto
209	© Mary Evans Picture Library
211	© Getty Images
212	© Norman Chan | iStockphoto
216 top	© Mostafa Hefni | iStockphoto